Looking Up!

Looking Up!

Finding Joy as You Read and Pray through the Bible

365 DAILY DEVOTIONS

Janet Holm McHenry

Our Daily Bread Publishing

Looking Up! Finding Joy as You Read and Pray through the Bible

Names have been changed to protect the identity of people whose stories are told.

Published in association with the Books & Such Literary Management, 52 Mission Circle, Suite 122, PMB 170, Santa Rosa, CA 95409-5370, www.booksandsuch.com.

Interior design by Michael J. Williams

ISBN: 978-1-916718-34-0

Printed in Europe
24 25 26 27 28 29 30 31 / 8 7 6 5 4 3 2 1

In memory of my friend June Varnum,
and to Pam Cheek and the thousands of Bible Girls
who have been reading the Bible with me for many years.

Introduction

IN A CONVERSATION with my friend many years ago, June and I realized neither of us had read all the way through the Bible. So we went to our local Christian bookstore and bought little pamphlets with a reading guide that would lead us through God's Word in a year. When we were done, we realized that while we had learned a lot, there was still much to discover and more spiritual growth to come. So we kept up that practice for many years, one I have continued to this day.

Perhaps you want to learn more about God and the promises he offers those who love him. Maybe you also have been longing for a little more joy in your life. *Looking Up!* has much to offer you!

- The title of each day is God's promise to you based on the day's Scripture reading.
- By reading the daily Bible passage, you'll cover the entire Bible in a year! The Bible reading will take about ten minutes a day, and you'll be amazed at how much you learn! In fact, reading the Bible for yourself will help you discover additional insights and gain new understanding about God and his love for you.
- The short devotional readings will teach a bit about the verse and passage and provide ideas to help you apply the reading to your own life.
- Brief Bible-based prayers will jumpstart your personal prayer time with the Lord.
- Each *Keep Looking Up!* thought will encourage your next steps.

I believe you'll find, as I did, that reading God's Word gives you a rock-solid foundation for your daily walk. You will grow in strength, wisdom, and the joy of the Lord as you see his promises fulfilled in his Word.

Blessings,
Janet Holm McHenry

JANUARY 1

God Brings Light to the Darkness

Read Genesis 1–4

And God said, "Let there be light," and there was light.
—Genesis 1:3 NIV

WHEN I WENT back to college to get a teaching credential, the work of memorizing terms and concepts was challenging for midlife me. *I don't think I can do this, God!*

I remember fretting over test prep one morning when a friend knocked on the door.

"God prompted me to stop," she said. "Can I pray for you about something?"

After she prayed, it was as though God shone a new light on my understanding. I suddenly knew how to study and what to study. And I passed that national exam with a great score.

When God created the world, the first thing he created was light. His words brought about light that overcame darkness. It's interesting that God created light before he created the sun and moon. Evening and morning existed before God put the sun into place. We have the opportunity to tap into God's light every single day—simply through the study of his Word. No matter how hard our situation may seem, his words can overcome darkness.

Lord God, your very words bring light into my life. Darkness has no power over me as I choose to turn toward the light of your Word. It breathes clarity and understanding as well as the testimony of character that you follow through with your promises. Thank you for your enlightening Word.

Keep Looking Up!

Every day we can walk in the light as we read God's Word.

JANUARY 2

God Wants to Walk with Us

Read Genesis 5–8

Noah was a righteous man, blameless among the people of his time, and he walked faithfully with God. —Genesis 6:9 NIV

DO YOU HAVE a walking partner? Over the years I've had many women who have walked with me as we prayed for the people whose homes and businesses we passed. While I walk at a pretty brisk pace, some have challenged me to push myself to a faster clip, while others have asked me to slow down. Walking together implies an agreement between friends—an agreeable direction, a compatible pace, and an agreed time of day. Prayerwalking implies a mutual, like-minded purpose for the walk.

Noah walked with God, Scripture tells us. In the genealogy in Genesis 5, he is one of only two men listed in the ten generations from Adam to Noah who walked with God (Enoch, his great-grandfather was the other). When we walk with God, we are going in a like-minded, compatible direction with an agreed-upon purpose in mind. We are, in fact, going God's way.

Lord, it is my heart's desire to follow you and your direction for my life and thus be an example of goodness to others who know me. Most certainly, I would love for your favor to fall on me, but a greater hope is that you find pleasure in all that I say, do, and even think.

Keep Looking Up!

God's favor is on us as we follow him.

JANUARY 3

God Is with Us, No Matter What

Read Genesis 9–12

I have set my rainbow in the clouds, and it will be the sign of the covenant between me and the earth. —Genesis 9:13 NIV

WHEN WE WERE engaged, Craig and I had an idealistic thought: we would write our own marriage vows. Our pastor said, "See if you can improve upon the vows in the written ceremony."

As we read the vows, we found the words made sense: "for richer for poorer, in sickness and in health . . . to cherish . . ." However, we decided to change one word. Instead of saying *vow*, we wanted to say *covenant* because that word meant we were binding ourselves not only to each other—through the thick and the thin—but also to God.

The rainbow is a beautiful reminder that God covenanted with man that he would never destroy all earthly life with a flood. And he keeps his promises. When he says he will never leave us, he means it. Real storms and figurative ones will come and go in our lives, but we can always know that God is with us—despite whatever is going on around us or even within us.

Lord, despite our failings, you chose to make an unconditional covenant not to bring about the destruction of life on the earth. Your rainbow is an everlasting sign of your good word. Thank you.

Keep Looking Up!

We can look beyond the storm to find God's gift of himself.

We Can Step Confidently into God's Provision

Read Genesis 13–15

Go, walk through the length and breadth of the land, for I am giving it to you. —Genesis 13:17 NIV

MIDLIFE MY HUSBAND made a huge transition: he left his law practice to raise hay and beef cattle. I remember the exact date we signed on the dotted line, because he found a notary public in the hospital the day after our third child was born.

"You just sign here," Craig said.

"You're sure about this?"

He assured me he had walked the hundreds of acres from corner to corner. "It is good land—some of the best."

Walking the boundaries is nothing new. When God showed Abram the land God was giving him, God told him to walk its length and breadth. We don't fully understand a piece of property unless we walk through it. We must experience the ground under our feet to grasp its value and challenges. Similarly, as we walk through life with God, we experience his provision, we see how he supplies for us, and that allows us to grow confident in belief that God is with us every step of the way.

Lord, when I feel buried, remind me to lift my eyes and look around—north and south, east and west. Help me to appreciate where I am right now and to boldly step into the land of opportunity you have given to me. Thank you for trusting me with possibilities.

Keep Looking Up!

Walking with God gives us confidence in his care.

JANUARY 5

God Sees You

Read Genesis 16–18

She gave this name to the LORD who spoke to her: "You are the God who sees me," for she said, "I have now seen the One who sees me." —Genesis 16:13 NIV

THE YOUNGEST OF six, Ezekiel, seven, sat on my couch in a pout, his bottom lip trembling. The other five were playing a game with my husband, Craig, their "Pop."

"Hey, buddy," I said, "want to watch a movie with me?"

He nodded, and we settled into cozy throws for a long winter's watch. Ezekiel smiled as I drew closer to him. He knew I had *seen* him—not yet as skilled as his older siblings in game strategies—and cared enough to tailor an experience for him.

God sees the unseen. Hagar also had been a victim of others' disregard. Her mistress resented the fact that Hagar could get pregnant, and Sarai mistreated her. When Hagar ran away, God found her and told her he had seen her misery. So she went back home and bore the child, Ishmael. And we learn later that God took care of her and her son, just as he sees us and provides good things for us.

Lord, you see me! You know my hurts and insecurities and fears. And you care about me. While I know that life can be hard and people can be unkind and even cruel, you see me and have good things for me. Therefore, I can run to you and gain strength from the fact that you care.

Keep Looking Up!

You and all your needs are important to God.

JANUARY 6

God Brings Laughter

Read Genesis 19–22

Sarah said, "God has brought me laughter, and everyone who hears about this will laugh with me." —Genesis 21:6 NIV

ME, A SCIENCE teacher. It was almost laughable, really, but there I was in an eighth-grade science class facing a boy with a rattlesnake in a pillowcase. A first-year English teacher, I was filling in for the science educator for a full ten weeks.

"Mr. Taylor gives us extra credit if we bring in roadkill," the boy said with a smirk. He knew he had me.

While I wanted to run, instead I laughed and pointed to the chest freezer next to my desk. "Just put that guy right in there."

Sometimes God puts us in the craziest of positions, such as an English teacher attempting to teach a science class or an eighty-nine-year-old woman named Sarah giving birth to her first and only child, Isaac, whose name means, "he laughs." Sometimes we laugh because situations or words are funny, but sometimes we shake our heads in wonder and laugh because God has just done the impossible . . . again.

And sometimes that laughter is the best medicine.

Lord, help me laugh at myself when I am taking life and my situation too seriously. Teach me to appreciate the humorous ironies and subtleties so that I find joy all around me. You created laughter, so may your Spirit well up laughter inside of me.

Keep Looking Up!

God brings laughter into our lives; we just need to look for its opportunity.

JANUARY 7

God Hears Our Prayers for Others

Read Genesis 23–25

Isaac prayed to the LORD on behalf of his wife, because she was childless. The LORD answered his prayer, and his wife Rebekah became pregnant. —Genesis 25:21 NIV

LAURIE JOINED OUR Bible study a few months ago, and because we pray for each other, she began asking for prayers for her homeless son, who was also drug addicted. In past years the family had taken him in, of course, but he always refused to abide by no-substances-in-the-house kinds of rules.

However, by the end of our eight-week session, she had a praise. "I talked to my son this week, and he said he had just made an appointment with a caseworker. Please pray he follows through. This is the first time he has ever admitted he needs help."

When we pray for others, we unite our heart with theirs as we lean together toward God, who loves that we go to him with our needs. And as we join in prayer and draw closer to him, God hears us.

Lord, hear my prayers for my loved ones. I see them hurting—and I hurt too. May our united hearts in prayer also unite with yours, Father.

Keep Looking Up!

Praying for our loved ones unites our hearts.

JANUARY 8

God Is in This Place

Read Genesis 26–28

When Jacob awoke from his sleep, he thought, "Surely the LORD is in this place, and I was not aware of it." —Genesis 28:16 NIV

THE FIRST TIME we ever saw the Sierra Valley, my husband, Craig, and I knew that God had led us to the place where we would raise children and live to an old age. We drove up what is called the Gold Highway over the Sierra Nevada to the top of the Yuba Pass to view the largest alpine valley in North America—a place I joke is just like Lake Tahoe, except without the water.

It was a holy moment standing there on the highway vista point, seeing a promised land of sorts where we would live—imagining snapshots of family gatherings and hikes and kids' ball games.

Jacob had a God-is-in-this-place moment too. In his dream, angels ascended and descended a heavenly ladder, and the Lord reiterated his promise for land and generations of offspring.

The truth is, however, that the Lord does live in all who believe in him through the presence of his Holy Spirit. So, yes, the Lord *is* in this place.

Lord, some moments seem especially holy, because I sense your presence and your promise to me, but I know that wherever I am, you are as well. May I always walk in a way that reflects your presence with me.

Keep Looking Up!

God inhabits those who love him.

JANUARY 9

God Provides Attention-Getters

Read Genesis 29–31

The angel of God said to me in the dream, "Jacob." I answered, "Here I am." —Genesis 31:11 NIV

WHEN I WAS a girl, my parents called us five kids in to dinner with a two-note whistle—a higher note followed by a lower one. Their whistles could carry across a couple backyards and even into the wooded area behind our home in upstate New York. And we would come running.

Similarly, God can get our attention in a variety of ways. We might have a health challenge that helps us refocus on wellness. We might also have a change of management in our workplace that creates a need to seek other employment.

Several times in the Bible, God simply calls out a Bible character's name, as he did with Jacob, his father, Abraham, and others. And each time the person responded, "Here I am." No matter how God delivers a wake-up call to us, the best response is to listen and heed God's direction.

Lord, thank you for the many wake-up calls you have given me over the years, because I know that each one has been for my good. May I always respond with "Here I am" and "Yes" to whatever you direct me to do.

Keep Looking Up!

God's wake-up calls are always for our good.

God Loves Our Reaching Out to Others

Read Genesis 32–35

But Esau ran to meet Jacob and embraced him; he threw his arms around his neck and kissed him. And they wept. —Genesis 33:4 NIV

ONE DAY MY friend Margot found herself completely cut off from her daughter, Naomi, which meant she also was estranged from her grandchildren. For three years she traversed a journey of healing and forgiveness, only to discover the impact her growing-up years had on her own mothering. As a consequence, Margot was able to walk away from her own codependent tendencies and into her identity in Christ.

When she understood her parents had tried their best, Margot was able to forgive them and then ask for and receive forgiveness from her daughter.

Twin brothers Jacob and Esau were estranged too. Jacob had cheated Esau out of his inheritance rights and feared Esau's reaction once Jacob returned home. But when Jacob asked for forgiveness, Esau's embrace erased their estrangement, and the brothers were united again.

Forgiveness is a defining quality of the Christian faith. When we ask for forgiveness, we choose to be more like Christ. And when we forgive, we choose to leave bad history in the past, offer grace to others in the same way God has forgiven us our sins, and make our best efforts at reconciliation.

Lord, thank you for the gift of your Son, Jesus, who paved the way for our forgiveness and modeled for us how to live free lives through forgiveness.

Keep Looking Up!

Taking the first step toward forgiveness is a leap in finding freedom.

JANUARY 11

God Gives Us Dreams

Read Genesis 36–38

He said to them, "Listen to this dream I had." —Genesis 37:6 NIV

WHEN PEOPLE ASK why I became a teacher, I tell them about my dream of touring a new housing development with children playing on rooftops and porches. But the children could not see that the homes were on fire.

I ran to the front of the bus and said, "Stop the bus! I have to get off!"

Within a week's time I had enrolled in graduate studies to become an English teacher.

There are different kinds of dreams. Our sleeping dreams can be kind of crazy. But then we also have human desires and hopes that we also call dreams. Sometimes our sleeping dreams impact the dreams we have for our lives. Like me, Joseph had a dream about the future. Unlike mine, Joseph's dream didn't sound like it would be nice for others. But he still bragged to his brothers, which made them resent him and sell him into slavery—which eventually led to their own rescue and the fulfillment of Joseph's dream.

If God is behind our dreams, he will help us see them to fruition.

Lord, thank you for inspiring me with dreams that have pushed me out of my comfort zone into places of personal fulfillment. I know you are leading me, and I can trust you for each step of the way.

Keep Looking Up!

When God gives us a dream, he helps us fulfill it.

JANUARY 12

God Raises Leaders

Read Genesis 39–41

His master saw that the LORD was with him and that the LORD caused all that he did to succeed in his hands. —Genesis 39:3

AT MIDLIFE MY dad had to start his career all over again. My mom's doctor had told my dad that Mom would not make it through another year in the climate of upstate New York with her severe asthma. So Dad shifted from managing a four-story department store to working as an assistant men's department buyer in a Phoenix store.

Starting a career over was not easy, but God helped him. A year later, our family moved to Albuquerque, and the next year Dad became a store manager in Sacramento. He also rose to lead three service organizations and his church board.

Leaders rise. Though Joseph was sold into slavery, God opened doors for Joseph to become second in command to Pharaoh, the Egyptian king. Imagine that—an unwanted prison inmate leading a country. Eventually he would save those who wanted his own destruction.

God raises leaders from all kinds of beginnings and through all kinds of circumstances.

Lord, give me the confidence and help me to rise to the calling that you have on my life, and may my work bring honor to you.

Keep Looking Up!

When the Lord calls us, he equips us.

JANUARY 13

God Helps Us Reach Out

Read Genesis 42–43

Deeply moved at the sight of his brother, Joseph hurried out and looked for a place to weep. He went into his private room and wept there. —Genesis 43:30 NIV

MY FRIEND MARTA found out she was a grandmother. Such news should be joyful, but she discovered her daughter had the baby a half dozen months ago . . . and had married a man Marta did not even know. Thumbing through pictures on social media, she pieced together an engagement, wedding, the baby's arrival, and birthdays and dinners and other milestones—milestones that weighed hard on her heart.

"I'm a grandmother," she said on the phone. "Now what do I do?"

"Reach out," I said. "You have nothing to lose, and you'll know that you've done what you can to break down the walls."

Doing the hard work of reconciliation can trigger a tug-of-war with our hearts. Joseph found that to be true with his brothers. But reaching out with loving gestures can heal even the greatest heart fractures.

Lord, it hurts when others shut me out. And often my gestures toward reconciliation are completely rejected. However, you are the great Restorer of people to yourself and of people to each other, so I trust you to bring about an outcome of healing.

Keep Looking Up!

Reaching out for reconciliation is worth the risk.

JANUARY 14

Forgiveness Is God's Work

Read Genesis 44–46

And now do not be distressed or angry with yourselves because you sold me here, for God sent me before you to preserve life.
—Genesis 45:5

AT A LOCAL fundraising event I was stunned to see my husband Craig laughing and talking with a man who had caused him great pain—and even significant financial loss. Later I asked him why.

He told me he had decided to forgive the man. "I just want to move on. Anger wasn't doing me any good."

When others hurt us, it's easier to allow the hurt to fester into anger, resentment, and bitterness. Even though Joseph's brothers were guilty of a horrific crime, he chose to forgive them. And God used Joseph to save the Hebrew people.

Releasing our hurt and anger can make room in our heart, mind, and soul to notice the greater work God may be doing through us.

Father, I know that through your Son, Jesus, my sins are forgiven. When I want to hold on to anger, help me release the whole situation to you and trust you for the outcome.

Keep Looking Up!

Because God has forgiven me, I can forgive others when they hurt me.

JANUARY 15

Trials May Have a Greater Purpose

Read Genesis 47–50

You intended to harm me, but God intended it for good to accomplish what is now being done, the saving of many lives.
—Genesis 50:20 NIV

YEARS AGO WE faced a literal trial. Six calves and an old bull bedded down in a remote part of our ranch during a two-day blizzard, got covered over, and died. A cranky neighbor reported the incident to authorities even before Craig knew, and a short time later he faced seven felony counts of animal cruelty.

The judge would not allow evidence and testimony proving Craig's innocence to be admitted, so jurors did not know about auction records and correct findings in necropsy reports. Also, the court didn't allow a veterinary school professor to testify. Consequently, Craig was convicted, and it took two years for the conviction to be overturned in appellate court.

Just as Joseph learned, we found during the years of injustice that clinging to God carried us through. And we found clinging to each other drew us closer—answering years of prayers for our marriage. God can use our pain for a greater good.

Father in heaven, I know that life here on earth will not be pain free, and I do not expect a lifelong reprieve from challenges. I just ask that you would use any suffering I may experience for your glory.

Keep Looking Up!

Seasons of struggle provide opportunities for character development.

JANUARY 16

God Is the Great I AM

Read Exodus 1–4

And the angel of the LORD appeared to [Moses] in a flame of fire out of the midst of a bush. He looked, and behold, the bush was burning, yet it was not consumed. —Exodus 3:2

ABOUT TWO WEEKS after my dad had passed away from ALS, grief finally settled over me. Initially, busyness filled days of helping to plan a memorial, notifying people, and writing obituaries and the eulogy. At home I sat quietly, staring at a basketful of sympathy cards.

I suddenly felt a nudge to go prayerwalking—a devotional practice I had begun seven months earlier. As I left home, I noticed a series of cirrus clouds layered one above the other—like musical score lines. They hung there as the sunrise intensified in a spectrum of yellows, pinks, and purples . . . a silent, heavenly song.

The notes of grieving quieted a bit with the sense that the Lord had given me a personal love song that morning. Such as with Moses's bush, God's burning greeting in the sky gave me the assurance that he was with me and would see me through the coming days and seasons. And he has.

Lord, thank you for your assuring presence through the grieving seasons of my life. Just as Moses could know you are the great I AM, I can too as I see your beautiful creation all around me, which inspires me to keep looking up!

Keep Looking Up!

God's creation provides reminders all around us that he exists.

JANUARY 17

God Pursues Relationship

Read Exodus 5–7

I will take you as my own people, and I will be your God. Then you will know that I am the LORD your God, who brought you out from under the yoke of the Egyptians. —Exodus 6:7 NIV

I WAS A college sophomore when I learned I could have a personal relationship with Jesus. I had always believed in God the Father, Jesus his Son, and the Holy Spirit, but the idea of God's choosing me for a personal relationship was new. That word, *personal*, kept ringing in my head when a man spoke of it, and faith suddenly made sense in that context: Jesus came to be my personal Savior so I could know the Father and have the Spirit of God living in me.

So I prayed, "Lord, I ask forgiveness for my sins and invite you to be my personal Savior."

From that moment I knew deeply in my mind, heart, and soul that God was not distant but was with me and had a purpose for my life.

Just as God pursued a relationship with the people of the Exodus, he still pursues one with us today.

Lord, thank you for your pursuit of a personal relationship with all mankind over the years of human existence. And thank you for your gift of Jesus, the yoke-bearer who carries the weight of my sins.

Keep Looking Up!

We are God's people, and he is our God—that's personal!

JANUARY 18

God's Fingerprints Are Everywhere

Read Exodus 8–10

Then the magicians said to Pharaoh, "This is the finger of God." But Pharaoh's heart was hardened, and he would not listen to them, as the LORD had said. —Exodus 8:19

IN MY FOURTH year of teaching, budget cutbacks led to my losing my job. As summer waned without another offer, I wondered what God had in mind. Then I learned two English teachers decided to retire . . . and a position opened up. The site principal hired me for the temporary spot, then the permanent position. Instead of a half hour commute, I was only ninety seconds from my school. Instead of being a half hour away from my kids, I was in the school with them.

Sometimes God's fingerprints are all over our circumstances. God led his people to Egypt to save them from a famine, then he guided them out when they were oppressed.

Even today when life's details fall into place or when a seemingly tough turn of events leads to something better than we'd ever imagined, we begin to see God always has a better plan. We simply have to wait for his perfect timing.

Lord, the circumstances of my life filter through your hands. Some of those situations might be wonderful; some might be hard. But I know you have a purpose for all of that, and I pray my witness honors you.

Keep Looking Up!

We are not victims of circumstances but vessels of God's grace.

JANUARY 19

We Can Memorialize God's Goodness

Read Exodus 11–13

> This is a day you are to commemorate; for the generations to come you shall celebrate it as a festival to the Lord—a lasting ordinance.
>
> —Exodus 12:14 NIV

WHEN I WORKED for a daily newspaper years ago, the editor explained that the paper would never print the expression "first annual." He said that an event is not annual until it has at least existed one year. "We don't know if it will be an annual event until it has occurred at least once before," he said.

But perhaps there is scriptural precedence for a "first annual" event. The Lord told Moses the Passover would be a memorial day for all the following generations. And the Lord even explained in detail how the Jews would later observe the Passover.

We too can memorialize special days in our lives when we have seen evidence that God has watched over and protected us. Just telling our stories of God's movement in our lives to our children and theirs can leave a legacy of faith.

Lord, there are countless days I can recall when I sensed your intervening hand so as to prevent disaster. And I am sure there are many more of which I never even knew. When those instances come to mind, may I remember to thank you and give you praise.

Keep Looking Up!

We can create memorial days that testify to the Lord's faithful protection of us.

JANUARY 20

God Fights for Us

Read Exodus 14–16

The LORD will fight for you, and you have only to be silent.
—Exodus 14:14

I HADN'T KNOWN a boy was bullying my son in high school until I heard the boy call my son names. Bullies typically keep their behavior under the official school radar, but I happened to hear the unkind remarks in the gym before a school assembly and warned the boy not to do it again. Or course my son was embarrassed when his teacher mom intervened, but protecting any student from bullying was my job.

God is our protector. When the Israelites saw that the Egyptians were about to overtake them, Moses assured them that the Lord would do battle for them. The Hebrews only needed to stop complaining and be silent before God. Despite their complaints, God parted the Red Sea for the Hebrews' escape.

The Lord does not want us to take abuse or cruelty from others, and we can trust him to show us how to defend ourselves and to help us deal with situations of injustice.

Lord, sometimes life is a battle. In those times of struggle, though, I will look to you in hopeful expectancy that you will fight for me in the heavenlies and bring about a victory on my behalf.

Keep Looking Up!

God will help us defend ourselves.

JANUARY 21

God Loves Arm Lifters

Read Exodus 17–20

When Moses' hands grew tired, they took a stone and put it under him and he sat on it. Aaron and Hur held his hands up—one on one side, one on the other—so that his hands remained steady till sunset. —Exodus 17:12 NIV

I WAS EXHAUSTED. I had taught my classes, coordinated hours of senior project presentations after school, and navigated the needs of my own four kids. As I drove home, I wondered, *What's for dinner?*

That question was quickly answered when I opened the front door . . . and smelled what seemed to be pot roast, affirmed with the dishes on the kitchen counter. My friend June had struck again. She always knew when to lend a helping hand.

We all grow weary at times. On those days we need arm lifters. In one of the Israelites' battles, they prevailed against the enemy as long as Moses kept his hands lifted. At one point when he grew weary, Aaron or Hur gave him a rock to sit on and helped Moses keep his hands up as he held the staff of God.

With the Lord's help, we can hold one another up with prayer or even pot roast.

Lord, thank you for those arm lifters who have held me up in tough seasons. Make me aware, Father, of those around me who need practical help or just encouragement to keep them going.

Keep Looking Up!

Even just a simple thinking-of-you note can encourage a friend.

JANUARY 22

God Gave Us Rest

Read Exodus 21–23

Six days you shall do your work, but on the seventh day you shall rest. —Exodus 23:12

I REMEMBER THE year my dad learned the department store he managed would open on Sundays. Boy, was my normally sweet-spirited father unhappy. Our family reserved Sundays for singing with the church choir, worshiping God, attending Sunday school, and relaxing with family fun. Never work or even shopping.

The practice of working on Sundays was a life shift of culture decades ago. But many, both then and now, are required to work on Sundays, such as my husband, who has to tend to and feed his beef cattle. No matter what day of the week, we can choose to set aside time for worship in community and for rest, reflection, and appreciation of all God has given us.

God gave us a day of rest as a gift for us to enjoy and worship him. We can withdraw from normal work routines and enjoy creation, just as he rested on the seventh day. Rest makes us whole again.

Lord, thank you for rest. May I be mindful of this weekly opportunity to pull away from the world and its work and cares, seek you, and allow physical restoration to settle over and into me.

Keep Looking Up!

Rest fills our empty reservoir when we seek God.

God's Glory Is Powerful

Read Exodus 24–27

In the view of the Israelites below, the Glory of GOD looked like a raging fire at the top of the mountain. —Exodus 24:17 MSG

FIRE ON THE mountain is not something new to us. Our county in northern California is 72 percent national forest, and we have lived through several major forest fires, including one that devastated one million acres of forest. Typically, those fires creep or race in jagged lines down and up mountainsides—fearful sights that bring loss.

I imagine awe and fear settled into Moses as he climbed up 7,497 feet of Mount Sinai to meet with the Lord God—while all others waited below, watching the fire-like glory of God. Watching a fire is humbling. It puts into perspective the power of God versus our own limited abilities.

I do not know why natural disasters occur. We have even experienced fire on our ranch property. It's hard and tough to recover from. But we have found that the same God of power is also our Comforter and our Strength for such times.

Lord God, into your glory you invite me. May I step willingly into your plans and your presence every single day—ready to display your glory to others around me.

Keep Looking Up!

We need not be afraid of God's powerful nature because he is also our Comforter and our Strength.

JANUARY 24

God Leads Us to Our Home

Read Exodus 28–30

And they shall know that I am the LORD their God, who brought them out of the land of Egypt that I might dwell among them. I am the LORD their God. —Exodus 29:46

SOME GET THEIR dream houses, but our first home was not dreamy. The hundred-year-old farmhouse in the middle of a wheat farm lay miles south of Fort Riley, Kansas, where my husband served in the army. The prior tenants painted shocking pink and dark turquoise over layers of peeling wallpaper and left dog messes in the enclosed porch. But we turned it into a lovely retreat away from the busyness of the large military fort.

While our homes may be restful, our best dwelling place is with the Lord. The people of Israel eventually learned that God had their best interests in mind when he led them out of slavery in Egypt. Yes, they would enter the promised land, but they also would learn that the Lord himself would dwell among them.

God leads us from place to place, but even when the surroundings don't look especially appealing, we can find our home in him there.

Lead me, Lord. Lead me to whatever place you intend for me to call home. And lead my daily walk, too, God—as you take me step by step to my eventual heavenly home.

Keep Looking Up!

Our best dwelling place is with God.

JANUARY 25

Time with God Is a Mountaintop Experience

Read Exodus 31–34

Thus the LORD used to speak to Moses face to face, as a man speaks to his friend. —Exodus 33:11

I LOVE HOSPITALITY. My favorite activity is having friends and family over for a good meal and rich, face-to-face conversation. We laugh together and get caught up on the details of each other's lives. Just a couple hours together can provide quality time for us to get below the surface hellos and how-are-yous to heart matters—for which we can support one another in prayer.

We can also enjoy God's companionship. Moses did life in partnership with the Lord God, who spoke to Moses on numerous trips on Mount Sinai. The longest of those visits was forty days and nights. You can learn a lot about a person in forty days of isolation together. The amazing thing is that God desires to meet with us just as he did with Moses.

Real friendships develop in person. Rich conversations ensue as we do life together. The same is true for our relationship with God as we seek his presence for direction and adoration.

Lord God, my heart is lightened when I meet with you. You bring clarity out of my confusion. You pass along peace to ease my anxiety. And you provide companionship when I feel alone. Thank you for your presence, God.

Keep Looking Up!

Alone time with God is like a mountaintop experience.

JANUARY 26

Many Hands Make God's Work Light

Read Exodus 35–37

All the men and women, the people of Israel, whose heart moved them to bring anything for the work that the LORD had commanded by Moses to be done brought it as a freewill offering to the LORD.
—Exodus 35:29

MANY YEARS AGO, friends of ours decided to completely renovate our little country church. Together, we refinished the floors and wooden pews, installed new light fixtures, repaired and painted walls, added wooden paneling, crafted wooden trim, and added decorative touches. It was a complete facelift—a delightful project as we all worked together on tasks for which we were best equipped.

That massive project proved to be a great example of how we can use our gifts and talents for kingdom work. This was true also when the Israelites created the tabernacle—the people's portable worship center—to the Lord's specifications. The people freely gave of their time, talents, and treasure.

We still can do that today. Sunday mornings in churches everywhere require many hands to provide music, sound, video effects, teaching, greeting, and more. And hearts become one as we work together.

Lord God, while I may feel I do not have much to offer a community of believers, I know that you have given me certain spiritual gifts and talents. Help me step out in faith and boldness to offer my service for your kingdom's work.

Keep Looking Up!

Serving others is an opportunity to be God's hands and feet here on earth.

JANUARY 27

Our Work Is an Offering to God

Read Exodus 38–40

That completed the work of The Dwelling, the Tent of Meeting. The People of Israel did what GOD had commanded Moses. They did it all. —Exodus 39:32 MSG

I CAN ONLY remember my kindhearted dad chewing me out as a kid a couple times. One of those times was when I had offered to do the dinner dishes and rushed through that chore, leaving a soapy mess and still-dirty counters behind me.

When Dad pointed out my unfinished job, he said, "When you do a job, do it right the first time."

It's easy to say yes to a volunteer job. The work seems noble at first and even perhaps exciting. But the responsibilities can grow tedious, and we can find excuses to slip away.

But the people of God were faithful to complete the tabernacle, and Moses took note that the people finished all of the work. The people who had continually criticized and fought with Moses finally worked together to accomplish a community worship center. Their work as an act of obedience was their offering to God. And so is ours.

Lord, I want to be a person who is good for her word, so may I seriously and prayerfully consider what I say yes to. And may my work be worthy of your name.

Keep Looking Up!

My work can be a love offering to the Lord.

JANUARY 28

The Lord Is Holy

Read Leviticus 1–4

And the priest shall make atonement for him for the sin which he has committed, and he shall be forgiven. —Leviticus 4:35

THINGS HAD NOT gone well the day before. A student had talked back to me—and that affected not only the tenor of the classroom but also my feelings. But shortly after I got to school the next day, the boy walked up with flowers. "I'm sorry, Mrs. McHenry. I shouldn't have mouthed off like that."

We chatted a minute. I said it was all right . . . and it really was. He didn't have to give me the flowers, but they showed he was truly sincere.

Before Jesus came to earth, God required the equivalent of flowers before he could forgive or accept anyone who had sinned (that's all of us). Since the unholy cannot approach the holy God, the people gave gifts of grain, oil, salt, and animals of various kinds. It was a tremendous burden but well worth the cost to approach our magnificent God. However, when Jesus went to the cross, his sacrifice made it possible for unholy us to approach our holy God. We simply need to repent of our sins, accept his gift of salvation, and put our faith in him.

God, when I only think of you as my friend, I can lose sight that you are the holy Lord Most High. May I ever be mindful of the gift you made of your Son, Jesus, and the sacrifice that he made in my behalf.

Keep Looking Up!

We can be thankful for Christ's sacrifice, which allows us to approach our holy God.

JANUARY 29

God Provides a Way for Atonement

Read Leviticus 5–7

In this way the priest will make atonement for them before the LORD, and they will be forgiven for any of the things they did that made them guilty. —Leviticus 6:7 NIV

I PLOPPED A giant poinsettia on Delores's desk in her history classroom.

"Wow! What's this for?" she asked.

"I just wanted you to feel welcome," I said. "I sensed I've not been kind to you since you started teaching here. I have missed my friend, your predecessor, and I failed to really see you and the strengths you bring to our faculty. I am so sorry, Delores. I want to be your friend and support you."

As the years progressed, we did become strong teaching partners—and Delores poured many kindnesses my way, including a hallway rally of students and teachers who cheered me during a hard season of grief.

When we atone for our sins, we make reparation—like a gift to a country after a war. We give of ourselves in confession and determine, with Jesus's help, to step into a different, better direction.

Lord God, when I falter in my faith and fall short, I know that I need to confess my sin. Help me recognize poor decisions before I get into a mess, so my life brings you honor and glory.

Keep Looking Up!

When we make mistakes, we can apologize and determine to do better, with Jesus's help.

God's Glory Shows Up with Blessings

Read Leviticus 8–10

Then Aaron lifted his hands toward the people and blessed them.
—Leviticus 9:22 NIV

A WOMAN BLESSED me in Lowe's a couple years ago. I was nursing a dislocated shoulder by keeping it in a sling, and she noticed.

"Could I pray for you?" Her smile invited me into instant friendship.

"Of course," I said.

She proceeded to ask God to not only heal me but also bless me. And today that shoulder is stronger than the other one.

We have the ability to bless others we meet as we are on the go—with a prayer, with quick "bless you" words, with kind conversation, and with simple acts of kindness.

When Moses's brother, Aaron, the priest, blessed the Israelites, they saw the sudden presence of God's glory. The people shouted for joy and fell face down in what must have been an overwhelming sense of awe.

We can be God's ambassadors by blessing others with simple kindnesses. It just takes a minute to brighten someone's day.

Lord, make me a blessing to someone today. Help me look past my own needs to see the needs of others around me and bless them with words or little helps.

Keep Looking Up!

Jesus can shine through me when I bless others.

JANUARY 31

Our God Is Holy

Read Leviticus 11–13

For I am the LORD who brought you up out of the land of Egypt to be your God. You shall therefore be holy, for I am holy.

—Leviticus 11:45

ALL FOUR KIDS nagged me during the three-hour trip to my parents' place.

"Can we stop for ice cream?"

"I want to look at the lake!"

"Mom, we need more snacks."

No was the answer each time.

As we approached one of the final crossroads, little Bethany said, "Mom, can we stop to see the cows?" An old dairy farm sat just beyond the intersection.

The others chimed, "C'mon, Mom!"

I sensed God nudging me to stop, and just as I touched the pedal, a car sped through the intersection right in front of us. The driver had run his stop sign, while I did not have one.

Moments like that make us stop and reflect. We get a glimpse of God's sovereignty, power, and holiness—his incredible presence. While accidents are a natural part of our rushing world, we will also experience times of his protection that help us better understand his greatness and sovereignty. This helps us make the right choices that will honor him.

Lord, I want to be my best for you. You are my Creator and my Savior. You are worthy of my worship. Help me choose rightly today, so that you are honored.

Keep Looking Up!

Holiness is choosing God's way.

FEBRUARY 1

Fasting Shifts Our Gaze to God

Read Leviticus 14–16

It is a Sabbath of all Sabbaths. You must fast. It is a perpetual ordinance. —Leviticus 16:31 MSG

WE HEAR OF all kinds of fasts—periods of time in which someone abstains from something, most often food or drink. Typically, people fast to lose weight—so the focus is on oneself.

Biblical fasts are different because the focus shifts to God and seeking his will. Fasting provides additional time apart from food preparation to pray for God's provision and power to be manifested through our lives. Recently, a group of prayer leaders in California prayed during the forty days prior to an election—seeking God's will for the state.

We can fast for many reasons: to seek freedom from addiction, to find a problem's solution, or to prepare for revival. I fast and pray when I need direction or when a loved one is struggling. Fasting helps us to focus less on ourselves and become more attentive to God.

It shifts our gaze from inward to upward.

Lord, you directed the Israelites to fast as part of a process of atonement. Guide my gaze from myself and my seemingly continual needs to focus on you as I pray and when I fast.

Keep Looking Up!

Fasting sets us apart from routines to focus on God.

FEBRUARY 2

God Wants Us to Honor Our Elderly

Read Leviticus 17–19

Show respect to the aged; honor the presence of an elder; fear your God. I am GOD. —Leviticus 19:32 MSG

MY HUSBAND, CRAIG, still misses Elmer—a lifelong rancher here in the Sierra Valley, who was a father figure for him. Elmer thought Craig was nuts for leaving his law practice and going into cattle ranching and hay farming. But when Craig had a question about cattle or equipment, he would talk to Elmer, who offered both fatherly and farmer-ly counsel.

Folks often discount the elderly and even overlook them. I've seen this when I take my mom to a restaurant when the waitress asks me what she wants. "Could you ask her?" I'll say.

But God's Word teaches us to demonstrate respect and to honor those advanced in years. We can do this by rising when they enter the room, listening to their stories, helping them with simple needs, and speaking kindly to them.

The elderly in our communities have a breadth of wisdom, and they love sharing their experience, memories, and knowledge.

Lord God, help me to tangibly demonstrate appreciation to the elderly you place in my life. May I have the patience to listen, kindness to help with their needs, and compassion to express value and respect to them.

Keep Looking Up!

Engaging a senior in conversation can show our respect and honor.

FEBRUARY 3

We Can Access God's Provision

Read Leviticus 20–21

But I have said to you, "You shall inherit their land, and I will give it to you to possess, a land flowing with milk and honey." I am the LORD your God, who has separated you from the peoples.

—Leviticus 20:24

SWISS DAIRYMEN SETTLED the Sierra Valley in the 1800s—probably because it looked much like their homeland. Today's descendants now raise beef cattle. Unlike them, my husband, Craig, is a first-generation rancher, and we quickly found out that ranching and farming are hard work.

The Bible says that God gave the Israelites a land flowing with milk and honey, which sounds easy. Except it probably wasn't. When I toured Israel, our guide said what was called "honey" in the Bible was more likely date sugar from the native date palms . . . the very tall date palm trees that covered long stretches of desert. I can only imagine how hard it was to retrieve the dates and then process them.

And so it goes in our lives as well. God provides the opportunity, but we harvest and honor his gift with our hard work.

Lord, thank you for leading me to opportunities that reap provision for my family and me. May I be mindful of your trust in my abilities and my sense of dedication to steward well your gracious gifts.

Keep Looking Up!

Abundance comes through the filter of God's fingers.

FEBRUARY 4

God Deserves Our Thanks

Read Leviticus 22–23

When you sacrifice a thank offering to the Lord, sacrifice it in such a way that it will be accepted on your behalf. —Leviticus 22:29 NIV

THE BIG MEAL was finally ready—meat sliced, potatoes mashed, salad tossed. But I said, "Okay, now I would like each of you to offer a prayer of thanks before you dig in."

The four kids' jaws and shoulders dropped, and there was more than one sigh. But prayers came out quickly. It was a bit manipulative of me—to require their sacrifice of thanksgiving before they could eat—but their prayers were sincere if not a bit hurried.

The book of Leviticus spells out the various duties for the Levites, those who were responsible for worship practices in the tabernacle, the Israelites' movable worship center. Offerings of livestock and field produce were made for many reasons—including thanksgiving.

Just as those offerings provided an opportunity to pause and recognize the Lord God, thanksgiving and praise are our opportunities today to remember God's gracious provision for everything and everyone in our lives.

Lord, thank you for the opportunity to pause in reflection for all the good in our lives—and even the struggles, too, as they bring us closer to you. May I ever be mindful of your grace-filled provision.

Keep Looking Up!

Being thankful is the easiest offering we can give.

FEBRUARY 5

God's Ways Are for My Security

Read Leviticus 24–25

Therefore you shall do my statutes and keep my rules and perform them, and then you will dwell in the land securely. —Leviticus 25:18

THE FIRST DAY of teaching was always a beast. I handed out the syllabus to each class and went through all the materials, routines, and rules. Eyes rolled. Mouths yawned. Bodies squirmed in their chairs.

However, soon those parameters to create a safe space geared toward inquiry and discussion became routines, and those juniors and seniors learned I would be their best advocate and co-laborer as they began to envision their post-secondary futures.

The Lord God set parameters too—laws for conduct and worship. Lots of basics had to be covered so the Israelites could understand that God was much more than their buddy and that laws helped create a safe community so they could work and fight as one nation for each other's benefit.

Some say rules are made to be broken, but if we consider God's rules, we see that they are there for our good.

Lord, I am thankful for laws—yours and others'—that are meant for my good. May I model compliance and obedience as a means to show respect for you and other authorities in my life, so that others see you through me.

Keep Looking Up!

I am safe and secure within God's sanctuary.

FEBRUARY 6

God Is on Patrol

Read Leviticus 26–27

> I'll set up my residence in your neighborhood; I won't avoid or shun you; I'll stroll through your streets. I'll be your God; you'll be my people. —Leviticus 26:11–12 MSG

EVEN THOUGH WE live on a state highway, I don't worry about safety. I don't always lock my car, and if I forget to lock up the house, I don't fret. Because the residents of our area look out for one another, a loose dog creates the greatest anxiety for this prayerwalker.

Ultimately, I can rest securely, knowing God is on patrol, not only in my neighborhood but also in my life. That does not mean I have avoided all accidents or unkind remarks. It does mean that I am God's child, and he promises to work things out for my good. He has taken up residence within me, so peace rather than fear controls my emotions.

I love the figurative image of God walking among his people. It not only implies safety and protection but also suggests companionship. He is not an aloof God who keeps his distance. He is loving and forgiving, and his residence with those who believe is a reassuring comfort.

Lord God, thank you for taking up residence in my life. You bring peace that passes all human comprehension, even in difficult circumstances. I trust in you through Jesus, your Son.

Keep Looking Up!

With God on watch, I can rest securely.

FEBRUARY 7

We All Count to God

Read Numbers 1–2

> Take a census of all the congregation of the people of Israel, by clans, by fathers' houses, according to the number of names, every male, head by head. —Numbers 1:2

DO YOU COUNT things? Or do you have someone in your family who does? I do. I think I got it from my father, who worked with numbers his whole life.

On field trips I counted students before we left school and before leaving our destination for school. Every person counted. I did not want to leave anyone behind.

The Lord told Moses to count the people before they went into the promised land—important for several reasons. The people had to settle in the various territories by family tribe. The leaders needed to know how many men could serve in the army. And perhaps the census also provided a written record for history's sake.

Still today, God counts his people, and then he counts the number of hairs on each of our heads. I count, and you count. We all count in his kingdom.

Lord, it encourages me to know that you count me as one of your own. You sought me, you revealed yourself to me, and you numbered me as your child. May I never lose sight of your care and love for me.

Keep Looking Up!

Each of us counts to God.

FEBRUARY 8

Ministers Are Special to God

Read Numbers 3–4

According to the commandment of the Lord through Moses they were listed, each one with his task of serving or carrying. Thus they were listed by him, as the Lord commanded Moses. —Numbers 4:49

MY BACK SURGERY was scheduled for six in the morning, and moments before I was wheeled into the surgical unit, I saw a familiar face.

Pastor Ron.

"How did you find me?"

His smile easily moved into a laugh. "It wasn't easy."

Somehow he had located me in the bowels of the hospital and gotten permission to step into the prep room to pray for me.

Church pastors have one of the most challenging jobs on this earth. They are tasked with preaching a brilliant sermon one or more times a week. They counsel those struggling with marriage and addiction and more. They keep staff and volunteers moving forward and encouraged. And they visit the sick and weary.

The Lord made special provision for such folks, the priestly tribe, the Levites. And today we have the opportunity and privilege to provide for those who minister to us.

Lord, may I ever be mindful of ways to support my church and its staff financially and emotionally. Those who serve you can be easily discouraged, even though they work so very hard. Make me aware of ways I can help.

Keep Looking Up!

A simple note of encouragement can lift up a discouraged pastor.

FEBRUARY 9

God Is the Blessing

Read Numbers 5–6

The Lord bless you and keep you; the Lord make his face to shine upon you and be gracious to you; the Lord lift up his countenance upon you and give you peace. —Numbers 6:24–26

PEOPLE HAD VARIOUS ways of not going stir crazy during the recent pandemic. I did yard work. Hacking away at shrubbery that should have been hacked many moons before. Trimming trees. Removing pine needles and other debris. Moving river rock into place over a wide expanse of the yard.

And while I did that work, which I prefer to call a *workout*, I sang a song called "The Blessing." Over and over I sang that blessing for each of our children, for our grandkids, and for other family members. The workout passed, the front yard began to look friendly again, and thankfulness replaced my woe-is-me mindset.

In one of the earliest blessings, God allowed his name to be placed over the people of Israel. His presence with them was the blessing . . . just as I prayed it would be for my family.

Lord God, your presence in my life is a privilege and a blessing for me. I pray that my loved ones too would understand that pursuing a relationship with you is the greatest joy that they can experience in their lives.

Keep Looking Up!

We can pray this blessing over our loved ones each day.

FEBRUARY 10

God Speaks to Us

Read Numbers 7

When Moses entered the tent of meeting to speak with the LORD, he heard the voice speaking to him from between the two cherubim above the atonement cover on the ark of the covenant law. In this way the LORD spoke to him. —Numbers 7:89 NIV

THE SPEAKER AT the women's retreat ended her presentation with a charge. "Go find a rock, sit on it, and wait until God speaks to you."

Kind of shaking my head, I headed out into the woods. Sitting on a large rock, I prayed, *Lord, now what?*

Not too long later I heard, *I want you to write for me*. It wasn't an audible voice, but an undeniable certainty in my soul: God had spoken to me. More than three decades later I am still pursuing that calling on my life.

God's Word is filled with stories about the Lord speaking specific direction to his people—from Adam and Eve in Genesis to John in Revelation. When we quiet our hearts, minds, and souls, and wait expectantly, God provides clarity through the Bible or through prayer. It's a posture that keeps us looking up!

Lord, thank you for the privilege of receiving direction from you for my daily life. I am willing and open to whatever you have for me to do. I trust you for the small steps as well as the larger leaps because you never lead me astray.

Keep Looking Up!

**When we quietly wait for God,
he directs our steps.**

FEBRUARY 11

God Is Our Guide

Read Numbers 8–10

Whenever the cloud lifted from over the sacred tent, the people of Israel would break camp and follow it. And wherever the cloud settled, the people of Israel would set up camp. —Numbers 9:17 NLT

WE JOKE ABOUT how we used to get from one place to another without navigational devices. Someday someone might look through our things and remark, "Wow, they used to put maps on paper?"

Yes, and those paper maps got us across the United States many times. Even when devices are not confusing, I say, "Just follow the signs." Sometimes, though, I've wished for a personal guide.

The Israelites had such a navigator: the Lord God. When the cloud lifted, the people set out. When it descended like fire at night, the people camped out. Moving more than a million people from Egypt to the promised land would have been about impossible except that the Lord provided a supernatural navigational system.

Even when circumstances seem to cloud our directional sense, prayer and God's Word can guide our steps.

Lord, keep me from wandering aimlessly. Help me know from day to day what you would have me do so I can proceed with confidence that only you can provide.

Keep Looking Up!

God can lead us right through our cloudy circumstances.

FEBRUARY 12

God Helps Us Delegate

Read Numbers 11–13

I will come down and speak with you there, and I will take some of the power of the Spirit that is on you and put it on them. They will share the burden of the people with you so that you will not have to carry it alone. —Numbers 11:17 NIV

I WORKED A full-time job teaching English. I took on numerous responsibilities in our church. And I had four kids—the oldest in driver's training, the youngest in potty training. As I sat at my desk one day after school, staring at the load of papers to grade, I knew I could not handle everything that week.

I rested my head onto my arms and prayed, *Lord, I cannot do it all. Please send help.*

Just then Mari walked through the door. "Mrs. McHenry, I was wondering if I could do something for extra credit."

I looked at her, and I looked at my stack of papers. "How'd you like to grade some papers?"

Moses too was overwhelmed with responsibilities more than once. Each time, though, God provided ways for him to delegate his work. From him we learn that we simply need to cry out to God and then humbly accept the help.

God, I don't know why I get myself overcommitted the way I do, but I often take on more than I should. When that happens, please help me admit I cannot do it all, seek out your help, and then be willing to accept that assistance.

Keep Looking Up!

We can simplify our lives by delegating work to willing helpers.

FEBRUARY 13

God Rewards Our Obedience

Read Numbers 14–15

If the LORD delights in us, he will bring us into this land and give it to us, a land that flows with milk and honey. —Numbers 14:8

MY OLDEST OFTEN wanted to have friends sleep over, and that was always welcome, with one condition: her room had to be clean. We didn't give out extra privileges if she hadn't met basic responsibilities. Grumbling was sometimes a response, but my husband and I held firm.

The Israelites grumbled a lot. They complained about food and water, and when God provided both, they complained for the lack of variety. Bottom line, they didn't trust God and didn't follow his direction. Consequently, God did not allow the first generation of people who had left Egypt to enter the promised land. This may seem harsh, but moving into territories that others occupied would require an army of men willing to follow the Lord's specific directions.

Sometimes in my life I'll sense that I'm not moving forward—that I'm only hitting frustrating roadblocks instead. When I recognize my own lack of obedience and discipline and change course, roads seem to open up again. Faithfulness keeps us moving forward.

Lord, I am sorry that I grumble and complain when I face obstacles. Perhaps they are there to teach me something or cause me to reflect inward. May my response always sync with your desires.

Keep Looking Up!

When we have a grumbling spirit, it's time for a heart check.

FEBRUARY 14

God Is My Portion

Read Numbers 16–18

I am your portion and your inheritance among the people of Israel.
—Numbers 18:20

DIVIDING UP DESSERTS among four children was always a challenge. Eventually I learned to have one kid cut the cake or pie and allow the others to choose before that person did. Each wanted their rightful portion.

Among the twelve tribes of Israel, there was one tribe that received no portion of land when the Israelites entered the promised land: the Levites. They were the priestly tribe that would never own property. Cities were reserved for them, but inheritance was never an issue—they could only inherit the responsibilities to supervise religious duties in the tabernacle, including offerings, cleansings, and dedication ceremonies. The Lord was their inheritance. While the others got land, the Lord was the Levites' portion.

The Lord is the best of anything in my life. Even without an inheritance of land or wealth, I have found he is enough, and he will take care of me.

Lord, you have blessed me with much—and for all that I have I am grateful. As I move ahead through the years, may my heart take less pleasure in the accoutrements of life and find that you are enough.

Keep Looking Up!

God is our portion!

God's Word Refreshes Us

Read Numbers 19–21

Then Israel sang this song: "Spring up, O well!—Sing to it!—the well that the princes made, that the nobles of the people dug, with the scepter and with their staffs." —Numbers 21:17–18

THE ATHLETES OF our high school of one hundred students travel long distances for games—often several hours. Over the years their parents and coaches have depended on the mom-and-pop watering holes along the way. We all need refreshment—physical and otherwise.

The weary Israelites experienced arduous travel—from well to spring to well on their journey through the desert to the promised land. More than a million people depended upon that water to quench their thirst, and finding water in desert lands was a continual struggle.

We may also feel as though we are journeying from well to spring to well. Without the daily refreshment from God's Word, we can feel spiritually parched if we attempt to wander on our own. But we can experience an oasis of renewal and strength when we read his Word.

Lord, just as water quenches my thirst and refreshes my whole body, your Word is delightful refreshment for my heart, mind, and soul. May that living water always provide just the encouragement and exhortation I need.

Keep Looking Up!

Following a daily reading plan in the Bible helps us navigate through life.

FEBRUARY 16

God Is Faithful

Read Numbers 22–24

> God is not man, that he should lie, or a son of man, that he should change his mind. Has he said, and will he not do it? Or has he spoken, and will he not fulfill it? —Numbers 23:19

I LOVED TEACHING classic literature to high school students. The issues and quotables provided ample opportunities to discuss important life questions relating to all kinds of subjects. One of my favorite quotes is found at the end of *A Christmas Carol* by Charles Dickens: "Scrooge was better than his word. He did it all, and infinitely more." The character Scrooge experienced a dramatic life change that caused him to shift from greediness to generosity. When we are good for our word, we do all we have agreed to do. When we are better than our word, we exceed our commitment.

God is good for his word, and this has been proven through his Word, the Bible. He fulfills his promises. His words and actions through the recorded interactions throughout the ages demonstrate his faithfulness to love us, forgive and redeem us, guide us, and have a relationship with us.

Lord, you have been faithful from generation to generation. I can see that in the stories of the men and women of your Word, so I know that you will continue to be faithful in my family's lives as well.

Keep Looking Up!

We can trust in God's promises.

FEBRUARY 17

God Evens the Score

Read Numbers 25–26

> To a larger group give a larger inheritance, and to a smaller group a smaller one; each is to receive its inheritance according to the number of those listed. —Numbers 26:54 NIV

SOME STUDENTS USED to tell me they were not good at math, but when grades were posted, some questioned the numbers. I never really assigned grades: I just let the computer do the math.

Equity is always a challenging concept, and such was true for the Israelites. Before they entered the promised land, God told Moses to take a new census of the younger generation who would enter the promised land. The larger tribes would get a greater proportion of the land, while the small tribes got a smaller proportion. Final decisions of placement were made by lot—by a flip of the coin, we would say. We can see this division for ourselves on Bible maps of the twelve tribes. Some areas are clearly larger than others.

We can get caught up in equity and justice issues, but ultimately our faith should lead us to a place where we trust God for the outcome. No matter how people treat us, God will even out the score . . . or grade.

Lord, I get frustrated when I am discounted as a person or even flagrantly slighted. I can trust, though, that you love me, value me, and watch over me.

Keep Looking Up!

When we experience inequity, we can trust God to work it out.

FEBRUARY 18

God Sees Injustice

Read Numbers 27–29

And the LORD said to Moses, "The daughters of Zelophehad are right. You shall give them possession of an inheritance among their father's brothers and transfer the inheritance of their father to them." —Numbers 27:6–7

THE FIRST TIME I felt discrimination as a woman I was twenty-seven and had been a staff writer at a company for two years when a young man was hired right out of college. When he asked me what I was being paid, I learned his salary was greater than mine, even though I had the same education and five years of work experience. Despite the inequity, I decided not to say anything.

The five daughters of Zelophehad felt a similar injustice. They stood to inherit no property because they were women. Moses and others in authority heard their case and then took it to the Lord in prayer. The Lord determined the daughters could possess their father's inheritance.

Simply because we are Christians does not mean we must suffer silently when we experience or view an injustice. We can advocate for ourselves or others, ultimately trusting God for the outcome.

Lord, you are the just judge, and even when life is not fair, I can pray for your intervention—either through the earthly channels or through the spiritual realm. You are trustworthy, no matter the outcome.

Keep Looking Up!

Respectfully speaking up often can effect change in unjust situations.

God Values Our Commitment

Read Numbers 30–32

This is what the LORD has commanded. If a man vows a vow to the LORD, or swears an oath to bind himself by a pledge, he shall not break his word. He shall do according to all that proceeds out of his mouth. —Numbers 30:1–2

OUR CHILDREN RECENTLY have been asking us how we have made our marriage last so long.

"Stubbornness," I joked.

"The covenant," my husband said.

We could have broken our marriage agreement with each other at different points of struggle, but ultimately, we knew we couldn't break our agreement with God. We have trusted God and as we've drawn closer to him, we have grown closer to one another.

It's important to be a person of integrity. Moses taught the people of Israel the importance of being careful of what they promised and then keeping their word once given. When we don't live up to our commitments—including following God—our actions affect not only how people view us but how others view God. Daily I can decide to represent God well with carefully choosing my commitments and then faithfully honoring my word. And being true to not only my Word but also God's Word brings contentment and joy.

Lord, help me choose wisely as I make commitments in my life—to family, friends, employers, my church, and more. I truly want my actions to match the words that come out of my mouth.

Keep Looking Up!

Instead of rashly saying yes to any request, it is prudent to pray first.

FEBRUARY 20

God's Road May Not Be Easy

Read Numbers 33–36

Take possession of the land and settle in it, for I have given you the land to possess. —Numbers 33:53 NIV

MOVING IS NOT for the faint of heart. It requires logistics, endurance, and a positive outlook. Sometimes it takes time to settle into a new community. We joke that we're still newcomers because we've only lived in our town for forty years. But we have proven ourselves as contributors through elected office, volunteer service, and our careers.

The Israelites had a tough charge. Yes, God had given them Canaan. But the promised land was not vacant; other people groups already lived there. The Hebrews would have to fight for God's gift of the land.

While we might expect God's perfect plan to fall easily into place, often that is not the case. We may have to study hard, take risks, be diligent to take the right steps, and work hard to prove ourselves. In the end, though, following the Lord takes us to the place he wants us to be.

Lead me, Lord, to the place in life you have for me—whether that is a career or a new place to live. I understand that the circumstantial dominoes may not easily fall down, but I am willing to work hard for whatever you have for me.

Keep Looking Up!

If God has led us to a place, the people there have a place for us.

FEBRUARY 21

God Helps Us Get Unstuck

Read Deuteronomy 1–2

You've stayed long enough at this mountain. On your way now. Get moving. —Deuteronomy 1:6 MSG

FOR MANY YEARS I felt stuck in a career rut. I wasn't moving forward, mostly because I was fearful and had not been disciplined. So that year I chose *grit* as my word for the year. Actually, the word I had in mind was *sisu*, Finnish for a combination of determination, tenacity, grit, bravery, resilience, and hardiness. To make it through tough winters, the Finns of years gone by had to have sisu. To make it through several tough goals that required a rapid accumulation of technical knowledge, I needed sisu too. I had been sitting too long at a mountain of inactivity.

We do have seasons of feeling stuck, but we don't have to let fear, perceived incompetence, laziness, or lack of vision keep us from achieving goals. Instead, we simply can put one foot in front of the other, seek the Lord's help, and step into the challenge he lays before us.

Lord, I have let mental and emotional mountains make me feel incompetent. Be my guide, speak courage into me, and help me chip away at whatever it is I need to do to move forward with my life.

Keep Looking Up!

One way to move forward is to start with the simplest task first.

FEBRUARY 22

God Equips the Called

Read Deuteronomy 3–4

You shall not fear them, for it is the LORD your God who fights for you. —Deuteronomy 3:22

LEARNING HOW TO teach English at age thirty-seven was a fearsome task. I process information through writing, so I did not excel in standardized tests. A journalism major, I found remembering authors' and characters' names and book titles for two national exams formidable.

As I was stewing about that one day, I heard a knock on the door. Roxanne said, "I was driving by your house when God told me to stop and pray for you." A half hour later, I felt assured I would pass the tests . . . and after studying for two months, I did.

God also called Joshua to a fearful task: to lead Israel into occupied land. But God was on the Israelites' side, so Joshua simply had to trust him. The same is true for us today. We can trust God to equip us for whatever he calls us to do.

Lord, for some reason you birth callings into me that are not in my comfort zone. But I also see that each time you equip me for those challenges. So I know I can trust you for whatever you ask me to do, because you are on my side.

Keep Looking Up!

God will help us conquer our fears.

FEBRUARY 23

Love God, Love Others

Read Deuteronomy 5–8

Love the LORD your God with all your heart and with all your soul and with all your strength. —Deuteronomy 6:5 NIV

MY DAD OFTEN said, "There should just be one law: be nice." He reasoned that covered all kinds of offenses—from traffic laws to crimes. He got that, he said, from what has been called the greatest commandment.

When Jesus was asked what was the greatest commandment, he said, "Hear, O Israel: The Lord our God, the Lord is one. Love the Lord your God with all your heart and with all your soul and with all your mind and with all your strength" (Mark 12:29–30 NIV). It encapsulates the first four of the Ten Commandments, which govern how we view and treat God. Jesus added that the second greatest commandment is "Love your neighbor as yourself" (Mark 12:31 NIV). If we truly love God, we will strive to love his people well.

If we only do one thing well, loving God is the best choice because everything else will spring from that love.

Lord, may I always put you first in my life because then all other priorities in my life will be ordered and handled well. And may others see your love for them in me.

Keep Looking Up!

We can live out our love for God by extending love and grace to others.

FEBRUARY 24

God Is Our Praise

Read Deuteronomy 9–11

He's your praise! He's your God! He did all these tremendous, these staggering things that you saw with your own eyes.

—Deuteronomy 10:21 MSG

I FOUND GREAT joy seeing our kids graduate from high school and college. While commencement is a perennial rite of passage event, the steps across the stage always seemed miraculous to me, one for which I always praised God. Despite some struggles, each one finished well and then marched into adulthood.

Passages are important. The end of the Israelites' wanderings was a historical turning point. A full generation passed while they traipsed in the desert and struggled to follow God. Crossing over into the promised land signaled a return to Canaan, the land God had given Abraham. Formerly a people enslaved without a homeland, they could praise God in their ancestors' homeland again.

Just as the Hebrew people found their God and their nation home, we too can always find our place and praise in him.

Lord, you indeed are my praise. Your wonderful works in my life are too many to recount, but when I start listing them mentally, I cannot help but marvel at your grace and your goodness. I praise your holy name!

Keep Looking Up!

Praising God for his faithful character is the best way to start a day.

FEBRUARY 25

We Are His Treasured Possession

Read Deuteronomy 12–15

For you are a people holy to the LORD your God, and the LORD has chosen you to be a people for his treasured possession, out of all the peoples who are on the face of the earth. —Deuteronomy 14:2

I WAS ALMOST always the last kid picked for kickball on the playground. However, when I was in high school, my PE teacher chose me as a leader. I then excelled and even started the first girls' tennis team. Knowing someone values you encourages you to live up to that value.

God chose his people Israel to be those through whom he would make himself known and to whom he would bring the Savior, his Son, Jesus. A human evaluation of this people would have left them on the sidelines. They had forgotten God. They didn't want to leave slavery. They continually succumbed to fear, complained, and disobeyed the God who was saving them. He loved them anyway.

Our value is not based on what we do. God sees us as his treasured possession simply because we are his creation. We are his, and he has chosen all who believe in him for his team.

Lord, that you see me as your treasured possession is humbling. I mess up all the time. I do that which I should not do, and I do not do that which I should. Thank you for all your mercies and your everlasting love.

Keep Looking Up!

We can choose to see others as God's treasured possession too.

FEBRUARY 26

God Provides

Read Deuteronomy 16–19

The LORD your God will bless you in all your produce and in all the work of your hands, so that you will be altogether joyful.
—Deuteronomy 16:15

MY RANCHER HUSBAND experienced the blessing of what he calls *manna* last year. In addition to raising Angus beef cattle, he also produces his own hay to feed them. With California several years into drought conditions, that meant the hay crop probably would not be abundant. Not to mention the grazing land would likely be sparse.

But a strange thing happened. A native rye grass appeared throughout his fields, filling in where other crops were leaner—which effectively also kept weeds at bay. His hay crop more than doubled as a result, allowing him not only enough feed for his cattle but enough to sell to others—a first in many years.

Some years can be lean financially, can't they? But as we trust in God, we can find his presence brings us joy—no matter the season or situation.

Lord, thank you for your provision for my family and me throughout the years. We are ever mindful that you are the great supplier and sustainer of our lives and give you honor and praise for all that we have.

Keep Looking Up!

We can choose joy in abundance but also in lean times too because we have Jesus.

FEBRUARY 27

God Fights for Us

Read Deuteronomy 20–22

The LORD your God is he who goes with you to fight for you against your enemies, to give you the victory. —Deuteronomy 20:4

I SAT SILENTLY while a student's mother screamed every awful word possible at me. My principal and another teacher tried to reason with her, and the grade sheets I had provided spoke volumes, but she wasn't hearing . . . or seeing . . . any of it. A couple years later I taught another of her children, and the mom was effusive with kind words. Time had taught her the truth about my teaching abilities.

Some battles of life feel immense, as though an army has come against us. Moses warned the Israelites they would see armies bigger than theirs and those armies were equipped with horses and chariots—none of which Israel had.

In those overwhelming situations we can take a deep breath, look up in prayer, and remember that the Lord Emmanuel—which means "God with us"—will advocate for us in whatever challenge we face.

Lord, when seemingly impossible situations come up in my life, I know that I need not fear or even panic because you go with me not just to keep me company but also to fight for me. So I trust in your battle plan.

Keep Looking Up!

Prayer is a deep breath of time that helps us trust God for hard things.

FEBRUARY 28

God Turns a Curse into a Blessing

Read Deuteronomy 23–25

The LORD your God . . . turned the curse into a blessing for you, because the LORD your God loves you. —Deuteronomy 23:5 NIV

"FATTY FOUR EYES."

"Can't you do anything right?"

"You'll never amount to anything!"

Words we remember from childhood can hang over us like curses, and it's true that even adults can say words that sting us to the core. However, we need not live into those words as though they were prophecies.

God's Word speaks truth about who we are and who we will become. The Lord canceled the words of Balaam, a false prophet, and instead spoke blessing over the people of Israel who, as God's chosen people, would walk into the land he had chosen for them.

Even when we hear unkind words spoken over us, we can choose instead to recognize those words are not true and believe that God loves us, he has chosen us, he walks with us, and he fights for us. And God says we are worth the fight.

Lord, thank you for speaking blessing over my life. May I remember the truth you write about my identity and allow those words to cancel any negative thoughts that may surface in my mind.

Keep Looking Up!

Using God's Word to speak truth into us cancels the power of unkind words.

Offerings Acknowledge God's Blessings

Read Deuteronomy 26–27

You shall take some of the first of all the fruit of the ground, which you harvest from your land that the Lord your God is giving you, and you shall put it in a basket, and you shall go to the place that the Lord your God will choose, to make his name to dwell there.

—Deuteronomy 26:2

GIVING BRINGS ME much joy. I visited a church recently and wrote a check for the offering. Some minutes later the pastor announced that it was Giving Sunday—the one day of the year when each family would receive a one-hundred-dollar bill to bless someone else. That was exactly the amount of my check!

The pastor said, "You bless us with your gifts. Bless someone God puts on your heart."

With the laws God gave the people through Moses, the Lord established the practice of giving out of our resources with the concept of first fruit offerings. He told the people to take some of their best harvest and give it back to the Lord. When we give to our church, charities, and other people, we are giving back to God for all he has given us.

Lord, you bless me continually with your daily provision of my home and food on the table. I delight in giving back to you a portion of what you have entrusted to me, and I pray it blesses my church and community.

Keep Looking Up!

Paying for the order behind you in the fast-food drive-through is fun!

MARCH 2

God Blesses Us

Read Deuteronomy 28–29

All these blessings shall come upon you and overtake you, if you obey the voice of the LORD your God. —Deuteronomy 28:2

SOME SAY, "YOU can't go home again." But we were delighted when our daughter, her husband, and two young toddlers did just that. She needed bedrest for her third pregnancy and then lots of support when the baby came three months early. All went well, and I loved the sound of little feet coming up our back steps.

I think my husband would agree that was one of our favorite seasons. Those small faces in our home daily for many hours were blessing upon blessing. We are thankful those two grandchildren and their four siblings still live near us.

When we obey the Lord, his blessings overtake us. Even in hard times, when we seek God daily and follow him, our perspective changes. Instead of listing obvious troubles, we can count blessings instead. Gratitude can overshadow those troubles if we simply call good things to mind. That is a looking up outlook!

Lord, the first blessing is that you love me and call me your own. May I never lose sight of that so that obeying you is a natural response. Thank you for the many ways you have blessed my family and me.

Keep Looking Up!

A sweet way to fall asleep is by counting our blessings.

MARCH 3

God Goes before Us

Read Deuteronomy 30–32

The LORD your God himself will go over before you.
—Deuteronomy 31:3

I WAS BAPTIZED in the Jordan River several years ago. Just a few steps into the river, it was already over my waist. But when the carp started nibbling at my feet, I began laughing and jumping to fend them off—certainly not the solemn, holy moment I expected! Our tour guide also chuckled.

Even in the fall, that spot along the river was deep and wide—and I imagined the formidable challenge it presented to the Israelites as they faced the prospect of crossing it to the promised land. But they had the best tour guide: the Lord God, who went before them and caused the waters to divide when the people stepped into the water in faith.

We are not alone when we face seemingly uncrossable rivers of hardship. God not only is with us but also goes before us as we navigate those challenging circumstances of our lives.

Lord, thank you for going before me as I step into and through the difficulties of my life. You are the best guide; help me to trust your guidance and follow in your footsteps.

Keep Looking Up!

To demonstrate our trust in God, we must take the first step.

MARCH 4

Secure in God's Hands

Read Deuteronomy 33–34

Oh, how you love the people, all his holy ones are palmed in your left hand. They sit at your feet, honoring your teaching.

—Deuteronomy 33:3 MSG

MY GRANDDAUGHTER FAITH is crazy about birds—wild and otherwise. She studies bird books and has a green-cheeked conure named Violet. On a recent walk she identified the names of a dozen different kinds of birds as we strolled through town. She has a knack for catching them too. Somehow they seem to know she is a safe haven.

The Israelites had to learn that they were in the Lord God's safe hands as they traveled to the promised land. Despite the fact that they continually complained and disobeyed God, the Lord led them, loved them, and did not abandon them in the desert.

We too are secure in God's loving hands. He knows us, seeks us out, loves us, and assures us. Even when the storms of life bruise our figurative wings, our Father comforts us.

Lord, just as you count the sparrows and watch over them, you count me as your own and take care of me. Keep me safe and secure in your hands, Father, and assure me with your presence.

Keep Looking Up!

One way to experience God's security is to look daily for his promises in the Bible.

MARCH 5

Recall God's Faithfulness

Read Joshua 1–4

When your children ask in time to come, "What do those stones mean to you?" then you shall tell them that the waters of the Jordan were cut off before the ark of the covenant of the LORD. . . . So these stones shall be to the people of Israel a memorial forever.

—Joshua 4:6–7

YOU PROBABLY RECALL a story or two behind some of the objects in your home. When my mother downsized from her large home to a senior apartment, she gave Finnish family tapestries to me. As I see them hanging, they remind me of our family trip to see family farm roots in the Upper Peninsula of Michigan. The hangings are a memorial to my father and his hard-working, faithful family.

Memorials are a biblical concept. Jacob erected a stone pillar in Bethel as the remembrance of a powerful vision. In today's reading Joshua orchestrates a memorial with men from the twelve tribes after they had crossed the Jordan River. Samuel will later establish a large stone he calls *Ebenezer*—"God is help"—as a memorial to God's goodness in military victory.

We too can recall God's faithfulness with simple objects in our homes: a picture, a decorative object, or even a simple stone, our personal Ebenezer.

Lord, all your merciful acts are worth remembering. If I filled my home with markers remembering all your works, there wouldn't be enough room for me! Help me recall your many acts of goodness as a means to dispel fear.

Keep Looking Up!

Photos are great reminders of God's hand on our family over the years.

MARCH 6

God Breaks Down Walls

Read Joshua 5–7

So the people shouted, and the trumpets were blown. As soon as the people heard the sound of the trumpet, the people shouted a great shout, and the wall fell down flat, so that the people went up into the city, every man straight before him, and they captured the city. —Joshua 6:20

WHEN I BEGAN prayerwalking many years ago, I prayed against the influence of substance abuse in our town. Several times, persons in one neighborhood were busted for drug manufacturing, so I walked through that area, praying. A couple years ago the development was sold, and the new owners leveled the abandoned, broken-down buildings. The dramatic, positive change of landscape surprised and delighted many.

God often prompts me to pray seemingly impossible things for people's needs but also for systemic issues in our community—broken families, substance abuse, apathy, prejudice. I have seen other answers to those prayer requests over the years, and while I should not be surprised, often I find I am. If God could cause the walls of Jericho to fall with trumpet calls and a great shout, he can topple negative walls in my own community . . . and yours.

Lord, thank you for big answers to my prayers, which always increase my faith and cause me to pray even bigger. Help me see impossibilities as possibilities. Remind me to give those situations prayerfully over to you and then wait expectantly for you to move.

Keep Looking Up!

We can gain confidence by remembering God's miraculous answers from the past.

MARCH 7

God Provides the Win

Read Joshua 8–10

There was not a word of all that Moses commanded that Joshua did not read before all the assembly of Israel, and the women, and the little ones, and the sojourners who lived among them. —Joshua 8:35

WHEN PROFESSIONAL ATHLETES win their championships, they splash Gatorade and champagne over their coaches and celebrate with victory parties and parades. Authors often post online photos of themselves as they sign their book contracts and release their new books. Musicians hold television celebrations of big anniversaries of their careers.

We love a good victory party, but perhaps there's a better way to acknowledge God's goodness to us. After the major battle against the king and people of Ai, Joshua built an altar to the Lord and wrote out a copy of the law that Moses had given him. Then Joshua read aloud all the words God had given them—not just to the men who had fought in the battle but also to the women, children, and others traveling with them.

God daily provides reasons for us to celebrate. And when we recognize where our help comes from, we'll be filled with thanksgiving and awe-filled respect.

Lord, every day I recognize the mercies you extend to me. As I celebrate the big and small wins, God, may I ever be mindful that they have filtered through your grace-filled hands.

Keep Looking Up!

Reading the Bible aloud can be a celebratory response to the victories in our lives.

MARCH 8

God Can Use Us at Any Age

Read Joshua 11–13

Now Joshua was old and advanced in years, and the LORD said to him, "You are old and advanced in years, and there remains yet very much land to possess." —Joshua 13:1

AT A RECENT writers' retreat, Mercy lamented, "I just turned fifty, and here I am thinking about writing a book. Am I too old?"

I smiled. "If God has put the idea to write a book into your head, you are not too old."

Joshua was of old age—seventy, eighty, or maybe older—when he led Israel into the promised land. Despite Joshua's age, God was not done with him. Fortunately, God determined how the land was divided among the twelve tribes and designated which cities belonged to the Levites. The supervision of the settlements of a million or more people would have been challenging for anyone . . . regardless of their age. Nonetheless, with God's help, Joshua continued to serve well into his senior years.

And the same is true for us today: the Lord is our coworker—no matter our age. With each decade of life, God has purpose for us and will equip us for fruitful service.

Lord, I understand there is no such thing as retirement for those who follow you. You call us, you give us gifts and talents to use, and you put passion into our hearts to have purpose-filled lives. So I can trust you in every season.

Keep Looking Up!

We can pray in all seasons that God will make our lives meaningful.

MARCH 9

God Pours Out Blessings

Read Joshua 14–17

She said to him, "Give me a blessing. Since you have given me the land of the Negeb, give me also springs of water." And he gave her the upper springs and the lower springs." —Joshua 15:19

WHEN WE WERE teens, my four siblings and I had lots of requests of our parents.

"Can I go to the dance?"

"Can I use the car?"

"Can I spend the night at [insert name]'s house?"

We found that if we could get our dad to say, "We'll see," that was pretty much a yes that required just a bit of hang time to find its fruition.

In the same way we asked our earthly parents for blessings, we also petition our heavenly Father for the desires of our hearts. Sometimes it's just a matter of asking. In today's reading Caleb had already given his daughter the land of the Negeb—which is still a desert and semidesert area. In order to make something of the land, she and her new husband, Othniel, would need water. So she asked her father, and he gave her not one spring but two.

God delights in blessing us with what we need—and often those blessings overflow in abundance.

Lord, I know that you are a good Father, who delights in pouring out blessing upon blessing. Therefore, I can ask boldly for your favor and that which I need.

Keep Looking Up!

Praying for God to bless us can be part of our daily prayer time.

MARCH 10

Stepping into God's Gift

Read Joshua 18–20

> So Joshua said to the people of Israel, "How long will you put off going in to take possession of the land, which the LORD, the God of your fathers, has given you?" —Joshua 18:3

THERE ARE MYSTERIES about my husband I will never understand. One is he delays opening gifts. Instead of opening a birthday or Father's Day gift in the morning, he waits until the very end of the day. His package will sit there, seemingly saying, "Open. Open. Open." But he says, "I'll do it later." So the giver has to wait to view the smiles of enjoyment and appreciation.

We can sense Joshua's similar frustration in Joshua 18:3—magnified by the immenseness of God's gift. The Lord had provided the land of Canaan to the people of Israel, yet they delayed in claiming it. Yes, it would involve a heave-ho of enemies who occupied the various territories, but God had helped the Hebrews achieve victory when the Amalekites attacked them in the desert. So they could take possession, knowing God was with them.

Because God promises to bring us good, we can confidently step into the gift God wants to give us.

Lord, forgive me my lack of courage or diligence or respect when I do not enthusiastically step into a new job or other opportunity you have given me. Help me recognize your gift clearly as something from you and assure me of the right steps.

Keep Looking Up!

We more clearly recognize God's provision when we are synced with his Word.

God Provides Rest from Struggle

Read Joshua 21–22

The LORD gave them rest on every side, just as he had sworn to their ancestors. Not one of their enemies withstood them; the LORD gave all their enemies into their hands. —Joshua 21:44 NIV

I THINK TEACHING made it hard for me to rest. Studies show that teachers are only second to air traffic controllers in the number of decisions made on a daily basis. One kid wants to go to the office. Another needs an extension on his essay deadline. Yet one more forgot his homework: "Can I turn it in tomorrow?" And that was typical for just the few seconds after class began. Every day provided a long list of problems . . . and I'm not even scratching the complaint surface. Friday at 3 p.m. spelled R-E-S-T.

After the Israelites' parents faced forty years of one struggle after another, the next generation stepped into and fought for the land the Lord promised them. And they finally found rest within their tribe's territory and from bordering peoples.

Struggles can preoccupy seasons of our lives, which can make us appreciate all the more those times of rest.

Lord, thank you for seasons of rest. May I not grow complacent or even turn away from you but instead testify to your faithfulness through the struggles to more greatly appreciate those sweet times.

Keep Looking Up!

Allowing hardships to fade into the woodwork helps us appreciate the present.

MARCH 12

A Mission Serving God

Read Joshua 23–24

As for me and my household, we will serve the LORD.
—Joshua 24:15 NIV

BEFORE WE HAD children, I pursued various needlework forms to keep myself busy in the evenings while my husband served in the Army: cross stitch, needlepoint, crewel, and crochet. When I was expecting our first child, I wanted to create something that would represent our family, so I made a cross stitch sampler of Joshua 24:15. That proved to be the last work I made, as time no longer remained once children started coming!

This statement is one of the very last that Joshua made to the people of Israel before he died. Some say these words sum up his faithful dedication to the Lord's calling on his life. Those in ministry often have a mission statement—a well-thought-out, formal summary of the values and aims of that person or organization. I've never regretted stitching Joshua's statement into fabric and hanging it on our wall. It's an excellent reminder that serving God each day is our family mission.

Lord, may each of my family members make daily choices to serve you. May there be no hesitating or quibbling or questioning that demonstrates a lack of trust or even rebellion. And may others be drawn to you because of what they see in us.

Keep Looking Up!

**Each day can start with a question,
"What would you have me do, God?"**

MARCH 13

God to the Rescue

Read Judges 1–3

> Then the Lord raised up judges, who saved them out of the hand of those who plundered them. —Judges 2:16

AT THE LAKE my last words were, "Do not go deeper than your waist."

Our two oldest had been taking swim lessons, gaining confidence each day. Because they could swim, they didn't want to wear life jackets, even though they hadn't proven themselves able to go distances. Earlier we had agreed they could go without the jackets if they followed my rule.

Even so, just moments later I heard, "Mom, help!"

The younger of the two had tiptoed just a bit too far into a drop-off. Seconds later I reached and rescued him.

This scenario pretty much sums up what we see in the book of Judges. The Israelites strayed from God, pursued evil, got themselves in trouble when enemies attacked, and cried out to the Lord for help. Then God raised a judge who rescued them.

Sometimes we follow the same pattern: complacency, sin, panic, repentance, and cries for God's help. Nonetheless, God, in his mercy, rescues us too.

Lord, I don't know why I make the same mistakes over and over. Despite my failings, you save me from my sin and even myself, helping me get back on the right track again. I will ever be grateful for your mercies!

Keep Looking Up!

A pause for reflection can help us make better choices.

MARCH 14

God Is Praiseworthy

Read Judges 4–5

When the princes in Israel take the lead, when the people willingly offer themselves—praise the LORD! —Judges 5:2 NIV

BREAKING INTO SONG was a natural for my parents when we traveled in the car. A word would trigger a musical response—with all of us joining them. My parents each had a quick wit, but I also think their singing served to keep us kids from fighting and driving our parents crazy.

Several in the Bible responded to good news with songs including Deborah, the only recorded judge who did just that. When God used her to secure victory over the Canaanite king, she sang a chapter-long song. The only female judge and the only one who was said to have been a prophet in the book of Judges, Deborah credited God for the resounding defeat of the enemy.

While some of us might not naturally sing a literal victory song, we always can pray our thanks to the Lord, who sees us through our struggles.

Lord, I can literally sing praises to you, because you see me through earthly battles that batter and exhaust me. You are good and your mercies endure forever. Therefore, I will lift your name on high in song and in testimony.

Keep Looking Up!

Singing along with recorded worship music is a great way to praise God.

MARCH 15

God Is Our Peace

Read Judges 6–8

Then Gideon built an altar there to the LORD and called it, The LORD Is Peace. —Judges 6:24

I STRUGGLED AS I prepped for teaching my first elementary classroom. A trained English teacher, I wasn't sure I could teach science, math, and even P.E. But my biggest worry was bulletin boards. Elementary teachers always have beautiful bulletin boards that wrap school children in a welcoming embrace.

Lord, please help.

Immediately a peaceful thought came to mind. My mom.

The next day my mom, a professional artist who had taught elementary school for nineteen years, drove three hours over the mountain pass to help me. She even created a giant brown paper oak tree, adorned with acorns with each student's name.

Sometimes we don't feel equipped for the job. As the weakest of the weakest clan, Gideon also felt unable to become judge and military leader of Israel. But God's assurance settled peace over him, just as God's peace today can overcome our doubts and give us peace.

Lord, again I learn through your Word that when you call someone to a difficult task, you provide the training or support or inspiration to complete that work. May I never question your calling but instead trust you every step of the way.

Keep Looking Up!

We can choose peace by studying God's faithful character.

MARCH 16

Cleaning God's House

Read Judges 9–10

Then they cleaned house of the foreign gods and worshiped only GOD. And GOD took Israel's troubles to heart. —Judges 10:16 MSG

NOTHING WAS GOING right. I had chipped a tooth. Two kids were sick. Worse, my husband and I were hardly talking. However, after a half-hour drive to the dentist's office across our beautiful mountain valley, I realized that I'd only been focused on myself. I could clean my mental house by changing my negative attitude to one that sees God's goodness and gives him praise.

With each judge the people once again would turn to God, clean house of their sins and idols, and then experience a period of peace and rest. The Israelites said, "We have sinned. Do with us whatever you think best" (Judges 10:15 NIV). After they got rid of their foreign gods, the Lord could no longer bear their misery and sent more help (Judges 10:16).

We can clean house and find joy in our lives again today by confessing our sins and leaving them behind us—serving God wholeheartedly.

Lord, I know my attitude can keep me from experiencing your peace. Help me recognize and confess sin quickly, so that I can clearly experience your presence.

Keep Looking Up!

We can sweep away a negative mindset by confessing our sin.

MARCH 17

God Works in Families

Read Judges 11–13

Then Manoah prayed to the LORD and said, "O Lord, please let the man of God whom you sent come again to us and teach us what we are to do with the child who will be born." —Judges 13:8

MY HUSBAND AND I went through childbirth classes for weeks, with many hours invested in perfecting breathing techniques during labor. Bringing that first child into the world did take more than fifteen hours, but we were prepared. What we *weren't* prepared for was parenting—the next couple dozen years ahead of us. We found, though, that prayer is the key.

That parenting principle is seen with Manoah, who prayed for his son, even before he was born. That baby was born and named Samson. Scripture tells us the Lord blessed him and then used him to defeat the enemy, the Philistines. Clearly, Samson was not perfect, but still God used him.

Our families today are admittedly not ideal either, not picture perfect, but with prayer God can use us within the context of our families and the greater community around us.

Lord, thank you for my imperfect family. Thank you for each imperfect person. Thank you for where you have placed me within my greater family. May I—may each of us—seek you on a daily basis, asking you what we should do for you and your kingdom.

Keep Looking Up!

We can pray daily that God will bless and help each family member.

MARCH 18

God Redeems Our Mistakes

Read Judges 14–16

> Then Samson prayed to the LORD, "Sovereign LORD, remember me. Please, God, strengthen me just once more, and let me with one blow get revenge on the Philistines for my two eyes."
>
> —Judges 16:28 NIV

BECAUSE OF ABORTIONS in her youth, my friend Rianna did not feel worthy of being a child of God. She knew Christ had forgiven her but she did not feel worthy of his love and sacrifice. One Sunday she confessed her past to her church family and felt not only forgiveness and love but also a new calling. Because she had spoken openly, others began sharing with her, which led to her starting an abortion recovery ministry.

God uses everything about us—good and bad. That was true of Samson, who lacked self-control in personal matters. Nonetheless, the Lord used him to destroy a pagan temple and a false god's followers.

It may be that our former failures—such as addiction or abusive behavior—enable us to minister to others with similar issues. God can always redeem our past.

Lord, you redeem my mistakes by allowing me to minister to others who have had similar experiences. Even if I only empathize and offer friendship, I can extend your amazing grace to someone who may be struggling. God, show me how I can serve the hurting.

Keep Looking Up!

The redemption of our past can start with a simple prayer.

MARCH 19

Godly Blessing Cancels a Curse

Read Judges 17–19

[Micah's] mother said, "God bless you, my son!" —Judges 17:2 MSG

IN HEATED INTERACTIONS with our kids when they were younger, words sometimes flew from both sides without thought. I didn't always respond well, but many times I'd answer, "Well, I love you!" I wanted to end the argument with positive last words instead of negative ones.

We learn a lot about God's grace and mercy during the time of the judges, a time when "Everyone did what was right in his own eyes" (Judges 17:6). In one incident that evidenced the every-man-for-himself behavior, the man, Micah, stole money from his mother but later returned it to her after he heard his mother's curse. When he admitted his crime, she blessed him, effectively exchanging her curse for a blessing.

A blessing can de-escalate a tense situation. It brings godly language into the room and can restore relationships.

Lord, help me live out a life that demonstrates your grace and mercy. Even when others are unkind, show me how to live in such a way that I extend kindness instead.

Keep Looking Up!

A verbal blessing can lighten someone's load.

MARCH 20

God Wants Us to Seek Him

Read Judges 20–21

Then all the people of Israel came out, from Dan to Beersheba, including the land of Gilead, and the congregation assembled as one man to the LORD at Mizpah. —Judges 20:1

THE TEENAGERS CONGREGATED around their buddy who had taken a bully's punch, and the two were exchanging words when I tapped the bully on the shoulder. He swung around and nearly slugged me. I had arrived just in time to prevent a fight precipitated by the desire for revenge.

An even worse situation is recorded in Judges. When terrible crimes occurred against a woman and she died, the people of Israel assembled together and sought revenge against the offending tribe of Benjamin. Great loss occurred, nearly enough to wipe out that entire tribe. Because people's hearts often did not seek the Lord during the time of the judges, they made poor decisions that proved costly.

But today we can learn from them. We avoid the path and costliness of sin when we seek the Lord before we react. Circumstances can bring difficulties, but when we seek him, he shows us the right way to respond.

Lord, sometimes I make quick judgments and poor decisions, which means I have faced some tough consequences. Instead, I want to take a big breath, seek you first, and consider a better response that reflects godly values.

Keep Looking Up!

A pregnant pause may be enough time to consider a godly response.

MARCH 21

God's Family Sticks Together

Read Ruth 1–4

But Ruth said, "Do not urge me to leave you or to return from following you. For where you go I will go, and where you lodge I will lodge. Your people shall be my people, and your God my God." —Ruth 1:16

IT WAS HARD to decide where we would settle down after my husband finished with college and then service in the Army. He wanted to live in a large mountain valley to start a law practice and buy ranch property, while I wanted to live by the ocean or a lake. However, after we saw the Sierra Valley in northeastern California for the first time, I agreed it was the place for us.

Deciding where to live was also a problem for Naomi and her daughters-in-law, Ruth and Orpah—all of whom had lost their husbands. Orpah chose to stay among her people in Moab, while Ruth chose to make Naomi and her Jewish people her forever family.

While our family lives may not be perfect and will probably experience tragedy, the story of Ruth and Naomi shows us how God's presence in relationships overcomes the toughest of circumstances that otherwise could create disunity.

Lord, I am thankful for family members who have helped us through the various ups and downs over the years. May I also be generous to family members and others when they experience loss, in recognition of the sacrificial gift of Jesus.

Keep Looking Up!

Faith can unify family.

MARCH 22

God Will Speak to Us

Read 1 Samuel 1–3

> The LORD came and stood there, calling as at the other times, "Samuel! Samuel!"
>
> Then Samuel said, "Speak, for your servant is listening."
>
> —1 Samuel 3:10 NIV

MY OLDEST HAS six kids, all of whom like to talk. One will tell you everything about birds. Another, new recipes. Yet another, his latest achievements climbing. But the oldest will sit down and say, "How's your day been, Nana?" And he's been like that since he could talk. Some people are simply interested in others and know the value of listening.

In the story of Samuel, we learn that when the Lord called out to him, Samuel thought it was Eli the priest instead. Three times Samuel ran to Eli and said, "Did you call me?" Finally, Eli realized it was the Lord calling to Samuel, and on the fourth time Samuel told God he was listening and asked him to speak.

God can still speak to us today. While we might not hear an audible voice, he does speak clearly through his Word.

Lord, I am embarrassed that I often do not slow down enough to hear your still, small voice. May I set aside time alone to pray, "Speak, Lord, for your servant is listening."

Keep Looking Up!

Reading God's Word helps train our ears to his voice.

MARCH 23

Worship Only God

Read 1 Samuel 4–7

So Samuel said to all the Israelites, "If you are returning to the Lord with all your hearts, then rid yourselves of the foreign gods and the Ashtoreths and commit yourselves to the Lord and serve him only, and he will deliver you out of the hand of the Philistines."

—1 Samuel 7:3 NIV

WHEN MY DAUGHTER married her husband, she had to change houses—not just shift from our house to one of their own, but also shift from being a San Francisco Giants fan to a Los Angeles Dodgers fan. Since the two teams are fierce rivals, differing allegiances could not sit together under one roof. That meant any T-shirts and fan gear had to go.

On a much bigger scale, the Hebrews learned that when they returned to God after their pursuit of other gods, they had to discard their former idols. They could not follow God and keep their idols too.

We get to choose whom we will worship. Shiny objects and other religions come from man's imagination, whereas the God of the Bible is the Creator of the universe and the one who has pursued a relationship with mankind since the beginning of the world. A relationship with God is an all-in proposition.

Lord God, I pray that my heart is not divided but instead fully committed to you. Give me your discernment to know if there is anything that reflects the worship of any object or other faith in my home that needs to be removed.

Keep Looking Up!

Objects that cause us to look up to God are worth keeping.

MARCH 24

God Wants Diligent Pray-ers

Read 1 Samuel 8–12

Moreover, as for me, far be it from me that I should sin against the LORD by ceasing to pray for you, and I will instruct you in the good and the right way. —1 Samuel 12:23

EVERY COUPLE WEEKS I get an email from a friend, asking how my sister-in-law is doing. When the family learned she had cancer, I contacted several different prayer groups to pray for her. It's assuring to know that some have her on an actual list for which they are praying on a regular basis—because I know those folks won't forget to keep praying no matter what happens.

When the judge Samuel gave his farewell speech, he indicated that while he would cease to be their leader, he would continue in his prophetic role. Even though Saul would be Israel's first king, any king would fall under the spiritual watch of God's anointed prophets, and as such, Samuel would continue to intercede for the Hebrews.

In the same way, God often brings people into our lives and asks us to continue praying for them even if we are no longer in regular contact. While it's challenging to keep track of prayer requests as we get them, we can always pray right at the moment when someone asks for prayer.

Lord, far be it from me that I should fail to pray for family, friends, and others when they ask me to pray for them. Others have blessed me greatly with their prayers for me, and I want to do the same. Help me establish a praying routine that provides me structure and accountability.

Keep Looking Up!

Writing others' prayer needs on sticky notes is an easy form of reminder.

God Works for Us

Read 1 Samuel 13–14

Maybe God will work for us. There's no rule that says God can only deliver by using a big army. No one can stop God from saving when he sets his mind to it. —1 Samuel 14:6 MSG

WE SHOULD NOT have won the basketball game the other night. Our school has all of one hundred students; the opponent, twenty-two hundred. The opponent's scorekeeper sitting at my side at the score table said, "Our freshman class is bigger than your whole town." But with focused excellence, determination, and quickness, our David-sized team beat the Goliath-sized one. As the official school scorekeeper, I had the privilege to write the final score: 87–50.

Repeatedly Israel won victories they should not have against bigger, better equipped, and more powerful enemies. The crucial element to any of their victories was the presence of the Lord. When the people put their faith in God and trusted him for the battle, they did not lose.

When we trust that God works for us, he will be our companion and guide and strength—no matter the outcome.

Lord, I know that adversity is always a part of anyone's life, and I do not expect that my years will be absent of those trials. I know, however, that you will work for me and see me through any of those circumstances.

Keep Looking Up!

Pray fervently, and remember that God is sovereign over everything.

God Looks on the Heart

Read 1 Samuel 15–16

The LORD sees not as man sees: man looks on the outward appearance, but the LORD looks on the heart. —1 Samuel 16:7

I GOT A call again this week from my mom's senior living place.

"We were wondering which medical facility your mother's appointment is with this week," the young girl said.

I took a deep breath. "Could you please ask her? She has a better memory than I do."

Our society often overlooks the elderly. Their outer shell isn't as strong or as attractive as a younger person's, and so others assume their mental sharpness is lacking too.

The world judges us largely by our appearance. King Saul was a handsome man, so Samuel, who had to anoint the next king, may have been looking for an equal in physical appearance. But the Lord told him not to consider outward appearance . . . and directed Samuel to choose David.

God understands our worth and calls us not because of how we look on the outside, but because of how we are on the inside.

Lord God, I obsess too much about my appearance, and often I judge others by theirs. Instead, I want to reflect your love, joy, and peace so that others see you in me.

Keep Looking Up!

We can improve our inner character by seeking God's heart.

MARCH 27

Friends Are God's Blessings

Read 1 Samuel 17–18

Then Jonathan made a covenant with David, because he loved him as his own soul. —1 Samuel 18:3

AS I SAT across the table from Kim in our very first meeting, I sensed that she would be my new friend. I was on the pastoral search committee, and we were interviewing her husband that day. In just weeks, Kim and I found we had a lot in common. Now, many years later, she is the first person I text when I have a prayer need.

David and King Saul's son Jonathan also instantly clicked. Jonathan was particularly devoted to David, despite the fact that Saul was threatened by David's many talents and popularity. Jonathan remained loyal to David even when Saul tried to kill David. In fact, Jonathan defied his own father and king to warn David.

True friends support and pray for each other in all seasons, good and bad. Their allegiance remains solid, despite how the world views them. They love each other as one's own soul.

Lord, thank you for my dear friends and their many kindnesses to me. May I be as faithful and caring a friend as Jonathan was to David.

Keep Looking Up!

Friendships are a two-way street and are fostered when we initiate contact.

MARCH 28

God Cultivates Friendships

Read 1 Samuel 19–21

Jonathan said to David, "Go in peace, for we have sworn friendship with each other in the name of the Lord, saying, 'The Lord is witness between you and me, and between your descendants and my descendants forever.'" —1 Samuel 20:42 NIV

AT LEAST ONCE a year my high school girlfriends and I get together for lunch. About a dozen of us have kept in touch, defying the expression, "There are friends for seasons of life." Instead, we believe we are friends *for* life. Through both celebrations and losses we have kept in touch and encouraged one another.

The friendship between Jonathan and David may be the strongest bond between two men in the Bible. Jonathan's commitment to David took precedence over his father's demands . . . and ultimately Jonathan paid the price, losing his life.

We may not be asked to give our life for a friend, but we can give of our time when a friend needs childcare, a meal, or a ride to chemo. Every season provides reasons to reach out to a friend.

Lord, thank you for the many friendships you have cultivated in my behalf over the years. Their endless kindnesses to my family and me have helped me weather tough seasons, and I am grateful. May I also reach out to them when you bring them to mind.

Keep Looking Up!

A simple text message could encourage that friend on your mind today.

MARCH 29

God Is Our Sanctuary

Read 1 Samuel 22–24

The prophet Gad told David, "Don't go back to the cave. Go to Judah." —1 Samuel 22:5 MSG

MY CLASSROOM WAS my cozy spot. I gave it homey touches, not only so students would feel welcome, but also so that it felt like home to me. Occasionally, though, I had to move out of that comfortable space to advocate for my students and our school. That involved going to school board meetings to make presentations for changes and funding—not something I enjoyed doing but usually was effective.

Sometimes we are called to shift out of our cozy spot. David had found that hiding in caves was effective to avoid conflict with Saul and his henchmen. But a prophet named Gad told him to go back to Judah where he would be thrown right into the conflict.

Struggles typically do not magically disappear; eventually we must face them head-on. However, in those conflicts we can trust that God is with us and will be our protection.

Lord, ultimately you are my sanctuary. I need not hide from the world and its problems because you will be my advocate and my protection as I walk through those struggles. Thank you for being my hiding place.

Keep Looking Up!

God is our sanctuary when struggles arise in our lives.

MARCH 30

God Gives Us Discretion

Read 1 Samuel 25–27

David said to Abigail, "Blessed be the Lord, the God of Israel, who sent you this day to meet me! Blessed be your discretion, and blessed be you, who have kept me this day from bloodguilt and from working salvation with my own hand!" —1 Samuel 25:32–33

JUST AFTER ELEVEN o'clock I heard a knock on the door. Two scared-looking teenaged girls stood there in the dark, asking for a ride home. "A bear just chased us down the street!"

That was believable because bears had been seen in our area for weeks, foraging through garbage cans.

After a few more questions that verified that one of them was a local girl, I drove them the few blocks to home. "Be safe," I said. "Bears may be the least of your troubles at this hour."

You never know who might show up on your doorstep, and that was true for Abigail. Despite the fact that her husband, Nabal, had not shown hospitality to David and his fighting men, she gave them ample provisions—an act of mercy that probably saved her and her husband's lives.

We need discretion when strangers ask for help, but God gives wisdom generously when we ask.

Lord, I do not want to live in constant fear of what-ifs. Instead, I will make smart decisions about my physical welfare and put my trust in you to help me discern when a situation is not safe.

Keep Looking Up!

"Trust but verify" is wise counsel for our own safety.

Sometimes God Says "Go!"

Read 1 Samuel 28–31

Then David prayed to God, "Shall I go after these raiders? Can I catch them?"

The answer came, "Go after them! Yes, you'll catch them! Yes, you'll make the rescue!" —1 Samuel 30:8 MSG

EVERY WEEK WHEN I taught school I had the same prayer, "Help me know what to teach, God, and help me do it better than last year."

Unlike other subjects with one textbook, English teachers have many to forge through in a year—a literature book, a grammar book, plus novels and works of nonfiction. It was impossible to cover everything in those texts, so I needed wisdom beyond my own to know what to do and how to be more effective each and every year.

Despite his military prowess, David found himself in a point of confusion too. When he and his soldiers returned home, they found the Amalekites had burned their community and taken their families. David's men even spoke of killing him. So David sought the Lord's counsel, and God said, "Go!"

While some days may feel like a battle zone, we can look to the Lord for our battle plan.

Lord, every day I need you. Every day I want to be more effective and avoid the missteps I create when I do not follow your guidance. Let me know, God, whether it's "no" or "go."

Keep Looking Up!

Prayer is the first step of any action plan.

APRIL 1

God Understands Conflicting Feelings

Read 2 Samuel 1–3

Then David composed a funeral song for Saul and Jonathan.
—2 Samuel 1:17 NLT

I RECENTLY ATTENDED a memorial for a man who had provided much conflict for many years, and there were few in attendance. When I asked someone later why, she said, "Some couldn't get over their resentments." While I had frustrations too, I attended out of respect for the man's position.

David could have cheered when Saul died in battle. But Saul was his king, his best friend's father, and his wife's father. David mourned because Saul served in all of those roles and also probably because his conflict with Saul brought about the death of his closest friend, Jonathan.

We may have conflicting feelings when bad things happen to people who have hurt us. That may have to do with the inability to bring about resolution or even redemption for the pain. But God can lead us into a season of healing and restoration of our own wholeness.

Lord, it is uncomfortable to have conflicting feelings about others who have had important roles in my life. As situations arise, help me understand the truth about those people and give me wisdom about how I should respond.

Keep Looking Up!

We can look beyond our own pain to comfort others in theirs.

APRIL 2

God Gives Us Ideas

Read 2 Samuel 4–7

And Nathan said to the king, "Go, do all that is in your heart, for the LORD is with you." —2 Samuel 7:3

WHEN MY HUSBAND was on the city council, he met a man who wanted to donate a huge, valuable collection to our little city museum, but the current building could not house even a portion of those artifacts.

Finding a new museum site became my husband's heart's desire.

I remembered that the school district had been trying to sell the closed middle school facility for many years. "I bet the district would sell that building for a dollar," I said.

All of that came to be true, and we have a spectacular museum now.

When we get ideas for good, often God has placed them within us. David realized that there was no permanent structure for worship, and he asked to build one. While the Lord was pleased, he said that responsibility would be set on David's son Solomon's shoulders when he became king.

When we are close to God, he blesses us with wonderful ideas.

Lord, thank you for the creative ideas you give me. Help me know how to prioritize them and how to carry out your work.

Keep Looking Up!

We can trust God's timing for project ideas he plants within our hearts.

APRIL 3

Compassion Is God's Idea

Read 2 Samuel 8–11

> "Don't be frightened," said David. "I'd like to do something special for you in memory of your father Jonathan. To begin with, I'm returning to you all the properties of your grandfather Saul. Furthermore, from now on you'll take all your meals at my table."
>
> —2 Samuel 9:7 MSG

MY FRIEND TRICIA and her husband adopted seven kids to add to their own three—all of whom they have homeschooled. They live out the biblical admonition to care for widows and orphans, because they also provide a home for Tricia's grandmother.

David had similar sympathies. When he was anointed king, he did not forget former King Saul's family and also provided for Jonathan's crippled son, Mephibosheth. While it would be understandable that David might feel obligated to care for his dead friend's son, David also inquired if any of Saul's relatives needed care. Despite the fact that Saul chased David for years with the intent to kill him, David still had compassion for Saul's family.

It's easy to allow hard feelings to remain and even fester when someone has hurt us, but the Christian faith is all about finding a better way—God's way.

Lord, you know that I can quickly call to mind the faces of others who have hurt me, but I do not want to do that anymore. I want to be the hands and feet of Jesus—bringing your compassion to those who need such a touch.

Keep Looking Up!

We tear down barriers when we offer kindness to others.

APRIL 4

God Can Redeem Our Sin

Read 2 Samuel 12–13

David said to Nathan, "I have sinned against the LORD." And Nathan said to David, "The LORD also has put away your sin; you shall not die." —2 Samuel 12:13

I COULDN'T TAKE back my words. They had flown out without my thinking—in a public setting—and hurt someone I loved and respected. Even though I later apologized and asked the woman's forgiveness, I've always wondered if she could forget my unkindness.

David's situation in 2 Samuel 11–12 was much more serious. He had abused his power as king, committed rape, and had the woman's husband set up for death in battle. Then he attempted to make things look good by marrying Bathsheba, who was pregnant. But the prophet Nathan knew of David's sin and confronted him. Nathan told him, "You are the man!" and told him the Lord would punish him. David and Bathsheba suffered great anguish when their child died, but later she gave birth to Solomon, who would succeed David as king.

Sin destroys lives, but our confessional response provides the opportunity for healing and God's redemption of those mistakes.

Lord God, I know that sin never plays out well. There are always hard consequences—sometimes affecting others I love. I want to respond quickly when I mess up, so that my sins do not damage the name of my Savior Jesus.

Keep Looking Up!

Asking forgiveness of God and others is the first step to breaking sin's power.

APRIL 5

God Is My Defense

Read 2 Samuel 14–16

And who knows, maybe GOD will see the trouble I'm in today and exchange the curses for something good. —2 Samuel 16:12 MSG

AT A RECENT soccer practice, a grandfather of one of the players started yelling at my eleven-year-old granddaughter. After a while, she said she found it hard to concentrate, so my granddaughter calmly walked over to the man on the sidelines and said, "Sir, you are making yourself look ridiculous." And she jogged back into position.

It's tough to maintain a calm demeanor when others are hurtling unkind words at us.

Although a clan member of the family of Saul threw a steady line of curses at David, David quietly tolerated the abuse. He did not have to prove himself because David knew he did not have anything to do with Saul's death.

If we keep our composure when someone else is having an emotional tirade, the situation rarely escalates and eventually the other person will look ridiculous.

Lord, it's a human reaction to respond defensively when someone attacks us personally. Sometimes I get emotional, and I just want to resolve the situation, but I know that usually words do not help diffuse things. Help me exercise restraint, God.

Keep Looking Up!

Silently praying Psalm 23 can calm us in emotional settings.

APRIL 6

God Understands Grief

Read 2 Samuel 17–19

The king was stunned. Heartbroken, he went up to the room over the gate and wept. As he wept he cried out, O my son Absalom, my dear, dear son Absalom! Why not me rather than you, my death and not yours, O Absalom, my dear, dear son! —2 Samuel 18:33 MSG

YEARS AGO I wrote about how prayerwalking helped me navigate the grieving process after my dad passed away from ALS. But one person made critical remarks about me because she said I whined too much about losing my dad. Ouch.

Grief is not weakness. When we express grief, it is not whining. And grief is not something that can be cut or short-circuited. When David learned his military commander, Joab, killed David's son Absalom, he grieved deeply. While Joab—also David's nephew—was a brilliant military man, he was short-tempered and judgmental. He criticized David for mourning his son, saying it humiliated those who had supported him.

Grieving helps us process our loss—and counselors say there are five (or more) stages of grief: from denial to anger to bargaining to depression to acceptance. For each of the stages, we can look to the Lord, who will offer comfort, grace, strength, and hope.

Father, loss brings a full gamut of emotions and intellectual wrestlings. Grieving reminds me that I am human. But then I recall that your Son, Jesus, was human too—and that he suffered all those same feelings. Ultimately, I am thankful for the hope that settles over me.

Keep Looking Up!

We are never alone in our grief because God is always with us.

APRIL 7

God Is My Refuge

Read 2 Samuel 20–22

He said, "The Lord is my rock and my fortress and my deliverer, my God, my rock, in whom I take refuge, my shield, and the horn of my salvation." —2 Samuel 22:2–3

OUR BUS ZIPPED along the freeway in Israel, headed for the Sea of Galilee. During one long stretch from the mountainous city of Nazareth, we saw cave after cave—natural indentations in the rock. Days later we viewed the caves at Qumran, where the Dead Sea Scrolls were found. At the end of our trip, we toured the back roads where David reportedly hid out from Saul. Caves clearly were hiding places for men and precious Scriptures.

When the Lord rescued David from his enemies, he sang a song to the Lord. David used imagery to describe the Lord as his rock, his fortress, his shield, and his refuge. His chapter-length song that is recorded in 2 Samuel 22 is a beautiful example of how we can praise God for his protection.

God is still our rock, fortress, and refuge who provides strength when we face troubles.

Lord, you are my rock and my fortress, my shelter where I can hide and where you give me strength. Thank you for your eternal love and promise of protection. May I always run to you when troubles come.

Keep Looking Up!

God is our refuge in times of trouble.

APRIL 8

God's Light Shines on Us

Read 2 Samuel 23–24

When one rules over people in righteousness, when he rules in the fear of God, he is like the light of morning at sunrise on a cloudless morning. —2 Samuel 23:3–4 NIV

I'VE WORKED UNDER some great bosses, pastors, and nonprofit leaders. Each has had certain strengths, and each made the job enjoyable. One school administrator used to joke, "School would be great—except for all those students!" Despite his tongue-in-cheek comment I knew he loved kids, and they loved him. A couple years later he got a position opening a new, large high school, and his first year there were no students as the facility was being finished. "My dream job for one year," he said with a smile.

It was David's hope that his leadership over Israel would bring light to the people. When leaders obediently follow the Lord, they display a peaceful countenance—which is not dependent upon circumstances. The wisdom they impart and the peace under fire they display make others' lives better.

Ultimately, when we bring the sunshine of love, joy, hope, and other positive characteristics into our surroundings, we reflect God's good character.

Lord, may your light shine on and through me, so that hope is spread wherever I go. May I not deflect that light with a critical spirit but refract and diffuse it into the dark spaces around me, where others need to know your love.

Keep Looking Up!

**When we trust and follow God,
his light shines through us.**

APRIL 9

Sharing God's Promises

Read 1 Kings 1–2

> When David's time to die approached, he charged his son Solomon, saying, "I'm about to go the way of all the earth, but you—be strong; show what you're made of! . . . Walk in the paths he shows you: Follow the life-map absolutely, keep an eye out for the signposts, his course for life set out in the revelation to Moses; then you'll get on well in whatever you do and wherever you go."
>
> —1 Kings 2:1–2 MSG

ENGLISH IS OUR family business. I was my daughters' English teacher, and both followed suit—almost laughable, considering teaching was the last thing I had planned on doing. In fact, our oldest is now doing my old job. I always find it delightful when my girls call for my advice about teaching strategies and curricular choices. "Be strong," I tell them often.

The passing of the mantel in the Bible happens several times, and in today's reading we see David give Solomon some final words. There were a few pieces of advice about military strategy, but those were prefaced by counsel to walk in God's ways according to the Scriptures. Prosperity would result if Solomon followed the Lord.

This promise is not a mathematical equation. We do not follow God's laws so as to receive favor. The favor simply results because we choose God. He himself is our reward.

Lord, your promises remain true, because when I read and follow your Word, it settles into my heart and that is reward enough. May the next generations in my family choose you and make your promises their own.

Keep Looking Up!

Sharing your testimony of God's goodness usually works better than sharing advice.

APRIL 10

Wisdom Comes from God

Read 1 Kings 3–5

> Give your servant therefore an understanding mind to govern your people, that I may discern between good and evil, for who is able to govern this your great people? —1 Kings 3:9

AS AN ENGLISH teacher I rarely gave exams. I felt the most important thing I could teach my students was how to think—how to analyze written works and communicate effectively about them. I felt the best way to demonstrate strong thinking skills is by writing, not regurgitating facts. If my students could think and write, they would be ready for the world.

When God said Solomon could ask him for anything, Solomon chose wisdom. Some now refer to Solomon as the wisest man who ever lived, evidenced by the wisdom books that are attributed to him in whole or in part: Proverbs, Ecclesiastes, and Song of Songs.

When we seek entertainment, we are satisfied for the moment. When we seek wisdom, we grow in understanding and maturity for the years to follow. Wisdom is a characteristic we gain through daily disciplines that include reading the Bible.

Lord, I see that wisdom starts with you, its author. Give me understanding as I read your Word. Increase my curiosity, so that ideas intrigue me for further study. And may your Spirit provide the discernment I need each day.

Keep Looking Up!

Underlining one important takeaway from your Bible reading daily builds your own arsenal of wisdom.

APRIL 11

Building God's Home

Read 1 Kings 6–7

Now the word of the Lord came to Solomon, "Concerning this house that you are building, if you will walk in my statutes and obey my rules and keep all my commandments and walk in them, then I will establish my word with you, which I spoke to David your father." —1 Kings 6:11–12

"HOW LONG DID it take to build our house?" our son asked.

My husband finished nailing some baseboard trim after we'd had replacement flooring installed.

"About a year," I said, looking at my watch. We were expecting company that evening.

My husband chuckled. "We're still building it."

It's true, isn't it, that a house is never done? There's always something more that needs to be fixed. That's true for the spiritual building of a family too. There's always something more from God's Word to teach.

One man in the Bible built two homes: King Solomon. One home—the temple—he built for the Lord in seven years. The other—a palace—he built for himself in thirteen years.

While we build physical houses, we also build a spiritual foundation within our family when we teach our children about how God establishes his Word in us.

Father God, I invite you to dwell in my home. I will open it to extend your love to others, so that they truly know you are the Lord of our lives.

Keep Looking Up!

When we live out God's Word, our children are more likely to as well.

APRIL 12

God Is Listening

Read 1 Kings 8–9

Yet have regard to the prayer of your servant and to his plea, O LORD my God, listening to the cry and to the prayer that your servant prays before you this day. —1 Kings 8:28

THE WEEK OF this writing, the football-watching world saw something different on national television. After a typical impact, an American football player fell to the ground, his heart having stopped. After he was carried off the field and placed in an ambulance, both teams spontaneously dropped to their knees in a circle together and prayed for him. The next day a national sports broadcaster prayed on live television for the young man, and millions across social media also said they were praying for him. Fortunately he awoke from unconsciousness three days later.

Our prayers can have effect because we have a God who cares and listens to us. When the temple was finished, Solomon prayed, asking God to hear his prayers and those of Israel. And the Lord responded that his covenant with the people would stand—if they obeyed.

While we who believe in God may not always see the answers we desire to our prayers, we can know God is listening. And knowing that can draw us closer to him.

Lord, I come before you first to thank you for the privilege of prayer. That I can appeal to the Lord of the universe is humbling, and I hope that each day my heart grows more closely to yours so that my prayers align with your heart.

Keep Looking Up!

Praying for others unites my heart with those for whom I pray.

God Delights in Us

Read 1 Kings 10–12

Blessed be the Lord your God, who has delighted in you and set you on the throne of Israel! Because the Lord loved Israel forever, he has made you king, that you may execute justice and righteousness. —1 Kings 10:9

WHEN MY SISTER was a toddler going through potty training, my mom would always say, "I'd be delighted," when my sister asked for a little help.

One day my sister simply said, "Mommy, come be delighted!"

The truth was that our mom didn't necessarily delight in the chore but did delight in each one of us. And she has lived out her faith with simple, loving acts done with obvious pleasure.

Our lives can be a testimony of God to others. This was true when the Queen of Sheba visited Solomon and noticed his great display of riches. She was impressed with all his wealth but also with how his servants demonstrated happiness in serving their king.

Wealthy or not, we too have the opportunity to display God's delight in us simply by displaying the joy, peace, and love of Christ through our demeanor and kindnesses to others. Even just a smile points others upward.

Lord, I want my life and my testimony to make a difference for your kingdom. Help me demonstrate humility, kindness, and compassion, so that others see you through me.

Keep Looking Up!

A welcoming smile demonstrates God's love through us.

APRIL 14

Pray to God for Others

Read 1 Kings 13–15

Then the king said to the man of God, "Intercede with the LORD your God and pray for me that my hand may be restored." So the man of God interceded with the LORD, and the king's hand was restored and became as it was before. —1 Kings 13:6 NIV

MAYBE YOU'RE LIKE I am. When people ask for prayer on social media, I pray for them. Sometimes I'll even see expressions such as "Could you send prayers to me?" That tells me that person does not know that we don't pray to other people; we pray to God.

But when we of faith pray for unbelievers, God certainly does hear our prayers and can heal the person for whom we're praying. This happened with Jeroboam, the first king of Israel's northern kingdom. When Jeroboam objected to a prophecy, God shriveled Jeroboam's hand as a means to turn him to God. And it worked. Jeroboam asked the prophet to intercede with the Lord to restore Jeroboam's hand, which is what happened.

Praying for those who do not follow God is important because of two things. First, answered prayer could trigger a faith response, and second, when others see our compassion, they are drawn to God's goodness they see in us.

Father God, build compassion in me. Help me see every single person as valuable in your sight and support them with prayer and loving acts. I do want to be your emissary in prayer.

Keep Looking Up!

We can stop at any time to pray for someone who asks for prayer.

APRIL 15

Choosing God's Side

Read 1 Kings 16–18

And Elijah came near to all the people and said, "How long will you go limping between two different opinions? If the LORD is God, follow him; but if Baal, then follow him." And the people did not answer him a word. —1 Kings 18:21

"HELP, MOM!" I heard through the kitchen window.

A few seconds later I could see the problem. Our three-year-old had climbed up on the fence at my parents' home and was sitting on the top rail of the horse arena.

"I'm stuck," she said as I approached.

"Were you trying to get in or were you trying to get out?" I reached out, and she jumped into my arms.

"I don't know," she said, running off.

The prophet Elijah noticed a similar problem. The people of Israel weren't sure what they wanted to do. Sometimes they followed God but were often enticed by the evil practices of the man-made god, Baal. And so Elijah made it clear that the people needed to choose.

Making a choice for God means we follow him day by day. We stop sitting on the faith fence, turn away from evil, and determine to follow where God leads.

Lord, I confess that sometimes I sit on a faith fence. Cultural allures draw me away from spending time with you, and I make choices that do not honor you. May I always stay on your side of the fence.

Keep Looking Up!

Making choices for God starts with seeking him each day.

APRIL 16

God Knows When We Hide

Read 1 Kings 19–20

> And when Elijah heard it, he wrapped his face in his cloak and went out and stood at the entrance of the cave. And behold, there came a voice to him and said, "What are you doing here, Elijah?"
>
> —1 Kings 19:13

I NOTICED THAT the school's storage closet door was slightly ajar, so I peeked into the dark, only to see a figure sitting on the floor.

"What are you doing here, Denton?"

"Just chillin'," he said without looking me in the face.

"Aren't you supposed to be in chemistry?"

He stood up and headed across the hall, with an under-his-breath grumble.

My questions were rhetorical because I knew the answers. He was avoiding a big test—one that my own kid also had feared.

Even responsible people find themselves hiding out to avoid circumstances. The powerful prophet Elijah hid out in caves away from the evil Queen Jezebel, who had soldiers out looking for him.

But we do it too, even though we know that hiding could make the situation even worse than if we faced life head-on. However, when we seek God, he will walk with us out of that cave and give us strength for whatever is ahead.

Lord, I can be such a procrastinator when I don't want to face difficult tasks. Give me the courage, God, to tackle the tough things of life and to trust you for the outcome.

Keep Looking Up!

When we face a difficulty, we pray for God's help.

APRIL 17

No Lost Causes with God

Read 1 Kings 21–22

Then the word of the LORD came to Elijah the Tishbite: "Have you noticed how Ahab has humbled himself before me? Because he has humbled himself, I will not bring this disaster in his day, but I will bring it on his house in the days of his son."

—1 Kings 21:28–29 NIV

JOHNNY HAD BEEN labeled a lost cause when he transferred to our high school. He had been shuffled from one relative to another—now with grandparents who were trying their best. His records showed deficient credits and poor grades. But he found his niche in our agriculture classes and went on to a tech school and a productive life.

The Bible has a seemingly endless series of lost causes in its kings of Judah and Israel. Ahab started out that way—marrying evil Jezebel and worshiping Baal. However, toward the end of his life, Ahab made a dramatic turn, humbling himself. And as a result, God reduced his punishment.

There are no lost human causes in God's eyes. Each person has value. Each one can turn to God and find acceptance, worth, and purpose. While we may have to live out consequences for our earlier decisions, we serve a God of second chances.

Lord, I have loved ones who stubbornly refuse to surrender their lives to you. It hurts, God, seeing them make poor choices and live without peace. But I know that you love them even more than I do, so I trust they will find their way to you.

Keep Looking Up!

We can hope and pray for those who are lost without God.

APRIL 18

God Gives Us Music

Read 2 Kings 1–3

> And when the musician played, the hand of the LORD came upon him. —2 Kings 3:15

GETTING THREE KIDS up, fed, dressed, and sent off with all their things was not easy on school days. Many times the exodus was accompanied with less-than-encouraging words from their dad and me. But somehow doing the same thing on Sunday morning was often a more difficult task—even with a couple more hours of slack. However, my frazzle would dissipate when church music began to settle peace back into my mind and emotions.

It's encouraging to me that the prophet Elisha also needed music to bring about clarity. In today's reading we see that Elisha turned to music to calm his soul when Judah's king Jehoshaphat asked for the Lord's counsel. And when the harpist played, Scripture tells us the power of the Lord came through Elisha with words of prophesy.

Often we have a cacophony of negativity from media and those around us that can seemingly drown out the promises of God we have hidden in our hearts. But listening to biblical worship music can restore a God-focused perspective.

Lord, thank you for the gift of music that often calms my heart, mind, and soul when the world is shouting negativity. Through music, lead me to a place of worship, trust, and peace.

Keep Looking Up!

Worship music can bring clarity and calm.

APRIL 19

God Always Provides

Read 2 Kings 4–5

When the vessels were full, she said to her son, "Bring me another vessel." And he said to her, "There is not another." Then the oil stopped flowing. —2 Kings 4:6

HAVE YOU EVER cried in the grocery store? I did once.

In the produce section I stared at prices, wondering how I could buy fruit for our family, which included four extra adults and two children. I couldn't. I didn't have enough money. So I took a deep breath and grabbed a couple bags of apples, praying they would multiply. At the end of that next week, we still had apples left, as others had generously given some more to us.

A widow in the Bible experienced God's multiplied provision when she poured oil from one storage jar to another. The oil just kept coming, eventually filling all the jars her neighbors had lent her.

Sometimes we have seasons of want, and sometimes we have seasons of plenty. In both we can trust that God knows our needs and will be with us through each of those times. Just his presence in our lives fills us to overflowing.

Lord, you have seen my family and me through some lean times, but when I look back, I see how you faithfully guided us . Thank you, Father, for your gracious provision in our lives.

Keep Looking Up!

There are no limits to what God can do!

God Fights for Us

Read 2 Kings 6–8

Then Elisha prayed and said, "O LORD, please open his eyes that he may see." So the LORD opened the eyes of the young man, and he saw, and behold, the mountain was full of horses and chariots of fire all around Elisha. —2 Kings 6:17

DON HASKINS, THE coach for Texas Western College's basketball team, led his underdog team to win the 1966 NCAA Tournament and made history as the first coach to use an all-Black starting lineup. People were uncertain of the team's chances, but the players prevailed against the cultural prejudices.

We can face all kinds of battles that seem stacked against us. This was true when the Arameans attacked the nation of Israel with a strong military force, horses, and chariots. However, God provided an even greater heavenly army with horses and chariots of fire that surrounded the city. He also struck the enemy with blindness. As a result, Israel prevailed.

Even when life seems completely overwhelming, God sees us in our struggles and is ready to fight our battles with us. He will also give us insight and the peace we need in the interim. We just need to ask for his help.

Lord, the struggles I face are real. However, I know that you see the situation too and can equip me and provide the support and wisdom I need for each step ahead. Thank you for fighting in my behalf.

Keep Looking Up!

One way to have God's insight for the struggles we face is to pray for him to open our eyes to his protection.

APRIL 21

My Example Matters to God

Read 2 Kings 9–10

The LORD said to Jehu, "Because you have done well in accomplishing what is right in my eyes and have done to the house of Ahab all I had in mind to do, your descendants will sit on the throne of Israel to the fourth generation." —2 Kings 10:30 NIV

MY MOTHER WAS an elementary school teacher. And my two daughters and I taught high school English.

My husband is a farmer and rancher, and both our sons went into the agriculture industry.

Children often follow what they know from their family background. There were two kingdoms of the Hebrews: in the north, Israel, and in the south, Judah. Biblical scholars agree that the Northern Kingdom did not have any good kings. King Jehu was no different. While Jehu wiped out Baal worship from Israel, he was not careful to follow God. And though the generations that followed Jehu came into power as God had promised, they were not good kings.

Daily we have opportunities to live out our faith in such a way that we bring honor to God and influence the next generations to put their faith in him, love him faithfully, and serve him.

Lord, may I be continually mindful that while I can count on your mercies, my witness and influence matter on a daily basis with those I love. Help me make right choices that point the younger generations to you.

Keep Looking Up!

When loved ones see us reading our Bible, they will be more likely to do so as well.

APRIL 22

We Are God's People

Read 2 Kings 11–13

And Jehoiada made a covenant between the LORD and the king and people, that they should be the LORD's people, and also between the king and the people. —2 Kings 11:17

WHO ARE YOUR people? Upon hearing that question, some might think of their family. And some think of their circle extending to friends, church folks, and business colleagues—they're the people in your inner circle. And the Bible says that the Hebrews who followed the Lord were his people.

The priest Jehoida made a covenant with the Lord confirming that the people of Judah and its king, Joash, would follow the Lord and be his people. As an immediate course of action, the people destroyed any form of worship that was not for the Lord. The king even posted guards at the temple of the Lord. And as a result, the Israelites had peace for a period of time.

When we also determine to be God's people and remove distractions and sins from our lives that would pull us from fully serving him, we too can experience joy that comes from no other source.

Lord, I want my entire family to be your people. Show me how to remove things and habits from my life that shift my eyes from you. I truly want to follow you.

Keep Looking Up!

When we follow God's leading in our lives, we demonstrate that we are his.

APRIL 23

God Rescues Us

Read 2 Kings 14–16

> The Lord had seen how bitterly everyone in Israel, whether slave or free, was suffering; there was no one to help them.
>
> —2 Kings 14:26 NIV

"I DON'T DESERVE this," Mark said.

I looked him straight in the eye. "You didn't hit Sam?" When the principal was gone from our site, I was the teacher in charge—meaning, I'd handle any discipline matters.

"Well, yeah, but he deserved it. He makes faces at me."

"Mark, if I hit every kid who made faces at me, all my students would have black eyes."

He nodded in understanding. And later Sam owned up to antagonizing Mark and asked if his suspension could be lifted. I told him no but said I appreciated his attempt to advocate for leniency.

God is the mercy giver. Even though the people of Israel were not following him and even though King Jeroboam was not either, God took mercy on them all and saved them.

We follow and serve God, who can rescue us.

Father, you see my suffering—often at my own hands—and you respond with your loving mercies. Thank you for helping me when I mess up.

Keep Looking Up!

Thanking God for his mercies is something we could do daily.

APRIL 24

God Is Trustworthy

Read 2 Kings 17–18

And the LORD was with him; wherever he went out, he prospered.
—2 Kings 18:7

MY FRIEND MARGARET once said she lives a "charmed life." She has had millions of books in print—some now reaching a second or even third generation of young women. But I know that despite what she said, life hasn't always been rosy. Like many of us, she's experienced job loss and health issues. Instead, her *perspective* was and is rosy—simply because she chooses to trust and follow God.

King Hezekiah was much the same. Despite seemingly insurmountable military challenges, Hezekiah prevailed because he trusted God, held fast to him, and did not stray from following him—even when others taunted him because of his faith (2 Kings 18:19–22).

Life may not always be charmed or rosy for us, but when we choose to trust, we know God fulfills his promise to be with us. And that's enough.

Father in heaven, the challenges I face right now seem to surround me from all sides. However, I know that I can look up to you and know you are present for these battles. I choose to put my trust in you.

Keep Looking Up!

While waiting for God to work, we can recount his faithfulness in the past.

APRIL 25

God Heals

Read 2 Kings 19–21

Turn back, and say to Hezekiah the leader of my people, Thus says the LORD, the God of David your father: I have heard your prayer; I have seen your tears. Behold, I will heal you. —2 Kings 20:5

WE PRAYED FOR a breakthrough in research and a miraculous healing for my dad when we learned he had developed amyotrophic lateral sclerosis—also called Lou Gehrig's disease. Despite some special treatment with a new drug, he was gone in less than five months.

Sometimes healings happen; sometimes they do not. King Hezekiah of Judah wept bitterly and prayed for God's touch on him when he was at the point of death. He also reminded God that he had walked faithfully with him and followed God with his whole heart. As a result of Hezekiah's petition, God gave him fifteen more years.

There doesn't seem to be a magic formula for healing. Some prayers are answered how we wish, and some are not. The one thing we can know is that when we turn to the Lord in times of illness, his presence blankets us with comfort and peace.

Lord, your Word is filled with testimonies of men and women you healed. Whether or not my prayers are answered, I will continue to trust you, because you are the Lord of my life.

Keep Looking Up!

Recounting Scripture strengthens our faith in the God who heals.

APRIL 26

God's Word Is a Blessing

Read 2 Kings 22–23

[Josiah] went up to the temple of the LORD with the people of Judah, the inhabitants of Jerusalem, the priests and the prophets—all the people from the least to the greatest. He read in their hearing all the words of the Book of the Covenant, which had been found in the temple of the LORD. —2 Kings 23:2 NIV

I HAD NEVER read the white leather Bible my parents had given me as a young girl until, as a college student, I asked the Lord to come into my life. Before then I had looked at the pretty colored pictures of Bible characters. But when I truly came to the faith on my own, the words jumped off the page and my life and purpose made sense for the first time.

God's Word is powerful and life changing. Josiah experienced the living Word when his high priest found the long-ignored Book of the Law and Josiah's secretary read it aloud to him. The words convicted Josiah, changed his thinking, and drove him to make a covenant before the Lord to walk after him and keep his commandments.

When we read through the Bible, we begin to get a glimpse of God's passionate and persistent pursuit of a relationship with us. That's life changing!

Lord, thank you for providing your Word, the Bible. Each day I see your love splashed all over its pages. Each day encouragement warms my heart. And each day I am affirmed and grow in my faith.

Keep Looking Up!

Reading a little of the Bible each day provides just the blessing I need.

APRIL 27

God Sees Leaders Too

Read 2 Kings 24–25

> Gedaliah took an oath to reassure them and their men. "Do not be afraid of the Babylonian officials," he said. "Settle down in the land and serve the king of Babylon, and it will go well with you."
>
> —2 Kings 25:24 NIV

AT THE WEEK'S end my son came into my English classroom, filled with complaints about a teacher.

"What are you going to do about that, Mom?" he said.

"I'm going to pray."

He made a face. "That's it?"

"Yes," I said, "because prayer is the most effective way to change people and change our situations. I'm going to pray for that teacher, and I'm going to pray for you because I think you can learn how to make the best of the situation you're in."

We know that we can have good leaders and bad leaders . . . and while we can't control them, we can control how we react to life. This was true when Jerusalem fell and the Hebrew people were exiled to Babylon. Even in a bad situation, the prophets said they could trust God and build their faith.

The same is true for us. We may not trust a leader, but we can always trust God and do the right thing.

Lord God, people have elected, work, and ministry leaders, and each of those persons is put in position of authority only because of your sovereignty. May I choose to grow under their authority, knowing you are ultimately in control.

Keep Looking Up!

Sending a card to a pastor, boss, or leader can make his or her day.

APRIL 28

People Count to God

Read 1 Chronicles 1–2

Israel's (that is, Jacob's) sons: Reuben, Simeon, Levi, Judah, Issachar, Zebulun, Dan, Joseph, Benjamin, Naphtali, Gad, and Asher.

—1 Chronicles 2:1–2 MSG

WHAT'S IN A name? Our name helps to provide our identity. My birth certificate name identifies me as my parents' daughter, but I'm also my aunt's namesake, as we have the same first and middle names. My married name ties me to the McHenry family, which we learned recently is part of the McDonald clan.

Names apparently were important to God, as genealogies occur many times in the Bible. Lists of generations start the book of 1 Chronicles, including the names of Jacob's twelve sons. While these records may seem tedious to read, they help us understand a couple things.

The first is that the Bible provides a reliable, historical record of the people who lived in biblical times. The other is that we can see that each person counted and still counts to God . . . just as I matter to God . . . and you do too.

Lord, while some of the names in the Bible seem different to me, I know that each person actually lived and mattered to you. I see that your Word is not just an inspirational book but also a historical record that helps me put my trust in it and in you.

Keep Looking Up!

One prayer strategy is to write down all your family members' names and then intercede for them.

APRIL 29

God Answers Big Prayers

Read 1 Chronicles 3–4

Jabez cried out to the God of Israel, "Oh, that you would bless me and enlarge my territory! Let your hand be with me, and keep me from harm so that I will be free from pain." And God granted his request. —1 Chronicles 4:10 NIV

JOHN ASKED OUR church group to pray he'd get a job for which he'd just applied. "I'm fully qualified," he said, "so I think I have a good chance."

I thought for a moment. "Which job did you apply to that you're *not* qualified for?"

"A big tech job at this other company, but I don't think I could get it."

"That's the one I'm going to pray for," I said.

Sometimes we may have a small view of God and what he can do in regard to our own life. Jabez, however, prayed big. He asked God to bless him, to expand his territory, and to provide his presence and protection.

We also can stretch our understanding of who God is by praying big. And when God answers those kinds of prayers, all the glory will go to him—well beyond the reach of our own abilities or qualifications. And as you might guess, John got the better job.

Lord, I know you can do anything, so I don't know why I limit my prayers to small requests. Help me pray big because I want others to see the magnificence of your generosity.

Keep Looking Up!

One step of faith is praying for something that is beyond our reach.

APRIL 30

With God We Win

Read 1 Chronicles 5–6

> They were helped in fighting them, and God delivered the Hagrites and all their allies into their hands, because they cried out to him during the battle. He answered their prayers, because they trusted in him. —1 Chronicles 5:20 NIV

MOST OF US have watched films of underdog teams that win the league championship. They're entertaining and inspiring. We've also probably heard fans say, "God is on our side." The truth is that both teams may have players and coaches who believe in God, and a winning team may not have any players or coaches who do.

We see an instance in today's reading when three of the Israel tribes came together to fight against several united enemies. Those God followers won the battle because they cried out to him during the fight and because they trusted in God.

When we cry out to God in our struggles of life, we are always the winner because we get to experience the presence of the holy God, who gives us strength and peace for our battles.

Lord, no matter what battle I may face, I know I can trust in you. You are bigger than the struggle. You are bigger than the enemy—human or otherwise. And you are certainly bigger than my fears. So I know with you I am a winner.

Keep Looking Up!

Praying aloud during a struggle builds confidence and a sense of God's presence.

MAY 1

God Ordained Music

Read 1 Chronicles 7–9

> Those who were musicians, heads of Levite families, stayed in the rooms of the temple and were exempt from other duties because they were responsible for the work day and night.
>
> —1 Chronicles 9:33 NIV

MY GRANDSON IS a wonderful vocalist. Just a teen, he sings continually. One evening he spent the night with us and watched a film about Davy Crockett with my husband. The next morning we heard him singing the theme song, word for word. And when he's in the car with me, he knows all the songs on Christian radio.

Historically the singers of the Lord's temple were greatly honored because they served him. Their work was leading the worship of the Lord God. Their home was God's temple. They had no other responsibilities than to be ready and available to offer the gifts God had given them—their musical abilities—to honor him.

People have differing ideas about what musical worship should look and sound like. But the purpose of worship is not to entertain or be entertained but simply to offer ourselves up to God in praise and song—no matter our abilities.

Lord, I lift up your name as the Creator and Sustainer of the universe. I sing of your goodness, grace, and saving mercies! You are worthy of all my honor and praise. May others see the glory of your creation and marvel at your works.

Keep Looking Up!

Singing worship music to God is a love offering.

MAY 2

God's Friendship Is Near

Read 1 Chronicles 10–12

> We are yours, O David, and with you, O son of Jesse! Peace, peace to you, and peace to your helpers! For your God helps you.
>
> —1 Chronicles 12:18

MY KINDERGARTENER CAME home from school one day with a sad expression on her face. When I asked her what was wrong, she said boys had been teasing her and she was "all done with kindergarten."

After I made her count on her fingers the names of those who were friends, she decided the friends outnumbered the enemies.

"I guess I'll be okay, Mommy," she said as she skipped off to her room.

The truth is even we grown-ups find that some people are for us and some seem to be against us. David found that to be true when he succeeded Saul as king of Israel. His support swelled and dissipated over the years after Samuel anointed him.

When we feel as though our friends have faded away, we can embrace the friendship of God that is always within reach.

Lord, I am yours. You are with me. I am grateful that you reach out to me as not only my Lord but also my friend. In times when I feel alone, please remind me that I can embrace the peace of your friendship.

Keep Looking Up!

A friend is often just a phone call away.

MAY 3

God Is Worth Celebrating

Read 1 Chronicles 13–16

Let the heavens be glad, and let the earth rejoice, and let them say among the nations, "The LORD reigns!" —1 Chronicles 16:31

WHEN A CALIFORNIA governor was installed in office, we attended the inaugural ball. I wore a bridesmaid dress, and my husband wore his dress Army blues. Because we don't dance much and because there were no chairs, we circled laps around the floor as we waited for the new governor to walk through the doors with his wife. Such occasions are worthy of celebrating.

The Lord God inaugurated the idea of celebrations: Sabbaths and festivals. When David finally reinstalled the ark, he made offerings and then musicians played harps, lyres, cymbals, and trumpets. After that, the people sang David's song of thanksgiving. The celebration was not designed to give glory to David, the new king, but to God, the King of Kings.

Celebration need not be reserved for certain calendar dates but can always be the center of our daily lives—because God is worth celebrating!

Lord God, you are worth celebrating every day. The moment I open my eyes in the morning I should say thank you and hallelujah for a brand-new day full of ways to serve you. Thank you for the gift of life with all its opportunities.

Keep Looking Up!

Find something today to celebrate with a friend or family member.

MAY 4

Humble People Appreciate God

Read 1 Chronicles 17–19

Then King David went in and sat before the LORD and said, "Who am I, O LORD God, and what is my house, that you have brought me thus far?" —1 Chronicles 17:16

THE GREATEST GENERATION produced some extraordinary people. They survived the Great Depression during their childhood and World War II and the Korean War as young adults. One of my uncles was a pilot in World War II, and another saved lives, receiving the Merchant Marine Distinguished Medal for heroism. I hadn't known of their accomplishments until recently because they were humble men.

Humility is a mark of God's people when they point others to the God who helped them instead of taking credit for themselves. David was such a man. The youngest son of a simple shepherd, he rose to be one of the greatest kings in the Bible. Although he wasn't perfect and made many mistakes, he knew his success was not of his own doing.

When we have the understanding that any success we have is only due to God's help, grace, and mercy, we sing his praises instead of our own.

Lord, I am very thankful—sometimes astonishingly so—for all you have done for my family and me. May I pour the overflow of your blessings on others, so that they too may know of your goodness.

Keep Looking Up!

A right perspective of God's greatness develops humility in us.

MAY 5

God's Timing Is Best

Read 1 Chronicles 20–23

Now set your mind and heart to seek the LORD your God. Arise and build the sanctuary of the LORD God, so that the ark of the covenant of the LORD and the holy vessels of God may be brought into a house built for the name of the LORD. —1 Chronicles 22:19

MANY YEARS AGO after my husband and I and our church friends had built our first homes, we realized our church was in disrepair. It was time to renovate our entire old clapboard church. Nothing on the inside of the sanctuary remained the same. Pews were refinished. Floors, sanded. Walls, repainted. Windows, doors, and wood trim, replaced. It was exhausting work but fun and rewarding.

David felt the same way—convicted that there was no house for God when David was building a glorious one for himself. But God told David his son Solomon should build the temple instead.

It's hard to wait on God's timing. When we get a great idea, we often want to jump ahead and make it happen. But sometimes God says, "Wait a minute." And later we find out that his timing is always better than ours.

Lord, you know how I like to get things done. It's hard to wait! Please override my enthusiasm when you know it would be best to wait for better timing.

Keep Looking Up!

Prayer is the best strategy when we're not exactly sure what to do.

MAY 6

God Uses Everyone

Read 1 Chronicles 24–26

Watch corresponded to watch. —1 Chronicles 26:16

IN A SMALL high school every teacher is required to pitch in for what are called extra duties: class and club advisement, dance and game supervision, student body activities. I was the senior class advisor and supervised their many activities: variety show/dinner/auction fundraiser night, senior trip, senior project presentations, awards banquet, and even the commencement ceremonies. It takes many hands to make things happen for young people.

The various tribes in Israel had duties for the greater good of David's kingdom too. Some were gatekeepers, with various divisions scheduled for the different watches throughout the day—assigned to the north, south, east, and west gates. Then others served as priests, musicians, and soldiers.

A society functions best when each of us participates, and this is true for the church as well. Each of us has value in God's eyes, and each can contribute to serve our community, church, and the Lord.

Lord, show me clearly how you can best use my gifts and talents to serve the Christian body and my community . . . and let me not wait until someone asks me. As I see a need, give me boldness to offer to help.

Keep Looking Up!

Churches always need one more volunteer.

MAY 7

God Finds Those Who Seek Him

Read 1 Chronicles 27–29

> And you, Solomon my son, know the God of your father and serve him with a whole heart and with a willing mind, for the LORD searches all hearts and understands every plan and thought. If you seek him, he will be found by you, but if you forsake him, he will cast you off forever. —1 Chronicles 28:9

MY HUSBAND IS a reader. When he was a college freshman, a young man of faith challenged Craig to read the Bible. So he took on that assignment and read the Bible from cover to cover. And he made a faith commitment without anyone else saying a single word to him. Craig sought God in those pages, and God built faith in my husband's heart.

Faith can blossom in several ways, but if we seek God, we will find him. That essentially was David's charge to his son Solomon, who would succeed him as king. He also gave Solomon all the instructions for building the house of the Lord, but David first told his son to serve God with his whole heart and a willing mind.

When we start with that kind of heart-and-mind focus, any earthly job or task God puts before us will honor him.

Lord, your Word is my starting place. It is my life instruction manual. It is my map. My faith daily is confirmed in its pages, and my heart grows toward you and heaven more and more each day as I take in your words. Thank you for your Word, God.

Keep Looking Up!

Memorizing a verse or passage from the Bible puts God's Word in our heart and mind.

MAY 8

God Gives Wisdom

Read 2 Chronicles 1–4

Give me now wisdom and knowledge to go out and come in before this people, for who can govern this people of yours, which is so great? —2 Chronicles 1:10

YOU'VE JUST BEEN charged with the most difficult job in the world. What do you do? Since 1933 a clergy member has prayed for each US president at his inauguration. And the president-elect has often attended an associated prayer service before the inauguration. As the expression goes, wise men still seek the Lord.

When Solomon was established as king of Israel, God told him he would give Solomon anything he wanted. Seemingly with little thought, Solomon asked for wisdom and knowledge to know how to govern. God granted his request and also poured out earthly riches on him.

The Lord's wisdom guides us, and while we can find wisdom through waiting-and-listening prayer, wisdom also filters to us from the pages of the Bible. As we read his Word each day, God can provide a yes, no, or not yet as we navigate the decisions of our lives.

Lord, I need wisdom for an important decision. I trust that you will guide me and will wait through the not-yet season until I hear your yes or no. I trust your Word to lead me.

Keep Looking Up!

God's Word provides the wisdom we need for daily living.

MAY 9

God Hears the Humble

Read 2 Chronicles 5–7

> If my people who are called by my name humble themselves, and pray and seek my face and turn from their wicked ways, then I will hear from heaven and will forgive their sin and heal their land.
>
> —2 Chronicles 7:14

AT A SCHOOL Christmas program I sat next to a former student—one who had cussed me out about twenty years earlier. I played peekaboo with one of his three little girls, and he told me about how much he loved being a dad. All was forgiven because, as a student, he had humbled himself and said he was sorry.

Relationships can mend when humility and confession are part of the equation. When Solomon had finished the temple, his work as king of Israel was not done. He was still responsible for teaching the people how to live a repentant, close walk with a holy God.

Closeness to God isn't impossible. It simply is a matter of humbly admitting our sins, praying for forgiveness, seeking God's presence and help, and turning away from the sins that trip us up. With God's help we can change our behavior when we're truly repentant.

Lord, I messed up. I am sorry and ask for your gracious forgiveness through your Son, Jesus. I need your help in making better choices and ask you to be with me and help me choose you rather than that which will interfere with my closeness to you.

Keep Looking Up!

God hears, forgives, and heals us when we humbly seek him.

MAY 10

People Notice God's Favor

Read 2 Chronicles 8–11

> Blessed be the LORD your God, who has delighted in you and set you on his throne as king for the LORD your God! Because your God loved Israel and would establish them forever, he has made you king over them, that you may execute justice and righteousness.
>
> —2 Chronicles 9:8

IT'S HARD TO be an elected official. My husband served as county supervisor for six years and as a city councilman for four years. Ten years of public office taught us that people rarely see what you've done—they usually see what they think is missing. However, he was able to achieve more than fifty different public works projects over his tenure—making a significant difference in the quality of life where we live.

Doing work well is a witness to others. King Solomon's wisdom and successes caught the attention of the Queen of Sheba, who, after her visit to him, understood that Solomon's achievements were a result of God's hand of blessing.

We need not accumulate a vast landscape of real estate and a thick portfolio to demonstrate God's favor on us. Doing good work can point others to God—no matter what our position is in our community.

Lord God, remind me to pray for the elected officials in my local area, state, and nation. They serve because you have allowed them to take public office. I pray their witness is strong, but that mine is as well.

Keep Looking Up!

Being a good witness for God can result from our diligent work.

MAY 11

God Watches over Me

Read 2 Chronicles 12–16

For the eyes of the LORD run to and fro throughout the whole earth, to give strong support to those whose heart is blameless toward him. —2 Chronicles 16:9

LIKE MANY YOUNG mothers I often felt lonely. I compared my life to the exterior of others around me—women who seemed to have better-put-together-on-Sunday selves and children. Depression often had a grip on me, and I cried behind closed doors. However, when I started prayerwalking—praying for the needs of others whose homes I passed—I began to understand the Lord's compassion for others. He saw others' pain and prompted me to pray, so I also knew that he saw me as well. And my depression disappeared.

Today's Scripture of focus reminds us that our omnipresent God is everywhere. His outstretched arms are ready to receive us and to carry us through the valley of struggles we face. Sometimes that help comes through walking, a friend, or medical intervention. But no burden is too great that he cannot lift. No problem is too complicated that he cannot solve. No feeling is too overwhelming that he cannot comfort. He watches over us.

Lord, you see me from the moment I wake up until the moment I lay my head on my pillow—and even through the watches of the night. I can rest in the assurance that you will see me through any difficulty I face.

Keep Looking Up!

We can be God's hands and feet to demonstrate his love.

MAY 12

We Set Our Face toward God

Read 2 Chronicles 17–20

Then Jehoshaphat was afraid and set his face to seek the LORD, and proclaimed a fast throughout all Judah. —2 Chronicles 20:3

WITHIN A MONTH'S time after our army son deployed to Afghanistan, four in his unit were killed. Fear struck me hard, and so I asked many to pray for him. For the next eight months I continued to send prayer updates and then saw in the news that a military policy had been changed so as to provide better protection for overseas troops like my son.

When King Jehoshaphat learned that three enemy tribes were bringing a multitude of warriors against Judah, the first thing he did was to pray. Then he proclaimed a fast so people from all the cities in Judah would join together to seek the Lord. And the Lord won the battle.

When we pray, we go to the commander in chief, the Lord God, who equips us for the battle.

Lord, help me not fall to the clutches of fear when bad news strikes. Instead, help me turn in the direction of you in prayer and expectation that as I stand firm and hold my position of faith, you will do the fighting for me.

Keep Looking Up!

Fasting helps our mind focus on God's faithfulness.

MAY 13

God Warns Us

Read 2 Chronicles 21–24

> Although the LORD sent prophets to the people to bring them back to him, and though they testified against them, they would not listen. —2 Chronicles 24:19 NIV

I WAS WARNED. The dentist said if I didn't use a night guard, my clenching in my sleep would take a toll. Sure enough, just months later one of my teeth crumbled. I expected an "I told you so" from my dentist, but he graciously repaired the damage.

Often we do get warnings in regard to our health or other matters. When Jehoida the priest died, various princes saw their opportunity to influence King Joash. Though the prophets warned the people, they would not listen and continued to worship idols. Eventually Joash's evil practices overshadowed his earlier good works.

The hopeful lesson for us, though, is that God wants us to draw near and stay close to him. He doesn't want harm to come to us. And he will guide us through the toughest of situations. It's just smart to pay attention to warnings.

Lord, often I ignore those nudges you so graciously give me. Thank you for sending those warnings. May I be diligent to take action when you send a warning.

Keep Looking Up!

God's Word has godly counsel for our everyday living.

God Equips Us

Read 2 Chronicles 25–28

But go, act, be strong for the battle. Why should you suppose that God will cast you down before the enemy? For God has power to help or to cast down. —2 Chronicles 25:8

WHEN FOUR OF my students were severely injured on a dangerous stretch of road (and a grandparent killed), I prayed, wondering if something could be done to widen the narrow highway. One of my students did research, surveyed the road, and discovered it was not graded properly. With that information I gave them an assignment: write formal letters to officials—each to a different person. We were ready to do battle!

Sometimes we have to fight for a cause. A godly advisor gave advice to Amaziah: go, act, be strong. Sometimes the Lord tells us to be silent and wait, and other times he tells us to take action. In both situations, we can know that God can equip us for what we need to do.

In our case my students testified at a public meeting with officials from across northern California. A year later a million dollars funded the road's reengineering and widening. God has the power to effect change.

Lord God, you know I do not enjoy conflict. And you know I would much rather sit back and let you handle the conflicts in my life. However, for those times when I need to put together a case and advocate for a need, I trust that you will equip me.

Keep Looking Up!

Memorizing God's promises builds courage for the struggles we face.

God Suddenly Provides

Read 2 Chronicles 29–31

Hezekiah and all the people rejoiced because God had provided for the people, for the thing came about suddenly. —2 Chronicles 29:36

DEEP BREATHS, I told myself. Deep breaths.

I was going car shopping and dreaded the process and probable price tag. The transmission on my eighteen-year-old car had died suddenly weeks before, so it was time for a change. As I sat there praying, the car I had hoped for drove suddenly onto the dealer's lot. And shortly after I purchased the car, an extra job suddenly fell into my lap to make my car payment.

When Hezekiah decided to repair the temple, much work was needed to restore its beauty and then collect the needed offerings, but all of those tasks, Scripture teaches us, came about suddenly.

Those "suddenly" kinds of gifts won't always fall into place, but knowing God is with us each day can provide the joy and peace we need to keep moving forward.

Lord, you know my earthly resources—my time, talents, and treasure. So I trust that once again you will suddenly provide exactly what I need.

Keep Looking Up!

We can be that "suddenly" blessing to someone else today.

MAY 16

Words Build Our God-fidence

Read 2 Chronicles 32–34

The people took confidence from the words of Hezekiah king of Judah. —2 Chronicles 32:8

I WAS FEELING self-conscious about my weight gain after a couple surgeries. But when I walked one day with a friend and expressed my frustration to her, she said, "You can do this!"

Just her little boost of encouragement motivated me to get healthier. And half a year later I had lost several dress sizes and felt great.

Kind words from a trusted friend can be confidence building—just what we need to tip the scale of the confidence we seek to make bold changes in our lives. King Hezekiah did that for the people of Judah. His confidence in the Lord's faithfulness toward his people spread into the ranks and gave them the boost they needed to go to battle against the invading Assyrians. With God's help, they won. They were full of God-fidence.

When we feel invaded by multiple problems, the prayers and kind words of others can help us rise up and win.

Lord, I feel invaded. One problem after another has dropped into my lap recently, and they're hard to deal with all at the same time. However, your Word is my confidence builder today, and I know you will help me.

Keep Looking Up!

Just a simple word of encouragement to someone in the grocery store checkout line could make her day.

MAY 17

God Persists

Read 2 Chronicles 35–36

The Lord, the God of their fathers, sent persistently to them by his messengers, because he had compassion on his people and on his dwelling place. —2 Chronicles 36:15

FOR A YEAR I watched one of my grandsons while my daughter taught high school. We did Nana School together: handwriting exercises, simple math problems, and art projects. But often he'd get restless and want to shift to something else. So his questions typically started with "Can I . . ."

Because I was working from home and had to maintain focus to get assignments done, often my response was "Later . . ."

But I knew that he would persist every ten minutes with the same request until I followed through.

God persistently pursued a relationship with his people in the Bible—through the patriarchs, judges, kings, and prophets, and then later through his Son, Jesus, and the disciples. It was his love and compassion that were behind such a passionate pursuit.

God still pursues us today, and we can understand that more fully as we study his Word.

Lord, I am so grateful for your persistent chase after me. Even on days when I don't feel I'm living up to my faith commitment, you extend your grace and beckon me to yourself. Thank you for your faithfulness to me, God.

Keep Looking Up!

Reading the Bible daily will develop perseverance in us.

MAY 18

God's Presence Produces Joy

Read Ezra 1–4

The people could not distinguish the sound of the joyful shout from the sound of the people's weeping, for the people shouted with a great shout, and the sound was heard far away. —Ezra 3:13

THE ARRIVAL OF troops returning from war prompts a joyful reaction. When my son's unit marched through the pavilion doors at an army fort on a cold February morning and stood in formation for a moment, one voice in the audience could not be distinguished from another in the mix of cheers and uncontrollable happy tears. The only comparison I could summon during those moments was the day of his birth—tears of joy—appropriate since his tour of duty in the Middle East was nine months.

Relief can unleash an emotional response. When the former exiles returned to Jerusalem from Babylon to rebuild the temple, their joy was an uncontrollable mix of joyful shouts and ecstatic tears. Their faith would again be practiced in the Lord's house.

Daily we can also experience that kind of joy when we remember that the Spirit of the Lord has found his home inside of us.

Lord, I find my joy in you. May I shout glorious praise and prayers of thanksgiving every day, because your Spirit lives in me.

Keep Looking Up!

Joy results from a daily awareness of God's presence.

MAY 19

God's Word Is Inspirational

Read Ezra 5–7

Ezra had devoted himself to the study and observance of the Law of the LORD, and to teaching its decrees and laws in Israel.

—Ezra 7:10 NIV

WHEN I STARTED teaching high school English, I had to teach units of study others had never taught me. Poetry is one that quickly comes to mind. So I immersed myself in studying poetry form and analysis—eventually creating a process students could follow to break down poetic elements and learn how to draw meaning from a writer's works.

Those who teach the Bible must study too. When the Hebrews returned to Jerusalem from exile and the temple was rebuilt, it was time to teach the people God's laws and guiding principles for their lives. Ezra, a teacher of the Law and a priest, devoted himself to studying the Scriptures so he could teach others about the Lord.

As we learn more about the Lord we love, we too can share what we have learned with others.

Lord, I love studying your Word. Each day provides new insight I've never noticed before. Thank you for those sweet treasures that encourage me and inspire me to encourage others as well.

Keep Looking Up!

We can use God's Word to inspire others in their faith journey.

MAY 20

Seeking God, Who Is Always Good

Read Ezra 8–10

The hand of our God is for good on all who seek him. —Ezra 8:22

THE RETREAT WEEKEND did not start out well. Three hours from home my car's transmission failed. Then after arriving at the retreat in my sister's mega-daycare van, I locked the keys in the vehicle. In the meeting room I sat on the floor with my dying cell phone plugged into an outlet, waiting for the car serviceman.

God, what is the good of all this?

Shortly thereafter one of the retreat organizers found me. Five minutes and a long prayer later, she said, "Well, God is good, and I know your presentations will go great." She was right on both accounts.

When we face challenges, the pieces may not come together perfectly. That's life, just as Ezra found with the temple reconstruction because of threatening enemies. However, because the people confessed their sins and humbly sought after God, good triumphed over evil.

Life is not perfect, but God is always good.

Lord, some days are an absolute mess with one difficulty after another. On those days I sometimes can't wait to put my head on my pillow and just sleep the bad stuff away. But I know that despite the fact that life is hard, you are good.

Keep Looking Up!

When frustrated, we can stop, drop to our knees, and pray to see God's goodness.

MAY 21

God Invites Our Prayers

Read Nehemiah 1–3

Then the king said to me, "What are you requesting?" So I prayed to the God of heaven. —Nehemiah 2:4

I FELT OVERWHELMED at my teaching job. In addition to the demands of being a full-time English teacher, I was also the only academic counselor, teacher-in-charge when the principal was gone, accreditation coordinator, scholarship federation advisor, newspaper advisor . . . and the basketball scorekeeper. My problem was saying yes too much, instead of asking God for his wisdom.

I should have followed Ezra's example. When he sensed the need to repair the walls and gates of Jerusalem, he went to the king to explain his concern. Then when the king asked him what was wrong, Ezra didn't immediately respond. He prayed. It would be a hard ask to seek permission to leave captivity for his homeland. But the king gave not only his approval but also his support.

When we have a hard question posed to us, a prayer pause will help us rightly frame our response.

Lord, I react and speak too quickly. And sometimes the words don't come out very kindly. Help me remember to pause for prayer instead of giving an immediate response, so that my words represent you well.

Keep Looking Up!

Praying "Guide my words" can help us respond with just the right thing.

MAY 22

God Protects Us

Read Nehemiah 4–7

We prayed to our God and set a guard as a protection against them day and night. —Nehemiah 4:9

THEFTS ABOUNDED IN our neighborhood some years ago. Someone stole a bicycle and a yard wagon from our driveway. So we began locking our doors—something we hadn't done in years. When I saw a woman pulling a child in my yellow yard wagon, I asked her where she got it. She said she'd bought it at a yard sale down the street. Sadly, even neighbors sometimes can't be trusted.

Nehemiah had some bad neighbors too. When they threatened his efforts to repair Jerusalem's gates and walls, he put several strategies into place. He positioned people around the walls by clans. Some would work, and some served as watchmen. Nehemiah also recruited all-day guards. And he enlisted the people in prayer.

God is the one who can stop Satan in his tracks. God protects us spiritually, emotionally, mentally, and even physically. But it's still a good practice to provide safe measures for our family.

Lord, remind me that prayer is the best strategy for protection. But I also ask that you give me discernment and awareness of how to be mindful of my surroundings. Thank you for protecting me, Father.

Keep Looking Up!

We spiritually lock our doors when we refuse to sin.

God's Joy Is Our Strength

Read Nehemiah 8–10

Nehemiah said, "Go and enjoy choice food and sweet drinks, and send some to those who have nothing prepared. This day is holy to our Lord. Do not grieve, for the joy of the LORD is your strength."

—Nehemiah 8:10 NIV

I THINK BOXES of tissues should be placed at the ends of every church pew (or row of chairs). Often the reading of the Bible and hearing a pastor teach its meaning touch my heart. The power behind those words convicts me and sometimes calls to mind God's great provision in my past.

The same reaction occurred when Nehemiah read the Book of the Law after the city walls and gates were restored. As the people had been in exile, they had not had the opportunity to hear God's law publicly read and taught. Hearing it then brought great emotion and tears. But that day was one for celebration, so Nehemiah told the people to enjoy the special food and drinks and to share with those who had none.

Choosing joy in emotional times provides strength that comes from God's sweet companionship. It doesn't negate the sorrow or regrets but helps us develop resilience.

Lord, the joy that wells up within me comes from you and is not anything I can summon. Thank you for your Word, which provides testimony after testimony of your love, care, and provision.

Keep Looking Up!

Recalling a sweet memory is one way to choose joy.

God Inspires Our Giving

Read Nehemiah 11–13

Remember me, O my God, concerning this, and do not wipe out my good deeds that I have done for the house of my God and for his service. —Nehemiah 13:14

WHEN I GOT home from teaching that day, there was stuff all over the living room, the kitchen was a disaster, and the kids' rooms were still a mess—with company coming for dinner! When I asked them why they hadn't done their chores as I had asked, the oldest said, "We just forgot."

Forgetting to do what we promised can put pressure on others. This was the situation Nehemiah discovered when the people forgot to give to the Levites, the priestly tribe. Because the priests then had to work to create their own food, the house of the Lord and related duties lay unattended. Nehemiah reminded the people to give, and he clearly felt some guilt and responsibility himself.

Giving to our church and Christian ministries is a gift of love and appreciation for all they do and all God has done for us.

Lord, you have given so much to me, and because I am thankful for all you do for me and all who work for the building of your kingdom, I can give a portion back to you. I can be faithful and generous to others because you are faithful and generous to me.

Keep Looking Up!

Giving from the heart allows others to fulfill their God-given calling.

MAY 25

God Calls Us to See Injustice

Read Esther 1–5

And who knows whether you have not come to the kingdom for such a time as this? —Esther 4:14

ALL I HAD done was volunteer to help with the National Day of Prayer. But then I got a phone call asking if I would consider serving as county coordinator. It seemed a daunting task, organizing a prayer event. But after a time of prayer, I sensed this was something God wanted me to do.

Sometimes we are suddenly thrust into leadership. Esther was quickly pushed into the role of queen of Persia and just as quickly was pushed to advocate for her people, the Jews. As queen, she was the one who could best influence her husband, King Xerxes, to allow the Jews to assemble and protect themselves and kill any who might attack them. She called on her people to fast (and presumably pray) for her, as she and her maids did also.

When we see injustice, we can ask God if he has positioned us in such a way to advocate for change. And then trust him for the results.

Lord, if I see an injustice and it creates a fire in me, perhaps you have positioned me for such a time as this . . . to try to make changes happen to help other people. Give me the courage to follow through.

Keep Looking Up!

One way to advocate for change is to write a letter to a public official.

MAY 26

God's Victories Are Worth Celebrating

Read Esther 6–10

For the Jews it was a time of happiness and joy, gladness and honor.
—Esther 8:16 NIV

OUR TOWN AND its people have been saved several times—from at least two major forest fires and multiple floods. Here in the Sierra, our county is 72 percent national forest, and we've witnessed the devastation that fire wreaks upon our neighboring forestland. Oddly enough, we see floods too—when warm rains follow heavy snowfall. So we love to celebrate the more peaceful seasons that follow those stressful ones.

Life is worth celebrating. After Queen Esther saved the Jewish people from being killed, her uncle, Mordecai, became second in command to the king. He established the festival of Purim to recall how mourning was turned into dancing. And the Jews began the annual celebration with good food and gifts—still practiced from one evening through the next day in the springtime.

Life has enough sorrow, so when there's good news, it's worth celebrating.

Lord, I celebrate life and family and friends. I celebrate faith and freedom. And I celebrate your Son's birth and resurrection from the dead. Thank you for all the goodness you pour into my life.

Keep Looking Up!

Faith-filled friends and potluck meals make the best parties.

MAY 27

God Sees Our Pain

Read Job 1–4

The LORD gave, and the LORD has taken away; blessed be the name of the LORD. —Job 1:21

IN ONE FELL swoop of cancer about nine years ago, I lost my sister, who was also my best friend. I still miss Nan every day, yet I am thankful for the delight God brought into the world through her sense of humor, gift of hospitality, desire for adventure, and faith-filled perspective.

Unfortunately, pain is a natural part of life. Job certainly experienced this. He lost his children, his health, and all his earthly wealth. While many of his responses in the book named for him were emotional, he continued to look to God for his answers. In his questioning he did not abandon God but instead sought answers from him.

When we question God, we are going to the right place. He understands our struggles with pain and loss because he loves us and cares for us. And God is bigger than any doubts we might have.

Lord, I know that there will be pain and loss here on earth because life is not perfect this side of heaven. Though I may struggle with questions, I will continue to seek you and hold fast to you as I walk those valleys with you by my side.

Keep Looking Up!

Writing out our laments can be therapeutic.

God Fulfills My Hope

Read Job 5–8

Oh that I might have my request, and that God would fulfill my hope. —Job 6:8

BECAUSE MY DAD always said "We'll see . . ." to our questions as kids, he and Mom named their place the Wheel C Ranch. They always had a hope-filled outlook on life, which fostered faith in us.

Like a loving father, our God inspires our hope, because he loves for us to go to him. Job had lost everything but his wife and his life, but he continued to go to God in complaints of prayer and to petition for understanding and relief from his suffering. His hope was not in vain, because although suffering will occur, God does not abandon us or fill us with false counsel as did Job's friends.

All of us will suffer. But those of us who follow the Lord will have his presence, comfort, and guidance to see us through those times.

Father, faith and hope are my choice for the hard times ahead because you are my guide and my help. I know that I will never be alone, and I am thankful you always welcome me and hear my prayers and petitions.

Keep Looking Up!

We can choose hope each day because our hope is in our ever-present Jesus.

MAY 29

God's Ways Are Not Our Ways

Read Job 9–12

With God are wisdom and might; he has counsel and understanding.
—Job 12:13

I DID NOT understand why we were going through such a painful trial in our lives. The final decision against us in a legal trial was difficult and would affect us for the rest of our lives. But on the worst day, outside the courtroom, a friend said, "Janet, look at your husband. He is a perfect example of a man who trusts in God."

As I looked at Craig, I suddenly saw him in a new light and understood that God had allowed that challenge in our lives. I accepted it as part of the answer to my longtime prayer that the Lord would make our marriage stronger.

God's ways are not our ways. While Job suffered greatly, he also knew that his own wisdom and understanding paled in comparison to the Lord God's. Just as Job learned to wait for God's timing and purpose, we can wait for his redemptive plan. God's ways are best.

Lord God, I understand that you give and you take away—that there's an ebb and flow of blessing versus struggle. I also know that there is a redemptive purpose to pain. Help me trust you even when I don't understand.

Keep Looking Up!

Posting Scripture verses throughout the house helps us focus on promises, not pain.

MAY 30

God Is Our Judge

Read Job 13–16

I would speak to the Almighty, and I desire to argue my case with God. —Job 13:3

WHEN I WORKED as a summer intern in the nation's capital, I learned that going to the top with a request often brought about quick, personalized attention. As my supervisors had instructed, I first answered letters that senators or congressmen had forwarded to that government office then I answered others sent directly.

This is true with other kinds of struggles too. When life deals out problems, we can go to the top: the Almighty God. Job had several counselors—all of whom gave unhelpful counsel. Job only wanted to plead his case to God rather than rationalize his situation to the people around him.

While friends and family and even professionals can help us at times, often a better strategy is to pray because we have a judge who understands and loves us.

Lord, you hear my case and know all the evidence of the situation I face. Help me see right from wrong, so I can do all that is expected of me in order to better handle what I am going through—trusting you for the ultimate decision.

Keep Looking Up!

Writing down prayer requests in a journal tracks God's gracious responses.

MAY 31

God Lives!

Read Job 17–20

For I know that my Redeemer lives, and at the last he will stand upon the earth. —Job 19:25

I BOUGHT A few things from an online auction house—a couple vintage cane-bottomed chairs and a wool rug. A couple days later I drove to redeem them—to pay for them and take them home—and we have been enjoying them ever since.

Redemption is an important idea in Scripture, and Job even calls God his Redeemer. He knew that God would redeem his life in at least one way. First, God might take away Job's pain on earth and restore the blessings he had lost. But ultimately Job said that even if his flesh was destroyed, he would see God (Job 19:26). It was a win-win situation: renewed life on earth or eternal life with God.

Every day of life on earth is a gift—given to us to enjoy and to acknowledge our Redeemer, Jesus. Even after life, though, we will meet him and experience the fullest blessings possible.

I know, God, that you are my Redeemer and that you live forever in heaven. Therefore, while I can appreciate the joys you offer here on earth, I know my ultimate fulfillment will be spent in heaven with you.

Keep Looking Up!

We can redeem seemingly lost days during suffering by finding ways to thank God.

JUNE 1

God Knows Our Days

Read Job 21–24

He'll complete in detail what he's decided about me, and whatever else he determines to do. —Job 23:14 MSG

WHEN YOU HAVE a parent who has passed away from an ugly disease such as ALS, at times you wonder how many more days you have left. But that kind of thinking takes my eyes off the wonder of the life God has given me this very day. I call that eye-shifting . . . and it can work for good or for not-so-good.

One Bible character who was good at eye-shifting was Job. While he wrote pages of laments pouring out the aches of his body, soul, and heart, he eventually shifted his eyes back to the truth of his situation—that God was still in control of Job's days, still good, and still worthy of praise and adoration.

Only God knows how many days are numbered for us. When we do an eye-shift from bad to good, we trust God for the gift of each and every day.

Some days, God, are just not fun. But I do not want to dwell in that hard mental space but instead do an eye-shift to all the blessings you have poured into my life. Thank you, God, for each day you give me. May I use them all well.

Keep Looking Up!

When days are difficult, we can shift our focus to God's goodness.

JUNE 2

God Is Wisdom

Read Job 25–30

And he said to man, "Behold, the fear of the Lord, that is wisdom, and to turn away from evil is understanding." —Job 28:28

"NEED SOME HELP?" I asked my daughter, who was trying to thread a needle in the dim light of her bedroom. She was working on a quilt for a 4-H project.

"No," she said, "I'll get it."

But she didn't, so she moved directly under the bright light of the nearby kitchen and accomplished her task in seconds. Soon she was sewing final stitches in the quilt hem.

Moving into the light of God's Word from the shadows of our own thinking lends understanding to our suffering. Job turned to the Lord to try to understand the whys behind his losses. Turning toward the Light away from the dimness of the world is a step in the right direction.

Wisdom is not elusive. God does not try to hide truth or direction or insight. When we seek the Lord, we are headed in the right direction.

Father, I see that developing wisdom in my life is not a secretive process. I simply read your Word, pray, and regularly spend time worshiping you.

Keep Looking Up!

God loves to give wisdom to those who ask for it.

JUNE 3

God Sees Our Steps

Read Job 31–34

[God] has his eyes on every man and woman. He doesn't miss a trick. —Job 34:21 MSG

THE PERFECT SEATS for our basketball games are at the score table. As the official scorekeeper for home games, I sit on the opposite side of the gym from the crowd—with no one to distract me or block my view. So when the young man went for a loose ball and fell, I could clearly see that his missteps might mean an ankle injury. And as we learned hours later, it was so.

God sees our right steps, and he sees our wrong steps. He sees everything we do, Job's friend Elihu argued, using that truth to imply that Job had made missteps in his life that brought about his suffering. But that assumption was not true because Job was a righteous man before God. Satan had brought about Job's suffering, and God permitted that suffering to prove Job's faithfulness.

God saw Job's steps, he gave them a stamp of approval, and faith won in the heavenlies!

Lord, I pray that if I am chosen as a soldier for the sake of heavenly battles, that I will prove faithful. In the meantime I ask that as you see all my steps during any given day, you will help me not walk on the wrong path but instead lead me in the right direction.

Keep Looking Up!

Knowing God sees us reminds us we have a guiding companion for our journey.

JUNE 4

God Is Sovereign

Read Job 35–38

Where were you when I laid the foundation of the earth? Tell me, if you have understanding. —Job 38:4

"MRS. MCHENRY, I'M not going to do this," Macie said. "I'm still tired from the weekend."

I stared at her for a few moments. Then I laughed out loud and said, "First, Macie, you're hilarious, and second, despite how tired you are, we are going to examine the common elements of Shakespearean tragedy today."

Some folks struggle with authority. They question government and law enforcement. They question decisions employers make. And some even question God. After Job had prayerfully petitioned God, the Lord finally answered him—reminding Job of God's unmatched, sovereign nature.

The truth is God is God, and we are not. That's a good thing, though, because we do not see the bigger picture of life. He is the Creator of the universe, and each of us is just one of his creations. We can know that our loving Lord knows what is best for us and will do it.

Lord God, you are sovereign over all the earth and the universe beyond it. You see the bigger perspective, whereas I just see my own situation. Help me exercise patience and trust so that I learn from the situation I am in.

Keep Looking Up!

**When we examine God's creation,
we get a view of God's greatness.**

JUNE 5

Forgiveness Is God's Idea

Read Job 39–42

The LORD restored the fortunes of Job, when he had prayed for his friends. And the LORD gave Job twice as much as he had before.
—Job 42:10

I DID NOT want to pray for that man. He had put my husband through a grave set of circumstances that spread over many years. While justice finally prevailed in our favor, I simply wanted to savor my righteous anger.

When people pile hurt upon hurt on us, the unkindnesses sting with their emotional weight. Job must have felt that, when three so-called friends and a younger whippersnapper criticized him unjustifiably. It's hard enough to suffer, but when our friends offer uninvited advice, we can also feel very much alone in our suffering.

What we see through Job's story, though, is that Job prayed for his "friends" when God asked him to. And God put them in their place and rewarded Job with blessings more than he had lost. Ultimately, justice is in God's hands, and because God forgives us, we will want to forgive others.

Lord, it's so easy to hang on to what I see as righteous anger. I mean, I'm right, and they're wrong! But you always ask me to forgive, and I know I won't have peace until I do. So I will trust you for the ultimate outcome because Jesus did too.

Keep Looking Up!

Sometimes forgiveness must be a daily practice.

JUNE 6

God Is Majestic

Read Psalms 1–8

When I look at your heavens, the work of your fingers, the moon and the stars, which you have set in place, what is man that you are mindful of him? —Psalm 8:3–4

I AM BLESSED to live in an isolated, rural mountain valley, where clear skies are typical. Light pollution is about nonexistent here, so "starry night" is not just a poster but something I can view from my front porch. The Big Dipper and Little Dipper are faithful evening companions, and I've seen a countless number of what we call falling stars—actually meteors that are vaporizing in earth's upper atmosphere.

Intentionally observing God's incredible creation is a humbling experience when we take in all its details. The blue-grays of mountain layers in the soft evening light. The swaying lines of migrating birds. The gurgle of a meandering creek and the kiss of a soft, blossom-scented wind.

David, the poet-king, took notice of the majesty of God's world and in comparison, wondered at the immenseness of God's love for humankind. God chooses us for his fellowship. And blesses us with his magnificent creation to enjoy!

O Lord, how majestic is your name in all the earth! That you are mindful of me, love me, and care about me is humbling indeed. May I also be mindful of your gifts of creation all around me and your gift of life to me.

Keep Looking Up!

Noticing the intricacies of nature is an act of worship.

JUNE 7

God Is Faithful

Read Psalms 9–17

I will give thanks to the LORD with my whole heart; I will recount all of your wonderful deeds. —Psalm 9:1

LYING FLAT WITH continuous pain from a herniated disc gave me time to think. I couldn't stand, sit, or even hold a book to read. On those days when my thoughts tended to focus on the pain, it became harder to bear.

Gratitude became a prayer practice I adopted. I would start with memories of childhood, rehearsing what I could remember and then giving thanks to God for them. As I moved through the history of my life, I was not as conscious of the pain, and time passed until surgery finally corrected the problem.

In Psalm 9 David writes that he remembers and gives praise for the Lord and his wonderful deeds. The Psalms model how to offer thanksgiving and praise. David notices God's character and praises him for specific traits. He also thanks God for the various ways he protected him. Praise and thanksgiving put God first in our lives.

Lord, you are my great protector and defender. You have held me up and walked with me through difficult seasons, and you are faithfully near me now. I can look confidently ahead because you are steadfast.

Keep Looking Up!

Counting blessings makes us grateful people.

JUNE 8

God Is Our Rock

Read Psalms 18–21

For by you I can run against a troop, and by my God I can leap over a wall. —Psalm 18:29

I HAD MANY students who were rock climbers. Ropes, carabiners, and belays were their gear, and their bucket lists were names of crags they wanted to climb. Our area in the Sierra is filled with exciting, solid-rock wall challenges, and my climbers laughed when I cringed at photos of them in places that appear entirely inaccessible.

With God's help we can not only face but also accomplish seemingly impossible tasks. David wrote confidently of God's help in Psalm 18. Throughout his life David often had to run for his life or hide from enemies from without or within.

Troubles might seem like an unscalable wall with no steps or an avalanche bearing down on us. But even when we feel physically and emotionally weak, God walks ahead of us and either knocks down those barriers or equips us to accomplish what we thought we could not. With him as our guide, we know we can trust him as our lead climber.

Lord, you see that mountain ahead that I must climb, but I do not feel equipped or strong enough for that scrambling. Be my lead climber, God, going before me so I have strong footings in my ascent over this problem.

Keep Looking Up!

We can trust God to help us when we face challenges.

JUNE 9

God Is My Shepherd

Read Psalms 22–27

The LORD is my shepherd; I shall not want. He makes me lie down in green pastures. —Psalm 23:1–2

MY RANCHING HUSBAND summers his beef cattle in pastureland bisected by a year-round creek. For the summer the cows and their calves have plenty to eat right next to the creek. But when fall comes, often the cows won't move over the hill to better grass on their own. So my husband asks our daughter to help move them to better grass with her horse.

Just as cattle might not be smart enough to move from dry stubble to green pastures, sometimes we might not either. We may feel stuck in a harmful relationship or even a bad habit. Rather than wait for a drastic turning point, we can turn to the Lord for his guidance and insight and provision for that new place in life that fills us not only with what we need but also with peace only he can provide.

We can trust our Shepherd to lead us.

Lead me, Good Shepherd. Take me from this stubbled, dry place of my life into those green pastures of your presence. I wander, God, and I get lost sometimes; help me to trust and follow you.

Keep Looking Up!

When we follow the Shepherd, he leads us to what is best for us.

JUNE 10

God Is a Joy Giver

Read Psalms 28–33

Weeping may tarry for the night, but joy comes with the morning.
—Psalm 30:5

AT THE END-OF-YEAR faculty meeting my principal started talking about assignments and plans for the next school year. And tears began to well up . . . because I wasn't going to be there. I had been laid off due to budget cutbacks. The days and weeks ahead were also gloomy. Even though I knew my job loss wasn't due to my performance, it was painful to explain the situation over and over again. I took it all to heart and felt misplaced shame.

However, the week before school started, I was offered another teaching job right in my small town. My commute went from thirty minutes to two minutes. My income increased. And eventually I taught all four of our kids.

God has a way of turning mourning into dancing. Some situations that seem dire put us in a position for something even better down the road.

Lord, there is a situation that has hurt me a lot, and I've tried to process how to accept and handle this. Help me be patient and wait for your redemptive answer and fresh new joy to replace the sadness.

Keep Looking Up!

Doctors say choosing joy even in hard places can lengthen life.

JUNE 11

God Is Good!

Read Psalms 34–37

Taste and see that the LORD is good! —Psalm 34:8

SEVERAL OF OUR grandchildren are picky eaters and look cross-eyed at me when I urge them to try something new. The rest are enthusiastic experimenters who will try anything once. They taste something before deciding if they like it, whereas the others will nix new foods based on the appearance.

Perhaps we once were like picky eaters in regard to our relationship with God—holding him at arm's length instead of learning about his good character. There are several ways we can "taste and see that the LORD is good." One is reading the Bible a little bit each day. Another is praying—asking God to help us with needs we have.

And still another is learning to trust him more each day—following the direction in his Word, giving up negative habits, and even sharing our faith with others. As we taste God's goodness, we will want more of him.

Father God, I want to feast on your goodness and grow in maturity of faith. I pray for diligence in daily disciplines that will help me learn more about your good character and leave behind that which drags me down.

Keep Looking Up!

Underlining Bible promises helps us more easily find them when we need them.

JUNE 12

God Thinks of Me

Read Psalms 38–42

As for me, I am poor and needy, but the Lord takes thought for me. You are my help and my deliverer; do not delay, O my God!
—Psalm 40:17

I NOTICED MY friend Chloe's distance one day—that she hadn't called or stopped by or even sought me out in church on Sunday mornings. We had been thick as thieves in many ministry events over the years, and I was missing her.

When I called and mentioned I hadn't seen her lately, she said, "You've been so down—it was depressing being with you."

I kind of gulped and threw out a quick apology, saying I hoped we could do something together soon.

While friends can come and go in our lives, the Lord is our faithful companion—even in our poor and needy seasons. He doesn't forsake us simply because we are heavyhearted. He loves us unconditionally, and we can always lean into his embrace. Friends will always disappoint us at some point in time, but the Lord sticks with us—through the thick and thin of life.

Lord, you see me, feeling all lonely and needy, and you sit with me in that life corner, loving me and encouraging me and pouring worth into me. I can always look up and find you smiling on me.

Keep Looking Up!

Instead of waiting for a friend to call, we can take the initiative ourselves.

JUNE 13

Seek God in Stillness

Read Psalms 43–49

Be still, and know that I am God. I will be exalted among the nations, I will be exalted in the earth! —Psalm 46:10

THE DAY SEEMED full of problems. The kids were bickering again. My work was spilling into and filling my evening. Unkind words spoken earlier in the day still echoed in my head. So I decided to give myself a moment away and stepped outside our home for a long look at the stars.

I didn't even pray much, just "Here I am, God." Ten minutes later God settled my tension with peace. And I headed back inside, better equipped for the challenges ahead.

Conflict is inevitable in families, in businesses, in schools, and even between nations. But the psalmist writes in Psalm 46 that God is our strength, our refuge, and our ever-present help in times of trouble. In those times of upheaval, if we can find a quiet moment away from the noise, doing so will help us collect our thoughts so we remember that God is with us and will help us.

Lord, as I consider you and exalt your name, the arguments pass away into insignificance. Nothing is more important than spending time with you, stilling my heart and allowing your peace to settle over my soul.

Keep Looking Up!

A prayer chair can provide a place of sanctuary.

God Forgives Us

Read Psalms 50–55

Create in me a clean heart, O God, and renew a right spirit within me. —Psalm 51:10

I HADN'T FELT right about my response to my student. When he loudly said I had lost his essay, I responded with a sarcastic comment, which only prompted an angry outburst from him. While others might have said my comment was justified, I knew I hadn't handled the situation well. So the next day I apologized to him in front of the class . . . and then he admitted he'd found his essay in his locker.

Having a clean heart doesn't mean we are perfect. It means we choose to please God rather than ourselves. The backstory of this psalm is that David took advantage of another man's wife and then attempted to cover up his own crime. When the prophet Nathan confronted him about his sin, David repented . . . and this psalm reflects his penitent posture.

Repentance, sincere apologies, and restitution help keep our hearts and lives clean.

Lord, help me turn from that which would drag me down and quickly repent when I mess up. If that means that I ask forgiveness of someone, may I do that quickly and make it right with that person.

Keep Looking Up!

An apology need not be perfect when it's sincerely expressed.

JUNE 15

God Is My Fortress

Read Psalms 56–61

Lead me to the rock that is higher than I, for you have been my refuge, a strong tower against the enemy. —Psalm 61:2–3

FOR A RECENT birthday my kids asked what kind of gift I wanted.

I said, "I want to hike with you to Castle Rocks."

On a cold spring day about a dozen of us hiked into the mountains just east of our small town up to a solid rock outcropping that looks like a castle rising toward the sky. I was the last one up the final steep incline. By then the younger ones were scrambling all over the formation with their look-at-me shouts. It was the best gift ever . . . with unforgettable views and memories.

Forts and castles were often built on hills—for vantage points against enemies. David hid out in protective caves that provided angles to see others approaching. Ultimately, though, God was David's refuge and advantage against anyone who could potentially harm him.

The Lord, our Rock, is still our best protector.

Lord, lead me to yourself, my rock and my refuge and my fortress. Protect me against anything that would do me harm. I often feel weak and need your tall-tower strength. Thank you for your steadfast faithfulness in sheltering me.

Keep Looking Up!

When we feel life is attacking us from all directions, we can pray for God to be our refuge.

JUNE 16

God Is the Best Parent

Read Psalms 62–68

But truly God has listened; he has attended to the voice of my prayer. —Psalm 66:19

ONE OF MY kids wanted to skip school that Friday for some fun activity with friends.

"No" was my quick and easy answer. "That's not a good example, since you're a teacher's kid, and your teachers work hard to teach you."

Just as parents have to say "no" or "not yet" or even "you've not been responsible lately," the Lord may have similar responses.

The Psalms are a great textbook on prayer. While we might have the tendency to make requests the central part of our prayers, we see from Psalm 66 that praise is important. And many psalms at least end with praise.

God is not an Instacart master—with immediate responses to whatever we want. He loves us and wants the best for us . . . but what's best may be different than what we expect. He is our heavenly Father, worthy of our praise.

Lord, I know I ask you for all kinds of things. And I know some of these requests are not made from a pure heart. But I know you want the best for me, so that is what I want also.

Keep Looking Up!

Beginning our prayers with praise puts our hearts into a posture of looking up.

JUNE 17

God Is Worth the Wait

Read Psalms 69–72

> But as for me, my prayer is to you, O Lord. At an acceptable time, O God, in the abundance of your steadfast love answer me in your saving faithfulness. —Psalm 69:13

I PRAYED DESPERATE tears for our legal case to go away—that I would wake up and find it was all a dream, or, rather, a nightmare. But the false charges played out as "guilty"—and my husband was convicted of criminal animal abuse relating to six calves that died in a two-day blizzard. Seemingly, God's answer was "no."

We walked in numb faith as we prepared an appeal and waited for the appellate court's decision, which overturned the conviction. God's answer was "yes"—we simply had to wait more than five years.

The Lord does answer us in his acceptable time. In the meantime we have the opportunity to cling to him, to grow in our faith, and to be an example of trust in the living God. He is our sovereign judge who reigns over all aspects of our lives.

Lord, I don't believe in blind faith because not only does your Word give testimony to your goodness and your faithfulness, I can clearly see your hand in my life. Therefore, I know that waiting on your answers to my prayers is an eyes-wide-open posture for prayer.

Keep Looking Up!

Time is never wasted when we ask God how to serve him while waiting.

JUNE 18

God Lifts Us Up

Read Psalms 73–77

When I tried to understand all this, it troubled me deeply till I entered the sanctuary of God; then I understood their final destiny.
—Psalm 73:16–17 NIV

I SHOULD HAVE gotten the job. The other applicants were fresh out of college, but I had a résumé full of experience and results. Nevertheless, the school district did not hire me but chose a fresh face instead.

I was mad at God. It wasn't fair. Why wouldn't he let me move on and start over in a new place? Why weren't my qualifications and experience considered?

Comparison is an awful trap that makes us question our value and even question God's judgment. The psalmist nearly got caught in that kind of struggle as he watched the wicked not only prosper but also harass the faithful who followed God.

But psalmists often use what the poets call a turn—a change of perspective toward the end of the psalm as they turn to trust God. We also can have a turn as we wait on God to lift us up and hold us in his embrace.

Lord, thank you for lifting me up from my pit of comparison. Use me, Lord, for your service so that others might see through me that faith works.

Keep Looking Up!

Even when the world pushes us down, God lifts us up.

JUNE 19

God Lives through Generations

Read Psalms 78–80

But we your people, the sheep of your pasture, will give thanks to you forever; from generation to generation we will recount your praise. —Psalm 79:13

MY PARENTS PASSED down several family traditions: singing in the car, celebrating birthdays in a big way, and going for drives on Sunday afternoons. The best one they passed down was attending and serving at their church. I have no memory of ever staying home from a Sunday service. Even one Christmas Eve when they couldn't dig our car out of the snow, they called a taxi to take us to the evening service.

Many times in the Bible the writers speak of the importance of passing down the faith to the next generations. Reading the Bible together, praying as a family, and attending worship services create a legacy of faith. And hopefully the younger generations will develop their own faith and praise God for his faithfulness.

Our actions and prayers can help younger ones embrace a life of faith that points others to Jesus as well.

Lord, life gets busy and it's easy to let the hustle take precedence over quiet time practices of Bible reading and prayer. May I be the example who models those disciplines in a joyful manner so that others pick up the faith mantle.

Keep Looking Up!

Putting Bible verses on sticky notes around the house keeps God's Word in our hearts and minds.

JUNE 20

God Is Our Strength Giver

Read Psalms 81–88

They go from strength to strength, till each appears before God in Zion. —Psalm 84:7 NIV

I HAD JUST had back surgery less than two months earlier before I traveled to an international prayer conference at the World Prayer Center in Colorado Springs. Fortunately, kind people helped lift my luggage. Unfortunately, I was still pretty achy by the first full day of the conference.

But I was greeted there by two organizers who said they wanted to pray for me. Here was their prayer from Scripture I will never forget: "Blessed are those whose hearts are on the highways . . . they go from strength to strength till each appears before God in Zion." With their kind, prayerful affirmation, I found that every time I needed a literal lift or a figurative one, God provided the strength I needed.

As we approach challenges, we also can pray the Lord's grace will carry us "from strength to strength."

Lord, you know my limitations. You know sometimes I feel weak and unequipped for the task. And yet whenever I have a need, I sense you have paved the highway for me, so that my travels through this wonderful life are not only doable but also grace filled.

Keep Looking Up!

Prayers can be incremental, asking God for strength for just one task at a time.

JUNE 21

God Is Our Dwelling Place

Read Psalms 89–94

Lord, you have been our dwelling place in all generations.
—Psalm 90:1

WHEN I NEED a quiet day away to think and hear from God, I head an hour south to a favorite dwelling place: Lake Tahoe. The largest alpine lake in North America and second deepest, Tahoe is barely behind the five Great Lakes in terms of volume and is well known for its clear, pristine waters. After a half day of staring at the blues and violets and the surrounding tree-covered Sierra mountainscape, peace and wholeness settle over my heart.

While our home and certain other special spots may be comfort zones for us, the Lord is always our dwelling place. In his presence we have peace, refuge, and protection. He counsels us and takes care of each of our needs. And God also gives us direction when we are confused or uncertain about our next steps.

One of the best things about the Lord is that, unlike all other comfort zones, he's with us all the time.

Lord, you are my dwelling place, my refuge, and my peace. Calm my heart. Guide my mind. Settle peace over my soul, for I trust in you.

Keep Looking Up!

Taking a retreat with the Lord refreshes the soul.

JUNE 22

The Generations Praise God

Read Psalms 95–103

Let this be recorded for a generation to come, so that a people yet to be created may praise the LORD. —Psalm 102:18

EACH YEAR I prepare a family newsletter and photo card to send to friends and family. A couple years ago I put those letters and cards into an album that I bring out when family visits. It has become a history of God's faithfulness to us as we are reminded of the joys as well as the struggles.

Thankfully we also have a record of God's faithfulness to his people from the beginning of creation until the coming of Christ and then through the acts of Jesus's followers. As we read the Bible each day, we become part of the generations who have found strength and wisdom—figurative daily bread that feeds our heart, mind, and soul for the calling God has placed on our lives.

Every day of opening God's Word can reveal new insights and new inspiration that help us rise above the difficulties of our circumstances to live grace-filled lives.

Lord, your daily bread has fed a countless number of Christ followers over the generations. May a people yet to be created continue praising your good name and share the good news that you love us and desire a personal relationship with us.

Keep Looking Up!

God's daily bread—the Bible—feeds the soul.

JUNE 23

God Is Very Great

Read Psalms 104–106

Bless the LORD, O my soul! O LORD my God, you are very great!
—Psalm 104:1

I HAD BEEN praying for years for God to favor and bless my family and me when one day, as I was reading the Bible, it occurred to me that perhaps I should instead shift to a posture of giving praise to the Lord and praying for *him* to be blessed. When I began that practice, I found that despite my circumstances, I too felt an outpouring of blessing.

The simple acknowledgment of God's greatness through the practice of praise blesses our souls too. We see God for his greatness, his creativity, his compassion, his grace, and more when we offer praise to him. Instead of focusing on what we think we lack and need and want, our eyes shift to Jehovah Jireh, which means "the Lord will provide."

His presence blesses us, because he truly is the great Provider—the one who blesses us with himself!

O Lord, I bless your holy name! You are good and your mercies endure forever. I give you all honor and glory and praise and look to and trust you for everything I need.

Keep Looking Up!

Praising God is just a matter of proclaiming his good character traits.

JUNE 24

I Testify to God's Goodness

Read Psalms 107–111

All of you set free by God, tell the world! Tell how he freed you from oppression. —Psalm 107:2 MSG

PUZZLED, MY FRIEND looked at me. "You don't seem worried about this situation. Why?"

I smiled. "I have seen God's hand provide for us over and over again. Why wouldn't he continue to do that?"

However, in earlier days I was a worrier. Finances, our kids, road travels in an old car—all of them provided ample reasons for nail biting.

But as years and then decades passed, I saw the Lord provide for us—even though the results may have been different than we wanted.

As God brings us through challenges, we have an opportunity to share his goodness with others with simple testimonies. When we know that he has furnished income to meet our needs, we can say, "God did it!" When our family experiences a surprise blessing, we can say, "God did it!" When we survive a hard season, we can say, "God did it!"

It's easy to weave our faith into conversations when we acknowledge the favor is from God.

Lord, as I look back over the years, I can see your footprints walking with me. Sometimes you held me close and sometimes you held me up. For all of that I give you thanks and praise.

Keep Looking Up!

Bringing God into our conversations points others to him.

JUNE 25

God's Son Is Jesus

Read Psalms 112–118

The stone that the builders rejected has become the cornerstone.
—Psalm 118:22

WHEN CRAIG AND I traveled in Israel, we visited Nazareth and Mount Precipice, which overlooks the Valley of Jezreel. You can see for miles in several directions. According to tradition, this is the setting where the people from Nazareth, Jesus's hometown, tried to push him off the mountain. The misguided crowd thought him insane for claiming to be the Messiah. But Jesus miraculously walked through the crowd away from them.

Some scholars believe hundreds of prophecies in the Old Testament point to Jesus's being the Christ, the Son of God. Today's verse is just one of them. Jesus did not aspire to his own greatness but instead pointed the way to the Father and the way of salvation for all who would believe in him.

Putting our faith in Jesus does not require a mountainous leap but simple steps toward him.

Lord, I put my faith in you. I confess that I am a sinner and seek your saving grace for my life. From this day I will trust you for every aspect of my life as I pursue a relationship with you.

Keep Looking Up!

Trusting Jesus each day creates a faith foundation.

JUNE 26

God's Word Guides Us

Read Psalm 119

Your word is a lamp for my feet, a light on my path.
—Psalm 119:105 NIV

APPLIANCITIS HIT OUR house badly this year. First our guest house refrigerator died, then the hot water heater, house fridge, and dryer. The microwave handle fell off, and the washing machine is now groaning too.

Making big purchases can be tough decisions, but we always sense God's help when we need that kind of guidance.

Even though the Bible obviously doesn't tell us specifically which appliance to buy, it's still the best map for the course of our day. It shows us guiding principles through the stories of many biblical people. Even through their mistakes we can learn what *not* to do. And we also grow in understanding and discernment from Jesus's life and his teachings, which always will guide us to the correct path for living.

Life these days offers many opportunities and choices—just as we find in an appliance department. But when we have God's Word in our hearts and minds, we can be certain the Lord will lead us.

Lord, sometimes I get confused about what to do. As I read your Word, help me learn to apply its principles to my life and trust more each day that you will help me make the right decisions.

Keep Looking Up!

When we ask God to teach us, he shows us how to apply his Word to our lives.

JUNE 27

God Is Our Source of Joy

Read Psalms 120–133

Those who sow in tears shall reap with shouts of joy! —Psalm 126:5

FOREST FIRES FREQUENT our area. One leg of the Dixie Fire started on the north side of our mountain valley—eventually burning over one million acres and wiping out a nearby community, Greenville. Homes and businesses were lost there and in other places. Yes, trees grow back, but wiped-out historic sites are never replaceable.

Much of the Hebrew exiles' history was also wiped out. When they returned from captivity in Babylon, they had to rebuild the temple and the walls . . . and presumably their homes and lives. But as they returned to their homeland, joy replaced their tears. They were home.

Greenville is rebuilding too, just as we can when we face great loss. God is always with us and sees us through our trials by fire. He is ready to help us reconstruct our lives as we seek him for our restoration.

Lord, you have seen my tears. You feel my heartbreak. You know of my disappointment and struggle to cling to you. May my tears turn to shouts of joy as I walk out of this valley season into fields of grace.

Keep Looking Up!

When life looks grim, we have the joy of God's constant presence.

JUNE 28

God's Love Endures Forever

Read Psalms 134–140

Give thanks to the LORD, for he is good. His love endures forever.
—Psalm 136:1 NIV

LIVING ON PROPERTY with a well, my parents often were concerned about whether the water table would hold up in seasons of drought. They were careful with water usage, but water is a precious commodity, and they hoped their well wouldn't run dry.

We may feel God's love runs dry sometimes. A job loss or a broken-down car or a serious illness can make you wonder if God cares. In those times reading the Psalms refreshes our parched souls. These pieces of poetry often were set to music or, like this one, used as a responsive reading. The Hebrews did not incorporate rhyme as a poetic sound device; instead, they used repetition and parallelism, which resonated the important truths the people needed to hear. The fact that Psalm 136 repeats "His love endures forever" is a signal that the truth is important enough for us to say it again and again.

God's well of love never runs dry because his love endures forever—even when we don't feel it.

Lord, you are good, and your love endures forever. Even when times are hard, even when I am hurt, and even when hope seems to fade from my view, I can still know that your well of love is endless.

Keep Looking Up!

Saying God's promises aloud can beat the blues.

JUNE 29

God's Grace Abounds

Read Psalms 141–150

The LORD is gracious and merciful, slow to anger and abounding in steadfast love. —Psalm 145:8

I STOPPED AT the stop sign, then looked left and right and left again. No cars, so I proceeded through the intersection . . . only to realize I had a near-miss to my right. And that driver had the right of way because she had no stop sign.

I meekly waved a thank-you and proceeded two blocks to the school, where I found out it was Lisa I'd almost hit. After my profuse apologies, she said, "Not to worry—I've made mistakes too."

I could never estimate the numbers of mercies given me—by others but also by the Lord. We all forget things, lose items, make mistakes, and hurt others—unintended or otherwise. This walk on the earth is only continued by God's gracious and merciful disposition. He blesses us when we don't deserve it (grace), and he forgives us when we should be condemned (mercy).

His love covers it all.

Lord, each new day is a gift of your mercy and grace, and I am so thankful that you are slow to anger and instead allow your love to cover all my mess ups. May I never take you for granted.

Keep Looking Up!

Thanksgiving keeps us mindful of God's graciousness to us.

JUNE 30

God Knows Best

Read Proverbs 1–3

Trust in the LORD with all your heart and lean not on your own understanding. —Proverbs 3:5 NIV

I COULD NOT understand why my friend did not get the teaching job. She was fully qualified and fully invested in the school and community. Someone from parts unknown got the job instead, and it just did not make sense to me. So I made my complaint—sticking my nose into business I should not have.

A day later I learned that the teacher who had received the offer decided not to take the position . . . which was then offered to my friend, who said she would work even harder than expected so as to earn the trust of those above her.

I often find myself leaning on my own understanding of what's right and not right, instead of leaning on the everlasting arms of the Lord. Trusting in him with all my heart means I believe his Word, wait for his sovereign timing, and listen to his direction.

Lord, I often rush ahead without asking you for your guidance. Forgive me, Father, for thinking my way is the right way, when you may have a different, better plan. Slow me down, and help me trust your sovereign plan.

Keep Looking Up!

A simple, silent minute of listening for God can help connect the mental dots.

God Gives Us Wisdom

Read Proverbs 4–7

> Get wisdom; get insight; do not forget, and do not turn away from the words of my mouth. —Proverbs 4:5

IT'S A SWEET comfort carrying around counsel my parents gave me.

"Fill your plate with different colored foods."

"Fall in love with your best friend."

"Call when you get home."

"Trust God for everything."

Some wisdom comes from experience, but other wisdom comes from God's Word and the sound counsel of others. I appreciate insights from others because learning by experience can be painful, can't it?

King David knew his son Solomon would become his successor one day, so he filled him with godly wisdom. Most of the book of Proverbs is attributed to Solomon. A proverb is a short statement of universal truth similar to a maxim or aphorism. These snippets of wise counsel are often phrased in a binary form—first a negative statement and then a positive one, or the reverse.

They are relevant, easy to memorize, and often help us think more deeply and make good choices for our lives.

Lord, thank you for all the wise counsel in your Word. It is so much easier to learn by reading or hearing those applicable truths rather than having to learn through hard experiences. May I walk through each day in wisdom.

Keep Looking Up!

Many enjoy reading one chapter of Proverbs each day of the month.

JULY 2

God Exacts Justice

Read Proverbs 8–11

Whoever walks in integrity walks securely, but he who makes his ways crooked will be found out. —Proverbs 10:9

WHEN WE WALKED out of the movie theater, my husband bent down and picked up three gold rings lying on the ground next to the curb—one with small diamonds, one the matching wedding band, and another of Black Hills gold.

My writer mind instantly went to work imagining an argument and an angry wife throwing her rings on the ground. What a loss, but what a find! But as we agreed, the next day I drove to the police station and turned them in.

Today's proverb teaches us that we are secure when we walk in integrity—which means doing the right thing. While keeping the rings would not have been a crime, we would not have felt good about doing that. God would give us the rings back if we were meant to have them . . . which is what happened several months later.

We can always trust God to do the right thing.

Lord, I see injustices all the time. I could get angry and bitter and resentful. But I know that ultimately you are responsible to bring about justice, so I can trust you for those situations.

Keep Looking Up!

The Bible has counsel for us about what is right and what is wrong.

JULY 3

Love Underlies God's Discipline

Read Proverbs 12–14

If you love learning, you love the discipline that goes with it—how shortsighted to refuse correction! —Proverbs 12:1 MSG

WHEN MY STUDENT turned in his final research paper draft, I quickly found that he had made no improvements to it at all. I had spent more than a half hour editing it, but he ignored my comments and simply turned in a newly printed copy of the old draft. Because he was unhappy with his low grade, he threatened me. As a result, the principal took disciplinary action against him.

This incident is an example of someone refusing correction. Today's proverb implies that when we are not willing to heed discipline for our bad behavior, there will be severe consequences. Yes, we are bound to make mistakes, but when we are defensive and argue about the fallout, we make the choice to not grow.

God loves us. Period. His gentle corrections are not pointless punishment. Instead, his course corrections are meant to help us repent, learn, grow, and draw closer to him.

Lord, it's tough to face consequences from mistakes I have made, but I want to be a better Christ follower, so I understand that means I have to own up to my wrong decisions and deal with the fallout.

Keep Looking Up!

A mature person admits her mistakes.

Gracious Words Point Others to God

Read Proverbs 15–17

Gracious words are like a honeycomb, sweetness to the soul and health to the body. —Proverbs 16:24

I WAS RUSHED to make another appointment, and the self-checkout line was long and slow. The young mom in front of me with two toddlers squished into the cart seat looked frustrated too.

"Cute kiddos," I said.

The mom muttered thanks, then really looked at me and smiled. "I love your earrings."

After a few more exchanges the line seemed to move more quickly, and soon we were waving goodbye.

We can extend kindness through simple, thoughtful words. I can hang on to a sincere compliment for an endless number of days, recalling it and its giver to mind over and over. Proverbs 16:24 says gracious words are like a honeycomb. It's true: kind words are something sweet for others.

It simply takes a quick reset to move from our own mental lists to notice the needs of others and offer a few thoughtful words.

Lord, I am quick to judge, criticize, and mutter something snarky. Instead, help me notice the needs of others around me and offer gracious words that express the empathy you would offer.

Keep Looking Up!

We can lighten someone else's day with a few kind words.

God Encourages Friendships

Read Proverbs 18–20

A man of many companions may come to ruin, but there is a friend who sticks closer than a brother. —Proverbs 18:24

ONE OF MY prayers for my kids was "Lord, may they have one good friend." Having lived in three different states in my junior high years, I had found it hard to make friends. But my own kids had at least one good friend when they were in school.

With so many electronics in our lives, we have fallen into behaviors that isolate us. We can have meetings, Bible studies, and even church in virtual settings. We can text instead of call. People rarely just drop by for a conversation.

But the proverb teaches us there is a friend who sticks closer than a sibling. We just have to find her! If we feel alone, we can ask someone to coffee or invite her over for lunch. Our future best friend may just be waiting for a friendly gesture from someone willing to share God's love.

Lord, may I be that friend who sticks closer than a sister. Nudge me to develop friendships by setting aside time to get to know someone and even reaching out to pray for her and encourage her.

Keep Looking Up!

Inviting someone over for coffee could be the start of a close friendship.

God Loves Us All

Read Proverbs 21–23

The rich and the poor meet together; the LORD is the Maker of them all. —Proverbs 22:2

TWO BROTHERS COME to church together each week. One is dressed in a suit and tie; the other in homeless layers. My friend, our pastor's wife, greets them both warmly with an embrace.

Then there are the men who come together in a van from the gospel mission, which helps them leave their addictions and seize ahold of the faith. Many become part of the wide team of volunteers who help in various ministries.

It does not matter who you are or what you've done: all are accepted into a personal relationship with Christ, and all are welcome to be a part of God's family. We may have perceptions that we have to look a certain way or have a big income to be welcomed into the church, but that is not true. We are all the same: God's creation, loved by him.

Lord, sometimes I feel pretty puny in terms of my significance in the grand scheme of life. I don't always seem to fit in. Help me adjust my sight to see what you see in me—your special creation and part of your family.

Keep Looking Up!

A warm greeting is a simple way to extend God's love to others.

JULY 7

God Can Speak Love through Us

Read Proverbs 24–26

The right word at the right time is like a custom-made piece of jewelry. —Proverbs 25:11 MSG

I SAVED THE sympathy cards after my dad passed away. On days heavy with grief, I read them again—both the printed sentiments and the handwritten notes. After the flowers had long faded away, those notes were a dear reminder of friends' care and prayers.

Kind words buoy our spirits just when we need them. God often brings to mind those many cards when I hear of others going through hard times and loss. So I keep a stash of thinking-of-you and sympathy cards. With a sympathy card I'll often include a vintage handkerchief.

I don't write things like "It's for the best" or "God's plan is always good" or "He's in a better place" because those sound sermon-like and are usually not received as comfort. Instead, I write, "I love you. I care. And I'm praying for you." And I hope those words are, as the proverb says, the right word at the right time.

Father, may the words I speak to others buoy them up, not drag them down. If critical thoughts come to mind, please keep me from expressing them, that encouragement and kindness may prevail.

Keep Looking Up!

A kind note can encourage someone experiencing grief.

JULY 8

God Gives Us Friends

Read Proverbs 27–29

Iron sharpens iron, and one man sharpens another. —Proverbs 27:17

"WHAT HAVE YOU been reading lately?"

"What are you studying in the Bible?"

"How is work going . . . and what are you learning from that?"

These are the kinds of questions a close friend often asks me when we get together. We recommend books to each other and like to discuss them afterward. She often knows a struggle I'm having and may give me a book that helps me think about how I could grow through the situation.

Friends like that sharpen one another. They truly make us better people mentally and emotionally—not just provide a light moment of entertainment. They not only are a safe, encouraging place but also challenge us and inspire our intellectual and spiritual growth.

Just as my knife sharpener makes my knives more effective, I hope I have that kind of effect on my friends.

Father, thank you for the many friends I have in my life who encourage me to be a better person by setting goals relating to personal and spiritual growth. May I also be an encourager and exhorter who looks for the best in others.

Keep Looking Up!

Discussing the Bible with a friend draws the two of you closer to each other and God.

Strength Comes through God

Read Proverbs 30–31

She is clothed with strength and dignity; she can laugh at the days to come. —Proverbs 31:25 NIV

OUR OLDEST TRULY lightens others' hearts. A working mom of six children, she exudes strength and confidence. The tone of her classroom is reflected in a sign posted on her front wall: "Get excited, people!"

While she works hard at teaching content, she also makes it fun. She would say life is for living, and that is a testimony to the fact that she is a heart attack survivor. Shortly thereafter, though, she was already asking the doctor if she could hike or climb or ride horses. That positive perspective comes from her unflappable faith in God. She works hard, loves hard, and expects that God will bring all things together for good as he promised.

When we put all our trust in the Lord, others can be drawn to the strength, dignity, and joy we demonstrate . . . and to the Savior we trust.

Lord, may I be the kind of person others turn to for companionship and help because they see your strength in me. May fear and worry be cast aside as I look to you for that kind of strength.

Keep Looking Up!

We can trust God for our future because we can rely on his strength.

JULY 10

God Is with Us in All Seasons

Read Ecclesiastes 1–4

For everything there is a season, and a time for every matter under heaven. —Ecclesiastes 3:1

RANCHING DEFINITELY HAS its seasons. Summers mean long days on farm equipment cutting, baling, and stacking hay—twelve or more hours a day. While most of my husband's cattle graze on pastureland alongside a creek, there still are some left behind to feed by hand.

Autumn means the cattle are back on the ranch, so he must daily lift tons of hay to feed them. When hay buyers come to the ranch, he also handloads tons of bales onto their trucks or trailers.

Winters are hard because freezing weather and snow mean challenges breaking up water for the cattle and breaking apart hay bales to get the feed spread for the cows and their calves.

Spring brings a little respite, with the cows back on pastureland and the fields not ready to harvest.

Hard seasons of life come and go, with times of joy and contentment providing satisfaction and growth. In all seasons God is good and is with us.

Lord, you have been with me through all the ups and downs of the various seasons of my life. You see my struggles and provide the strength I need to lift up those cares to you. And you sprinkle springs of refreshment no matter what season I'm in.

Keep Looking Up!

Recounting God's history in our lives helps us weather tough seasons.

JULY 11

God Is in All Seasons

Read Ecclesiastes 5–8

> On a good day, enjoy yourself; on a bad day, examine your conscience. God arranges for both kinds of days so that we won't take anything for granted. —Ecclesiastes 7:14 MSG

DON'T YOU LOVE those "We were so poor…" stories your parents or grandparents told you?

We could share some with our children too. My husband says, "We were so poor, we only had homemade bread." But I have a hard time sympathizing with him on that one!

I could say, "We were so poor, we only had homemade clothes." But some might think that means one-of-a-kind designer wear!

The truth is most of us probably have faced financial struggles at some point in our lives, whereas other times the money worries faded.

God is in both seasons—plenty and want—but we can feel his favor in either time simply by recognizing he is with us and will provide for the needs we have. There will always be uncertainties in life, but expectation of God's goodness—no matter what—can make uncertainty morph into hope.

Lord, instead of living in fear of what-ifs, I will choose to allow expectant hope to frame my outlook. Yes, there will be tough times. But I know my faith is not in vain, and that your presence will bless me in good and bad seasons.

Keep Looking Up!

We can be expectant in prayer by boldly asking God to provide.

JULY 12

God Generates Good Ideas

Read Ecclesiastes 9–12

Cast your bread upon the waters, for you will find it after many days. —Ecclesiastes 11:1

WHEN ASKED HOW she decided what to write, my friend Ruth said she sent many book proposals out and simply waited to see what came back.

This is a good example of one interpretation of what it means to "cast our bread upon the waters." There are several other interpretations as well. Some say it deals with commerce—that sending grain out could mean increased business. Others say it relates to charity—that as you give without expecting anything in return, your good act will multiply benefits to others, and you may see benefits at some point. Isn't God's Word interesting?

In any case we are inspired here to take risks—to step out of our comfort zone to explore opportunities that God puts on our heart and mind. God's ideas are always worth casting out on the waters.

Lord, I have so many ideas! Help me know which are good ones to pursue and which are ones I need to set aside. I dedicate all my work to you. May it bring you honor.

Keep Looking Up!

We can trust God to give us good ideas.

JULY 13

God Says You Are Beautiful

Read Song of Solomon 1–4

You are altogether beautiful, my love; there is no flaw in you.
—Song of Solomon 4:7

"BEAUTY IS IN the eye of the beholder," the saying goes. I am blessed my husband believes I am the most beautiful woman in the world—though I am decades older than the teenager he fell in love with. When I mentioned this to a friend of ours, he laughed—clearly he had not yet found his love.

We all have such a love—the Lord God who fashioned us into his intricate creation. Citing another saying: God does not make junk. While our culture has standards that define beauty, the God who made us did not make mistakes with our eyes, hair, nose, mouth, or other parts of our body.

God's love for us is unconditional. When our skin falls into creases and our hair thins, those physical things do not matter to him. And that's the kind of love we can demonstrate to others.

Lord, you call me beautiful. While I may not feel I fit into that description, those feelings do not negate the truth: you created me perfectly. Your love for me is unconditional. May I also demonstrate that kind of love, Father.

Keep Looking Up!

Seeking friends who love you for who you are brings freedom into your life.

JULY 14

God's Love Never Ends

Read Song of Solomon 5–8

Many waters cannot quench love, neither can floods drown it.
—Song of Solomon 8:7

"I HATE YOU!" my child screamed from the bedroom. "You never let me do anything."

"But I love you anyway," I said.

And then the bedroom door slammed. A good sleep later would bring an apology to the surface up through those feelings.

The Song of Solomon is a poetic song about the passion between a man and a woman in their pursuit of one of God's best gifts: love. Solomon wrote of unquenchable love—a love that would endure many waters such as that of the sea (Psalm 107:23). That kind of love cannot be quelled or suppressed or snuffed out. It will endure and rise above floods of troubles that can creep into a relationship.

What this means for us is that when we fall in love, we then commit to demonstrate the kind of love that lasts because God's love never fails.

Lord, your love fuels me for the relationships around me—my family and friends. May I be the kind of person who demonstrates a love that never fails.

Keep Looking Up!

We can pray for God's help to love others when they're not so lovable.

JULY 15

God Cleans Us Up

Read Isaiah 1–3

Come now, let us reason together, says the LORD: though your sins are like scarlet, they shall be white as snow; though they are red like crimson, they shall become like wool. —Isaiah 1:18

I AWOKE TO the sound of the phone ringing.

"Janet, are you coming to school today?" It was our office secretary.

I glanced at the clock: 8:05. School had started five minutes earlier.

"I'll be right there." I had not fallen sleep until after 4 a.m., mentally rehearsing my agenda for that day's field trip—taking seniors to the university library to do research. I threw on clothes, grabbed my makeup bag and a hairbrush, and got to school less than five minutes later.

But all day—and days beyond—I felt like a failure.

We all fail, don't we? We may even wonder how God puts up with our flaws. But he does. When we repent and ask Jesus to forgive our sins, he sees us as clean as freshly fallen snow or a just-washed lamb.

I learned a lot about grace that day—receiving it so as to give it.

Lord God, thank you for sending your Son, Jesus, to be the sacrifice for my sins. While I know I'll still mess up, help me navigate this earthly journey.

Keep Looking Up!

When others make mistakes and we're quick to judge, those are good times to remember the mistakes we've made and extend grace.

JULY 16

God Will Call Us

Read Isaiah 4–8

And I heard the voice of the Lord saying, "Whom shall I send, and who will go for us?" Then I said, "Here I am! Send me." —Isaiah 6:8

AS A COLLEGE senior I sensed God's call to work for a national campus ministry, so I filled out the application and got it ready to send. But all the uncertainties held me back, and I did not follow through. I lived with regret until my midthirties, when I finally prayed, "Lord, use me. Send me wherever you want me to go."

A short time later I sensed God's call to write, and here I am today, sharing this with you.

God called his prophets like Isaiah to preach repentance to the people. A calling is God's summons to a person to a certain profession or avocation for the purpose of serving him. We are called to God, but God has also given us many gifts to use to further his kingdom.

A simple way to find your calling is to pray as Isaiah did, "Here I am! Send me." And then wait.

Lord, here I am. Send me! Use me for your kingdom's sake. I offer up all the gifts and talents you have given me. I am open to your leading.

Keep Looking Up!

God will equip you for whatever call is on your life.

JULY 17

God Is Worthy of Praise

Read Isaiah 9–11

For to us a child is born, to us a son is given, and the government will be on his shoulders. And he will be called Wonderful Counselor, Mighty God, Everlasting Father, Prince of Peace. —Isaiah 9:6 NIV

I GREW UP singing in a church girls' choir. While I am now an alto, I used to sing the high soprano parts as an adolescent. I also sang in an adult choir as a young adult, and we altos would joke that anyone could join the sopranos, but they had to fill out an application to sing in the alto row.

One of my greatest choral challenges was singing parts of Handel's Messiah. One choir director threw many of its pieces into our Christmas program at church just a week before the performance—because everyone else already knew it! I didn't, but I stumbled through anyway.

The Scripture quoted above forms the basis for one piece in *Messiah*. The prophet Isaiah wrote many messianic prophecies—this verse is just one that refers to the future Messiah, Jesus.

The coming of our Lord is worth our praise, our worship, our song!

Lord God, all of the prophecies your prophets spoke about your Son, Jesus, came true. You truly are my Wonderful Counselor, Mighty God, Everlasting Father, and Prince of Peace!

Keep Looking Up!

Our great God is worthy of our praise!

JULY 18

God Comforts Us

Read Isaiah 12–14

And you will say in that day, "I thank you, God. You were angry but your anger wasn't forever. You withdrew your anger and moved in and comforted me." —Isaiah 12:1 MSG

I FELT BAD immediately after I talked back to my mom as a high school kid. I felt even worse when my dad lectured me. I had hurt one person and greatly disappointed another. So I apologized, and their forgiveness came immediately.

God is like that good parent. When he sees our mistakes, he gets angry because when we sin, we are choosing three things: to disobey him, to walk away from him and his presence and guidance, and to serve as a bad example to others. And yet when we seek his forgiveness, he withdraws his anger, moves in close to us, and comforts us.

Let's think about that again: the Lord comforts us in our repentance, even though our behavior kept us from his presence. Just as good parents understand children will make mistakes, our God extends mercy to us and even gives warm reassurance that affirms we are indeed his children.

Lord, thank you for your endless mercies that welcome me back into your embrace again and again. I am sorry that I do not always represent you well. May I call to mind the pain my mistakes bring about—and make better choices.

Keep Looking Up!

Owning up to mistakes helps us experience God's comfort.

JULY 19

Look Up to God

Read Isaiah 15–19

In that day man will look to his Maker, and his eyes will look on the Holy One of Israel. —Isaiah 17:7

BEFORE I MADE a public choice to follow Jesus as my Savior and Lord, I had thought faith was all about attending church and performing certain religious practices. I hadn't understood faith is about having a personal relationship with God. My history had told me I had to do all the right things, but what the Lord wants is simply relationship.

Through Isaiah God teaches the people that what they take to the altars doesn't matter and what they make for God with their hands doesn't matter. What does count is that we look to him for everything—for our supply of what we need, for our daily bread of encouragement, for our hope in the everlasting, and for the strength we need.

The difference is a shift from doing to being. What we do is less important than a moment-by-moment focus on looking up to him for direction for our lives.

Lord, I am a doing kind of person. I do this, and I do that. But my performance means less to you than my presence with you. Help me slow down, God, and worry less about fulfilling expectations you do not lay out for me, so I can see and experience your glory.

Keep Looking Up!

A good question to ask yourself is this: Why am I doing this?

JULY 20

God Places Watchmen

Read Isaiah 20–24

For thus the Lord said to me: "Go, set a watchman; let him announce what he sees." —Isaiah 21:6

I AM BLESSED with several friends I see as accountability partners in my life. They are strong students of God's Word and provide sound counsel to me when I need it. They ask good questions like, "Are you doing too much?" or "Are you staying healthy?" And they challenge me to fully use my gifts and to think more deeply.

Cities such as ancient Jerusalem used to have watchmen. These men took turns patrolling the city walls throughout the day and night to look for possible military threats to the city. They were essential figures who helped protect the people.

Today we may have those guard-type figures in our lives—family members, friends, work peers, or church friends. Watchmen watch out for us, warn us in kind and honest ways when we're falling astray, are available when we need help, and encourage us to follow God.

Lord, you have placed certain watchmen in my life . . . and it may also be that I am such a person to someone else. Thank you for having my back. Thank you for cautionary advice others give me. May I pay attention to those you've placed in my life.

Keep Looking Up!

Accountability can encourage us to be stronger in our faith.

JULY 21

God's Word Is Plumb

Read Isaiah 25–28

And I will make justice the line, and righteousness the plumb line. —Isaiah 28:17

A PLUMB BOB is an essential tool for builders. A heavy weight hanging from a string, this tool determines a vertical reference line that helps carpenters keep framing level. It's a useful tool that has been around for thousands of years.

I have an antique, solid steel plumb bob that hangs in my office. It belonged to my grandfather Max, passed down to me from my mom. Grandpa Max was a carpenter who built homes and furniture for people during the Great Depression. He and my grandmother lost their home during that era, but he continued to find work from people who still had money.

My mom used it to hang wallpaper because walls aren't always exactly vertical. You need to keep things straight and true.

God's Word teaches us that he is straight and true. He is just and righteous. His standards determine what is right and what is not. While the world's values change with the shifting wind, we can look to the Lord to find truth.

Lord, your Word is my reference point every day. I thank you for how it keeps me vertically aligned with you and your will. May I use your Bible as a tool to learn more about you.

Keep Looking Up!

Daily searching for truth in God's Word keeps us plumb.

JULY 22

God Waits with Mercy

Read Isaiah 29–31

Therefore the Lord waits to be gracious to you, and therefore he exalts himself to show mercy to you. For the Lord is a God of justice; blessed are all those who wait for him. —Isaiah 30:18

I GLANCED IN the rearview mirror. A police car was right behind me with flashing lights.

I was late, so I had been pushing it.

The officer came to my window. "What's your hurry?"

"I have to file these papers for my husband by five o'clock."

"What's your husband do?"

I took a deep breath. This might not go well. "He's an attorney."

After the officer recovered from his laughing fit, he gave me a ticket: "excessive fuel waste." Fine: five dollars.

Just as that officer was merciful to me, our God in the heavenly courts is gracious to us. He knows we will mess up. And because he is a God of justice, he allows us to face the consequences of our actions . . . but mercifully embraces us again and again.

That kind of love is excessive . . . for which we always can be grateful.

Lord, I cannot thank you enough for the unending mercies you extend to me. That you wait for my heart to align with yours is humbling. May I not take that lightly.

Keep Looking Up!

Those who receive mercy can discover how to give it to others.

JULY 23

God Is There for Us

Read Isaiah 32–34

God, treat us kindly. You're our only hope. First thing in the morning, be there for us! When things go bad, help us out!
—Isaiah 33:2 MSG

OUR YOUNGEST WAS five days old when I got a call that our oldest had been in a horse accident and was on the way to the hospital, unconscious. With no car, I cried out to God for wisdom and help. By the time I got to the hospital, our daughter was awake and the doctor was stitching up a large gash on her forehead. A few days later she was back in school and performed in a play that evening.

In this world we will have trouble— the Bible tells us we were born for it. We can't completely avoid illness or accidents unless we stay in a locked room. Instead, life is for living—riding those crazy horses, skiing down hills, starting a business.

The one constant in our lives is God. He is with us in times of joy, and he is with us in times of struggle. He is with us every day.

Lord, you are my only hope. In this struggle called life, you greet me in the morning, see me through my day, calm my anxious heart in the evening, and provide the rest I need. I will keep looking up to you in times of trouble.

Keep Looking Up!

When trouble arises, prayer is our best first response.

JULY 24

God Provides Streams in the Desert

Read Isaiah 35–37

Water will gush forth in the wilderness and streams in the desert.
—Isaiah 35:6 NIV

AS YOUNG MARRIEDS we decided to tackle what is called The Loneliest Road in America, US Highway 50, which bisects the middle of Nevada. Though we were without air-conditioning in our car, we were ready that early summer with ice water and peanut butter and jelly sandwiches. Hundreds of miles passed without services, but we did see patches of green. There were streams in the Nevada desert.

We sometimes may feel we are wandering in wilderness places. There may be a sense of discontent and uncertainty . . . or that our souls are completely parched and even empty. We may have some kind of loss or deep disappointment in someone we trusted. Grief may be swallowing us whole.

When the Israelites wandered in the desert, they often cried out to God for water. And he always provided. When we cry out to God to water our souls, he will always refresh us.

Lord, in this desert season I need you. I do not need anything the world can superficially provide. Instead, I need the refreshment only you can pour over me. I look to you in hope that never fails, Father.

Keep Looking Up!

We can always find refreshment in God's Word.

JULY 25

God Provides Strength

Read Isaiah 38–40

They who wait for the Lord shall renew their strength; they shall mount up with wings like eagles; they shall run and not be weary; they shall walk and not faint. —Isaiah 40:31

TWO MONTHS AFTER a major surgery, I was approached by my high school seniors to see if the class could hike up the mountain to refresh the paint on the large white *L,* which stands for our town, Loyalton. Locals call the mountain Elephanthead because of its shape, which also means it's very steep.

After praying, I knew the Lord would give me the strength for each step. And I made it, paint can and brush in hand—which we all carried to paint the rocks that formed the *L.* I wasn't among the first to reach the spot, but I did beat two asthmatic girls!

So much of what we daily face may appear to be like a mountain climb—an impossible ascent to a nebulous destination. But God will supply all the strength we need for each step until we are at that mountain peak looking back at our trail.

Lord, the impossible looms in front of me like a steep mountain. I am not sure I have the ability or strength to accomplish what I face, but I trust you for every step of the process.

Keep Looking Up!

A faith journey requires just one step after another.

JULY 26

The Lord Leads Us to Refreshment

Read Isaiah 41–43

> I will open rivers on the bare heights, and fountains in the midst of the valleys. I will make the wilderness a pool of water, and the dry land springs of water. —Isaiah 41:18

JUST PRIOR TO writing this, California had experienced many years of drought. So it was not a surprise that a year ago, I wrote a short prayer request next to the above verse: "For California, Lord . . . please!"

When the snowpack reached more than 200 percent of normal—over fifty-six feet of snow—officials declared the drought over. The rivers are running strong, and reservoirs that provide water all year long for agriculture and homes are full.

We may feel as though we are in an emotional or spiritual drought. Bills may be piling up. Relationships may be hurting. God may seem distant. But when we feel dry and empty, we can turn to the Lord to fill us with his love and his refreshment. He is always our source of hope that waters our soul.

Lord, I am walking through an arid season that seems endless. The difficulties come one after another like an endless desert. Lead me to your springs of life that never run dry.

Keep Looking Up!

God's Word provides refreshment in dry seasons.

JULY 27

God Equips Us

Read Isaiah 44–46

I equip you, though you do not know me, that people may know, from the rising of the sun and from the west, that there is none besides me; I am the LORD, and there is no other. —Isaiah 45:5–6

STRAIGHT OUT OF college with no computer experience, I was hired as a technical writer/editor for a large software company. In that capacity I edited proposals and reports relating to multi-million-dollar projects. It was scary. I knew where commas should go and how to match up subjects and verbs, but often I was reading way above my knowledge level. Gradually, though, I began to notice patterns of language and could deduce meaning of concepts in their context.

New challenges like that are intimidating, but God can equip us when we make the decision to listen to God and do the hard tasks in front of us. In this prophecy from Isaiah, we learn God anointed Cyrus, the king over both Assyria and Babylon, to defeat his enemies and later to rebuild Jerusalem for the Jewish exiles.

Just as nations watched God use even a nonbelieving king, others will notice when we gracefully navigate the challenges we face.

Lord, I feel so unequipped sometimes and just want to hide. But because you created me, I know you can also help me develop each of the skills and all the knowledge I need for the work I face today. I give you the glory, God.

Keep Looking Up!

God will guide those willing to learn.

JULY 28

God Remembers Me

Read Isaiah 47–49

Behold, I have engraved you on the palms of my hands.
—Isaiah 49:16

I TEND TO forget things—my phone, my keys, appointments. So, I write everything down. When a friend asks for prayer, I put that request on a sticky note. And if I'm going to be on the go that day, I will write that person's name on the palm of my left hand. I would not want to forget her needs.

Unlike me, God never forgets his people. He knows each of us by name. He counts the hairs on our head. And the Bible tells us he engraves us on the palms of his hands. We are continually before him as we work, sleep, and go about the mundane tasks of our days. He sees us and is concerned about that which we are concerned.

So although we may feel forgotten by even the loved ones in our lives, we can always know our heavenly Father never forgets us.

Lord, I feel forgotten—as though I were the last person on anyone's list. In fact, I often wonder if anyone cares or remembers me. But I know I am so important to you. I am engraved on your hands. Thank you for remembering me, Father.

Keep Looking Up!

Knowing God remembers us helps us understand our value to him.

JULY 29

God's News Is Good News

Read Isaiah 50–52

How beautiful upon the mountains are the feet of him who brings good news, who publishes peace, who brings good news of happiness, who publishes salvation, who says to Zion, "Your God reigns." —Isaiah 52:7

MANY YEARS AGO I began reading through the Bible each year with one objective: to find good news from God's Word that would encourage others to look to the Lord God for wisdom, for help, and for encouragement. I wanted to lift up others by sharing God's love and grace for them.

How sweet it is to share the good news of God's gift of salvation given through his Son, Jesus. Each of us has a faith story—how we learned God is real, that he loves us, and that he desires to have a personal relationship with us. Just telling the story of the difference faith has made in our lives can bring about a life-changing decision for someone else. We don't have to sugarcoat the gospel message. All we need to do is explain the good news that God reigns—in the heavens and on the earth.

Lord, I don't know why I make a big deal out of sharing my faith. I just need to share my story—the good news of how you have loved me and cared for me over the years. I pray that my story can help others know that you indeed do reign.

Keep Looking Up!

We can bring God into our daily conversations with others.

JULY 30

The Lord Makes Us Whole

Read Isaiah 53–56

But the fact is, it was our pains he carried— our disfigurements, all the things wrong with us. We thought he brought it on himself, that God was punishing him for his own failures. But it was our sins that did that to him, that ripped and tore and crushed him—our sins! He took the punishment, and that made us whole. Through his bruises we get healed. —Isaiah 53:5 MSG

I DID IT again the other day—made a sarcastic comment to my husband, bringing about silence and a mile of isolation between us. He had made a simple request, and I overreacted . . . from a place of feeling overwhelmed. He didn't know my frustration when he asked how to do something on the computer.

The truth is, despite the fact that we are God's children and heaven-bound, we will still fail here on earth. Thankfully, as this prophecy about Jesus reminds us, he took the punishment for our sins, and in doing so, he made a way for us to have a relationship with a perfect God. From the Father's perspective I stand in the shadow of Christ—in an eternal judgment sense, the Lord sees the perfect sacrifice, Jesus, instead of the mess-up me.

And for that gift I am eternally grateful.

Lord, thank you that by Jesus's wounds I am forgiven of all my former and future transgressions. I am grateful for Jesus's sacrifice and will strive to live into a growing sense of his perfect gift.

Keep Looking Up!

Remembering Jesus's sacrifice can steer us away from sin.

God Loves a Giver

Read Isaiah 57–59

If you are generous with the hungry and start giving yourselves to the down-and-out, your lives will begin to glow in the darkness, your shadowed lives will be bathed in sunlight. —Isaiah 58:10 MSG

IT'S HARD TO avoid panhandlers at corners and store parking lots. But then again, it's hard for them to avoid their tough circumstances. While giving money is controversial, I do when I feel the Lord directs my attention their way. I also distribute plastic lunch bags with granola bars and a bottle of water.

Some proverbs in the Bible speak to the importance of working for a living, but other parts, such as this passage in Isaiah, encourage generosity for the poor. Giving doesn't make us holier than others, but it solves my heart dilemma because I always wonder if the person with a sign will make it through another cold evening.

I have regretted passing beggars without so much as a glance, but I have never regretted giving. While I can't end poverty, I can help one person at a time.

Lord, please lend me your wisdom about how to give to those in need. Poverty may perpetuate itself, but I can help one person at a time. Teach me how I can be generous and make a difference.

Keep Looking Up!

Just a granola bar and a bottle of water could help a hungry person.

AUGUST 1

The Lord Sets Us Free

Read Isaiah 60–63

The Spirit of the Lord God is upon me . . . to proclaim liberty to the captives, and the opening of the prison to those who are bound. —Isaiah 61:1

WHEN I WAS in junior high school, a boy called me "fatty four eyes." Those words stuck with me for many years until I embraced a personal relationship with Christ. Our Savior freed me from a prison of negative self-talk and continual striving to earn others' love.

The beauty of the Christian walk is that we can tell others the story of how Jesus has helped us step away from shame, mistakes, and addictive behaviors. We can be honest about how we've turned from our messed-up sense of identity into the fresh air of freedom. We can come alongside our friends in their struggles by striving to help them embrace faith and find liberation from a history of negative self-perceptions.

Think about this: the Spirit of God lives in us! As we increasingly believe the good news that sin no longer has power over us, we are set free!

Father God, I believe I am liberated from the chains of mistakes or emotional misperceptions about my identity. I believe that they no longer have power over me. And I will share your good news to encourage others to look to you for their freedom.

Keep Looking Up!

Speaking of our freedom in Christ could inspire others to seek him too.

AUGUST 2

God Is the Potter

Read Isaiah 64–66

But now, O LORD, you are our Father; we are the clay, and you are our potter; we are all the work of your hand. —Isaiah 64:8

MY FRIEND SUZANNE is a potter who makes beautiful objects such as mugs, jewelry, and art objects. Some of her creations come from reclaimed clay, which consists of the discarded scraps from trimming or throwing the objects on her potter's wheel. While some might just throw out those clay pieces, she recycles them to make other pieces. Messes are given second chances and can become masterpieces.

God is the first artist. He created the world, including you and me. As years of our lives passed, though, we may have become cracked or chipped—imperfect—the result of being separated from our Creator. But when we accept God's gift of salvation through Jesus, he reclaims us and refashions our mind, heart, and spirit into a beautiful new creation.

Each day we have the opportunity to allow the Potter to work on us and through us to make us stronger and better equipped to serve him and others.

Lord, you are the potter, and I am the clay. Mold me into the person who will best represent you. Thank you, God, for second chances. Remake me into your useful vessel for your kingdom's sake.

Keep Looking Up!

Transformation begins when we give ourselves to God.

AUGUST 3

Age Doesn't Matter to God

Read Jeremiah 1–3

But the LORD said to me, "Do not say, 'I am too young.' You must go to everyone I send you to and say whatever I command you."

—Jeremiah 1:7 NIV

STRAIGHT OUT OF college, I didn't have enough experience to apply for a writing or editing job, so I applied to be a technical typist—work I'd done a lot during college.

But my future boss said he wouldn't give me that job. "I'm going to make you an editor instead." He also chewed me out for underestimating my abilities. Lesson learned.

The young may feel unqualified for God's calling. But the more senior of us may feel our time has passed. Jeremiah thought he was too young and unknowledgeable. But the Lord reassured him he would put his words into Jeremiah's mouth. The young prophet didn't need to worry because God would give him the words. Jeremiah just needed to follow God's leading.

No matter our age, God will guide us when we say "yes" to him.

Lord, I often do not feel equipped or capable to perform an assignment, but I do know that if you have provided the opportunity for me, you will not leave me high and dry. I trust you to help me.

Keep Looking Up!

Saying "yes" to God is the first trusting step.

AUGUST 4

God's Plans Are Best

Read Jeremiah 4–5

> If you swear, "As the LORD lives," in truth, in justice, and in righteousness, then nations shall bless themselves in him, and in him shall they glory. —Jeremiah 4:2

I'M A BIG planner. I have a spiral calendar noting all my appointments and obligations, and I use a bullet journal to set daily work and personal goals. But sometimes I realize I haven't put God first. I have sought out what I want for my life and sort of just asked God to go along with me.

Ultimately, we live for God, and that means that we look to him each day for whatever he has set out before us. God teaches in this passage that when we promise to follow him, we are committing to live for truth, for justice, and for righteousness—so others are drawn to him. He wants us to set aside anything that would take his place—especially the pursuit of anything that takes our focus off him.

When we repent, we will find ourselves blessed because we are living in God's goodness.

Lord, you live and reign over this earth, and I pray that my promises and oaths and yeses are first to you. You are the priority for my life. Use me to spread your goodness everywhere I go.

Keep Looking Up!

Repentance is requisite to a close relationship with the Lord.

AUGUST 5

Traveling with God Is Best

Read Jeremiah 6–8

> GOD's Message yet again: "Go stand at the crossroads and look around. Ask for directions to the old road, the tried-and-true road. Then take it." —Jeremiah 6:16 MSG

WHEN RESTRICTIONS EASED on meeting together during the pandemic, my husband and I had a choice. We could continue watching church services online or we could go back to attending in person. While it was sure convenient to stay home in our pj's on Sunday mornings, we chose to worship in our church building.

Faith practices are continually changing. While some people are resistant to change, others may find prior generations' practices old-fashioned and not relevant to today. But the Lord encourages us in this passage to pause and look around. What will help us grow into more faith-filled, mature people? What will challenge us to become stronger so that when we face adversity, we will be able to walk through it? Where will we have the support when we are weak?

We get to choose at those crossroads. And God promises rest when we choose his way.

Lord God, thank you that your Word always provides counsel for those times in my life when I am uncertain about which choice to make. Bottom line, I choose you, Father, because traveling with you is always the best.

Keep Looking Up!

Traveling with God is easier with his road map: the Bible.

AUGUST 6

We Get to Boast about God

Read Jeremiah 9–11

> Let him who boasts boast in this, that he understands and knows me, that I am the LORD who practices steadfast love, justice, and righteousness in the earth. For in these things I delight, declares the LORD. —Jeremiah 9:24

AS SOON AS the words were out of my mouth, I knew I should not have said them. I was complaining again about one of my kids to a friend who was experiencing yet another year without a child. My whining was probably hurtful to her.

Everything I have is from God, so it does not make sense for me to raise a flag to myself. People seem to respect others who are beautiful or successful, but God has other standards for human value. As his creation, we are already loved and have worth. Years ago moms and grandmas used to carry small photo books of their kids—called brag books. Now we have cell phones with photos. But if I had a brag book, it should say, "God did it!" and "God knows and loves me!"

I can delight in what delights the Lord: love, justice, and righteousness.

Lord, may I never be hesitant about boasting about your goodness. Your steadfast love astonishes me. Your justice is always right, and your righteousness is indisputable. You are worthy of my praise—in my prayer closet as well as in public.

Keep Looking Up!

We need not be shy about sharing God's goodness.

AUGUST 7

God Fills Us

Read Jeremiah 12–14

Yet you, O Lord, are in the midst of us, and we are called by your name; do not leave us. —Jeremiah 14:9

HAVE YOU EVER felt you were in a personal drought? As though everything was just drained from you and nothing was flowing in?

I did one year when I had three kids, worked in our office, and drove three hours to attend grad school weekly. Pursuing my teaching credential, I was gone for three days each week. I hustled on weekends for housework and kids' needs. When I found out someone close to me was not making wise decisions, the little in my reservoir evaporated.

Some days we may wonder how we will make it until bedtime, much less a whole season. Yet Scripture teaches us that God is not distant. In fact, he is in the midst of us, sustaining us day by day and giving us the strength we need for each and every task.

I found that to be true. Because we are called by his name, he does not leave us dry.

Lord, I feel depleted sometimes, unable to do one more thing. And I'm not proud of the emotional reactions I can have when stretched. But my failures just show how much I need you and the graceful filling you provide for the moment.

Keep Looking Up!

We have the assurance that God is in our midst.

AUGUST 8

God's Words Are a Delight

Read Jeremiah 15–17

Your words were found, and I ate them, and your words became to me a joy and the delight of my heart, for I am called by your name, O Lord, God of hosts. —Jeremiah 15:16

I FOUND A surprise this weekend when I was cleaning a closet: two boxes of classic books. While I have no remembrance of their entering our home, I deduced they came from my mother-in-law's estate. Many were well over a hundred years old—classic literature as well as children's story anthologies. A treasure of a find, many are now displayed throughout our home.

Can you imagine what it would be like to suddenly come upon a Bible after never seeing it before? Perhaps reading God's Word is a new practice for you . . . and you are finding great joy in swallowing it bit by bit. If we truly comprehend that God's words lie on each page, reading it is quite a delight—a meal of wisdom and history and teachings and encouragement.

Studying the Bible every day can fill us up for whatever lies ahead.

Lord, may I remember to read something from your Word each day. I need that fuel and admonition to keep my gaze looking in your direction.

Keep Looking Up!

Joy is better understood by reading the Bible.

God Rescues Us

Read Jeremiah 18–21

Sing to the Lord; praise the Lord! For he has delivered the life of the needy from the hand of evildoers. —Jeremiah 20:13

THE MAN IN a black sedan ran a red light, just missing me, but then turned around and started following me. *Lord, help me,* I prayed. *Give me wisdom about what to do.*

God helped me immediately, because I knew just what to do. Not wanting a confrontation in a defenseless place, I drove a half dozen miles to my brother-in-law's home, where he was working in the front yard, and dashed up to stand next to him. The man pulled up, screamed at me, and drove away.

Chances are, at some point in our lives we will need rescuing. Whether we face a dead car alongside the road or an angry stranger, we need God's protection—either from someone else or a God-given angel in disguise. Prayer is our distress signal.

And praise is our response when the Lord delivers us from evil.

Lord, thank you for answering my distress signals. I probably do not know the number of times you deliver me from those who would do me harm. But I trust that you will answer me and be with me during times of worry.

Keep Looking Up!

God always answers those who ask for wisdom.

AUGUST 10

God Is at Hand

Read Jeremiah 22–24

"Am I only a God nearby," declares the LORD, "and not a God far away?" —Jeremiah 23:23 NIV

IN OUR LOCAL thrift store I recently found a lovely wooden sculpture of Mary and Jesus for just a dollar or so. When I looked up the sculptor in online sources, I found the sculpture's value ranged over a hundred dollars. It was worth more than I had thought.

While we might not have high esteem for affordable items, that kind of perspective is not transferrable to our almighty God. Some people during Jeremiah's time worshiped ordinary, handmade, wooden idols. While we follow a God who is personal, close, and accessible to us, the Lord's words to us in Jeremiah 23:23 are a good reminder that he is also the Creator of everything on this earth as well as the Lord Most High who designed the universe. He is not only near and accessible, he is also priceless beyond measure.

That kind of outlook makes us reverence him more and humbles us to honor, love, and serve him well.

Lord, you are the almighty God. You created the heavens and the earth. May I never forget that you are the Creator and I am your created one.

Keep Looking Up!

Praise helps us keep in perspective how great our Lord God truly is.

AUGUST 11

God Restores

Read Jeremiah 25–27

I will bring them back and restore them to this place.
—Jeremiah 27:22

NOT INFREQUENTLY A student would come to me and say, "I'm checking out today. I'm moving." Sometimes families moved for work, but sometimes the teenager was being shifted to another parent or grandparent.

Whatever the case, it was always hard, because I got attached to my students and wanted to make sure they would be okay. So I would give them my email address and say, "You can always come back."

Historically, God restored his people Israel after they were exiled to Babylon. Today's verse refers to the promise of restoration during a time when the nation was falling. Decades later God fulfilled his promise and brought the people back.

Personal setbacks are unavoidable. We may experience job loss, an auto accident, or health challenges. But the Lord will bring us back and restore us to a place of peace, no matter the outcome of the situation.

Lord, you are a God who restores. In any life challenge I know that I can look up to you and trust you for the outcome—drawing me to yourself for the calm, peace, and contentment that only you can provide.

Keep Looking Up!

A personal setback is only temporary when we trust God for our lives.

AUGUST 12

God Gives Us a Hope-Filled Future

Read Jeremiah 28–30

"For I know the plans I have for you," declares the LORD, "plans to prosper you and not to harm you, plans to give you hope and a future." —Jeremiah 29:11 NIV

WHEN MY FRIEND Jenny's husband left her for another woman, Jenny was devastated, of course. She lost her home, comfortable financial provision, and, oddly enough, even some of her family, who blamed her for the situation.

Some years later, though, she found herself working full time in ministry and engaged to a man who loved God and her.

When the people of Israel were torn from their homes and livelihoods in Jerusalem and taken to Babylon, the Lord wrote them a love letter of sorts. He told them to build homes and settle down in exile, to marry and have children, and to seek the peace and prosperity of their new city. When they sought God with their whole heart, he would bless them and restore their losses.

Even when life seemingly crumbles, we can still trust the Lord, who gives us assurances for hope and a future.

Lord, I call on your name from this present place of heartache. I feel ripped apart from everything that was dear to me. Show me, God, your plans for my future. I am ready and waiting, listening for your voice.

Keep Looking Up!

When we seek God, he gives us hope for our future.

AUGUST 13

God Makes Us One Heart

Read Jeremiah 31–32

> I will give them one heart and one way, that they may fear me forever, for their own good and the good of their children after them. —Jeremiah 32:39

I MET SEVERAL women at a conference many years ago. We were raising kids and figuring out our ministry lives. One friend volunteered to keep us connected through email, and we updated each other on work and other needs, praying for each other. We called our group One Heart, and we became one heart as we prayed for one another.

People who follow Jesus can be of one heart and mind as they seek the things of God and support one another. Jeremiah prayed for the Jerusalem exiles headed for Babylon. With all the uncertainty ahead, they must have been afraid. But Jeremiah relayed God's covenant to them that they still would be God's people, and God would give them one heart so they would stay glued together as a nation within that foreign nation.

Despite our distance, friends and family can also be of one heart as we serve God, wherever we are.

Lord, make me one heart with you and with others in the faith you bring into my path. Help me pray faithfully for others and be a comfort and support for those in need. May we grow closer to each other as we grow closer to you.

Keep Looking Up!

Reaching out to a friend in need today could truly bind her heart to yours.

AUGUST 14

God Will Answer Us

Read Jeremiah 33–36

Call to me and I will answer you and tell you great and unsearchable things you do not know. —Jeremiah 33:3 NIV

ONE OF THE hardest parts of losing my dad to ALS was that I was off on a student trip the day my dad passed away. When I arrived home late that evening, my husband said, "Just stay packed. Go see your dad." But after the long drive there, my brother met me and said, "He's with God! He's with God!"

I was hurt that God would let my father slip away without my saying goodbye and telling him I loved him. But later I learned his quick release was God's gift of mercy. He was losing his ability to breathe.

Our earthly questions may seem unsearchable. Why do the good die young? Why did my marriage fail? The Hebrews didn't understand why they would have to go into exile. But God promised to be with them, hear their prayers, and give them understanding.

To this hope we can always cling!

Lord, when I do not understand the unsearchable, I still can trust that you are with me, you are for me, and you will help me understand that which I cannot. I trust you for each season ahead.

Keep Looking Up!

Often we can find the answers to our questions in God's Word.

AUGUST 15

God Has the Answers

Read Jeremiah 37–39

> King Zedekiah sent Jehucal the son of Shelemiah, and Zephaniah the priest, the son of Maaseiah, to Jeremiah the prophet saying, "Please pray for us to the LORD our God." —Jeremiah 37:3

IN AN INTERVIEW a magazine editor wanted to know more about prayerwalking—what it was, how God answered prayers, and how the practice connected me with my community. At first she acknowledged she didn't know what she believed about the Christian faith but was intrigued. However, after hearing stories of answered prayer, she asked me to pray for her sister, who was struggling as she raised her two teenagers.

Isn't it interesting that people who do not profess a faith in Jesus ask us for prayer? Perhaps they're just curious; perhaps they figure they'll try anything. Zedekiah was the last king of Judah before Jerusalem fell to the invaders. An evil king, Zedekiah may have wanted a god who would stamp YES on every request without his obedience.

But here's another thought: sometimes when a friend asks us to pray, it can be a first sign of faith. So we pray for them.

Lord, help me not to overanalyze people's motives when they ask me to pray for them. Help me not judge them or their requests. Instead, guide me to see them as you do and share my love by praying.

Keep Looking Up!

Praying aloud for someone teaches them how to pray.

AUGUST 16

God's Will Is the Best Prayer

Read Jeremiah 40–43

Jeremiah the prophet said to them, "I have heard you. Behold, I will pray to the LORD your God according to your request, and whatever the LORD answers you I will tell you. I will keep nothing back from you." —Jeremiah 42:4

FOR ABOUT TWENTY years I have been coordinating our church's prayer ministries, to include our prayer warriors team that prays for requests that come through the church. It truly is amazing to me how many of those requests God answers. What a gracious God we serve! Of many, though, I never hear the end result—and wish I did because those answers to prayer are like a steak dinner to a hungry rancher.

The most effective prayers are those that ask for God's will to be done in our lives. In today's verse Jeremiah addresses the commanders of a remnant who had stayed in Judah. These leaders were essentially asking for God's blessing on a bad strategy that God himself had not ordained and would not approve. And he did not rubber-stamp their plans.

God delights in answering the desires of our heart when we align our heart with his.

Lord, as I allow the world to influence what I think I need, often my prayers are motivated from a misplaced sense of what I deserve. Change that in me, Father, so that I want what you want.

Keep Looking Up!

The most effective prayers come from a posture of "Thy will be done."

AUGUST 17

In Love God Disciplines Us

Read Jeremiah 44–46

> Fear not, O Jacob my servant, declares the LORD, for I am with you. . . . I will discipline you in just measure, and I will by no means leave you unpunished. —Jeremiah 46:28

ONE OF OUR grandkiddos got in trouble the other day doing something that could have significantly hurt him. Though he admitted his offense, I dished out a timeout.

"I love you, buddy," I said.

Head bowed, he said, "I know."

We also can be as reckless, then plead with God to rescue us. Even though Judah had aligned itself with Egypt—against God's counsel—and then found itself in a bad position when Egypt lost to the invading Babylonians, God promised to preserve his people. Though they did not escape exile, God preserved them and eventually sent them back to Jerusalem.

While it may seem God has placed us in a disciplinary timeout, those circumstances can provide space to reflect on God's parental love and care for us—always for our good.

Lord, even in this place of timeout, you are with me. I trust you for the larger picture of protecting me from my own mistakes. So I thank you again for your endless mercies.

Keep Looking Up!

God's discipline is for our good.

God's Justice Reigns

Read Jeremiah 47–48

How can it be quiet when the LORD has given it a charge?
—Jeremiah 47:7

MY FRIEND MAXINE attended the memorial service of a man who had been unkind to her in many public settings. Someone asked her why.

"He served in a position of respect," she said. "He was in a position of authority over me, and I heard he had committed his life to Jesus."

In the end those who hurt others are in God's hands. The Philistines had provided continual military harassment to Israel, so the sword of the Lord came down on them.

When we face opposition from another individual, it is challenging to put our faith into action and respond with Christlikeness—grace, integrity, and self-control. If situations become abusive, certainly it's important to report that kind of activity to a person in authority. But simple conflicts with ornery characters we can hand over to God for him to implement his justice.

Lord, you reign over my life, and you reign over the whole world. For uncomfortable situations that I find myself in, I look to you for the eventual outcome. I trust your sword to protect me.

Keep Looking Up!

God's justice is worth the wait.

AUGUST 19

God Calls Us Together

Read Jeremiah 49

> I have heard a message from the LORD that an ambassador was sent to the nations to say, "Form a coalition against Edom, and prepare for battle!" —Jeremiah 49:14 NLT

OUR DAUGHTER HAD been moving heavy livestock panels when she suddenly felt ill. When she made it into their house, she fell to the floor in pain. We called upon a coalition of friends and family to pray. Hundreds around the country joined together for her benefit. Later in the hospital doctors said it was a heart attack, caused by intense physical stress, but the next day she was released from the hospital and soon she was riding her horse again.

We are stronger together. In Jeremiah 49 the Lord continued his judgments on nations neighboring Israel and ordered the people to form a coalition and ready for battle ahead.

Of course, we always want to be in unity with other believers, but there are many times in our lives the Lord may have us join together for his work: health concerns, church projects, and national and other crises. Together we can be ready.

Lord, you brought me into your family, and it is a privilege to pray with and for my faith family. May I always be mindful of ways to support those of the faith—honoring your mission that we gather ourselves together for any battle ahead.

Keep Looking Up!

Prayer is a battle weapon—especially when joined with others.

AUGUST 20

God Pleads Our Cause

Read Jeremiah 50

Their Redeemer is strong; the LORD of hosts is his name. He will surely plead their cause, that he may give rest to the earth, but unrest to the inhabitants of Babylon. —Jeremiah 50:34

OUR PROBLEMS SEEMED small compared to others' struggles, but when our car and two appliances all failed within a week's time, frustrations mounted. Then when one company would not make good on a guarantee for a two-month-old product under warranty, I went straight to the top. After mailing a letter to the company CEO, three days later I got a phone call saying the company would be happy to help us.

Sometimes we fail to remember we can go right to the top. We serve creation's CEO—the Lord Most High. The God who told the people of Israel and Judah that he would deliver them from their enemies will also help us today. When we are confused, we can pray for direction. When we are ill, we pray for healing. When we experience injustice, we can plead our cause with our heavenly Judge.

Lord, sometimes my problems seem to mount up into a stubborn mountain that I can't seem to climb or break down. I won't ask that my frustrations just disappear but instead ask that you help me face those problems, one by one, and turn them to rubble.

Keep Looking Up!

When we pray, we go right to the top: God!

AUGUST 21

God's Got This

Read Jeremiah 51–52

The LORD is a God of recompense; he will surely repay.

—Jeremiah 51:56

"BUT IT'S NOT fair, Mom!"

I agreed with her. The punishment from her teacher wasn't justified, as another student had taken her assignment and copied it without my daughter's consent.

"But God knows," I said. "He will catch up with that girl someday."

As time passed, the truth came out. I always told my kids that sometimes we do not get things we deserve, but other times we receive blessings we don't deserve.

We see this in the Bible too. Even though the people of Judah did not follow God, they cried out to him for help when Babylon invaded. Even after their disobedience, God promised he would restore them to their homeland. And he did.

When we find that life isn't fair, we can do what we are humanly able to in order to correct the situation and then put it in God's hands. We don't have to worry about it anymore!

Lord, you have heard my cries of "But it's not fair!" And you know when I allow unfairness to stir anger and bitterness in my heart. Help me turn over the problem to you—then I need not worry about it anymore.

Keep Looking Up!

Looking up prevents our bitterness when life isn't fair.

AUGUST 22

God Hears Our Cries

Read Lamentations 1–2

As each night watch begins, get up and cry out in prayer. Pour your heart out face-to-face with the Master. —Lamentations 2:19 MSG

"I'M SORRY," HE said. "I won't do it again."

I just stared at the young man standing in front of my classroom desk. "But you did do it again." He was always late with his work.

"I promise I will turn everything in on time from now on."

I smiled as he walked away. Time would tell.

But we mess up too, don't we? We make the same mistakes. We complain, gossip, eat too much, say unkind things. Each time we tell God: *I promise . . .*

The book of Lamentations begins with the writer's heart cries on behalf of his people who have lost their homeland and identity as a people and ends with repentance. The fall of Israel was due to the people's disobedience in following other gods.

When we mess up, we have the opportunity to repent—to turn from that wrongful mindset and behavior and turn toward God for his forgiveness. He will always hear our cries!

Lord, I messed up again, and as much as my regret hurts, it hurts even more knowing I have disappointed you. Forgive me, God, and help me to make better choices for myself and your kingdom's sake.

Keep Looking Up!

Kneeling in prayer can physically depict our submission to God.

AUGUST 23

God's Mercies Never End

Read Lamentations 3–5

The steadfast love of the LORD never ceases; his mercies never come to an end; they are new every morning; great is your faithfulness.
—Lamentations 3:22–23

I COULDN'T BELIEVE it. Despite my many failures to water the seeds I'd planted in late spring, I had California poppies and other new wildflowers growing in an otherwise bland corner of my backyard. I'm not the best nurturer of plants; when a friend gives me one, I jokingly say last rites over it. To me, if anything blooms in my yard, it's another example of the Lord's great mercies.

Having an ongoing sense of God's immense love and endless mercies should keep us in continual thanksgiving and praise. Even when times are tough—as the exiled Hebrews experienced—we can sense the Lord's compassionate presence and guiding hand. Though God had allowed the Israelites' exile, he promised his steadfast love and constant mercy.

Every new morning gives us the opportunity to bloom under God's faithfulness—as we embrace both the Son and the rains of life.

Lord, great is your faithfulness. Your love goes on and on, never ceasing, and your mercies are endless. Each new day you pour new blessings over me and even provide rest for my soul. Thank you for your faithfulness.

Keep Looking Up!

Rising with a "Thank you, Lord!" is a great way to start the day.

AUGUST 24

We Can Stand before God

Read Ezekiel 1–4

He said to me, "Son of man, stand on your feet, and I will speak with you." —Ezekiel 2:1

"WHAT HAPPENED?"

The young man sitting in front of me in the school office hung his head and mumbled. I had stepped in again for the principal.

"Mark, look me in the eye, please."

Slowly raising his head, he said, "I'm embarrassed I got into a stupid fight. I don't do stuff like this."

Like that young man in the office, we often feel insignificant in the presence of the Holy God. We understand the limitations of our humanity. There is a sense of space between the Lord in heaven and us on earth. But God calls us to him, just as he did with Ezekiel when he said, "Son of man, stand on your feet."

While we cannot look into God's face until we are with him in heaven, we can look up and know that we have the privilege of standing in his presence—only because Jesus died for our redemption.

Lord in heaven, that you call me to stand before you to receive your call on my life is humbling. May I never forget that you are the Holy God, and I am your creation. Thank you that you beckon me to yourself.

Keep Looking Up!

Letting go of false shame helps us approach our Holy God.

AUGUST 25

God's Wake-Up Calls Are Good

Read Ezekiel 5–8

And they shall know that I am the LORD. —Ezekiel 6:10

I HAD A wake-up call some years ago—a health wake-up call. I had been tolerating joint pain and breathlessness upon exertion, but when my knee gave way going down some stairs, I knew I needed to do something. The very next day I began walking for my health and praying for my community as I passed homes and businesses.

A wake-up call is a good thing—much better than an emergency or 911 call! Unfortunately, even though the Lord—through the prophets—had warned the people to return to him, they did not. Part of their wake-up call was the exile in Babylon. During that exile, Ezekiel was God's spokesman, declaring that God is their Lord.

The good news is just as the people of Israel can have a change of heart, so can we! We can leave our place of disobedience or even just disinterest and run into the arms of the Savior who welcomes and loves us!

Father God, thank you for your gentle reminders that you are the Lord, you care for me and my welfare, and you want me to stay close to you for my own sake. Increasingly, I sense your love for me and want to follow you.

Keep Looking Up!

A change of heart is demonstrated with obedience.

AUGUST 26

God Changes Our Hearts

Read Ezekiel 9–12

> And I will give them singleness of heart and put a new spirit within them. I will take away their stony, stubborn heart and give them a tender, responsive heart. —Ezekiel 11:19 NLT

I HAVE A friend who collects heart-shaped stones. They are a reminder of God's love for her, and she says that she finds them out walking or hiking just at the right moment when she needs that kind of encouragement.

No matter where we are, we can know God loves us. Even when the exiled Hebrews were scattered among the nations during their period of exile, the Lord said, "I have been a sanctuary to them for a while in the countries where they have gone." Even when their hearts were stonelike, God was still on a path of pursuit for a relationship with them.

Transforming our hearts from a stony, stubborn character to one that is tender and responsive is not hard. In fact, it can be a simple matter of pouring out our confession to the Lord and offering our open hands for whatever God has for us.

Lord, I do not want a heart of stone. I want a soft, malleable heart that bleeds when you are grieved and swells with your overflowing joy. And may my heart touch others with your love.

Keep Looking Up!

A tender, responsive heart says yes to God.

AUGUST 27

God Vows to Love Us

Read Ezekiel 13–16

I made my vow to you and entered into a covenant with you, declares the Lord God, and you became mine. —Ezekiel 16:8

A TALL, HANDSOME man stood before me and said, "I, Craig, take you, Janet, to be my wife, and I covenant before God and these witnesses to be your loving and faithful husband in plenty and in want, in joy and in sorrow, in sickness and in health, as long as we both shall live."

I said the same thing, and there we were minutes later, married, with almost nothing in the bank account and a whole lot of student debt. But that didn't matter. We were in love and we had promised—no, covenanted—to be faithful to each other. And we have!

Married or not, we have a loving Pursuer and Partner—the Lord God, who has covenanted to love us. When we commit ourselves to the Lord, we are his and he is ours. Even when we are not faithful and run after the next glittering object of fascination, God loves us and calls us his own.

Lord, you covenanted to love me, and I became yours. I choose faithfulness too. I choose to love you, honor you, and serve you.

Keep Looking Up!

As we mature, our love for God should grow.

AUGUST 28

Choosing God Is Choosing Life

Read Ezekiel 17–18

Make a clean break! Live! —Ezekiel 18:32 MSG

I RECENTLY RAN into a friend from the past. Although I had known she had wrestled a lot with addiction, she looked fantastic—which is exactly what I told her. She acknowledged her former struggles and said, "I'm now ten years sober."

When I asked how she had achieved that amazing record, she said, "I made a clean break. I chose Jesus and decided to live."

God gives us the gift of choice, which we find in the book of Ezekiel. Even though there is a lot of language about warnings and even condemnation, the bottom line is clear: just like the people of his time, we can make a clean break with whatever keeps us from God. We can turn in a new direction and choose a new heart and spirit that will be in sync with his. That simple decision will bring us new life!

Lord, I choose to not only know you but also have a relationship with you, which means I also choose to take delight in the things that delight you.

Keep Looking Up!

We truly live by following the Lord God.

We Are God's Favorite Offering

Read Ezekiel 19–20

What's more, I'll receive you as the best kind of offerings when I bring you back from all the lands and countries in which you've been scattered. I'll demonstrate in the eyes of the world that I am The Holy. —Ezekiel 20:41 MSG

I LOVE BABY photos—anyone's. Newborns with their squinty little eyes. Sleepy ones snuggled in a soft receiving blanket. Cute little ones with milk on their faces. They're all beautiful, and I don't mind at all when my friends show off the newest addition to their family.

I think God is a little like a proud parent or grandparent—I see hints of that in a section of today's reading. He cannot wait for his children of Israel to run back to him, so the watching nations can see how they reflect his goodness. We, his people, are his favorite.

Just like children should exhibit the best qualities of their good parents, we can reflect God's goodness too. In our Christian walk, we can show others that God exists when they see his likeness in us. When we are faithful and kind and exhibit integrity, other folks will be drawn to the God we emulate.

Lord, I offer myself to you. Cleanse me of anything that obscures my witness. Purify my sight so I am only drawn to things that are of you. Draw me to yourself as I surrender myself to you each day.

Keep Looking Up!

When we look like God, others see his likeness in us.

AUGUST 30

We Can Stand in the Gap with God

Read Ezekiel 21–22

I looked for someone among them who would build up the wall and stand before me in the gap on behalf of the land so I would not have to destroy it, but I found no one. —Ezekiel 22:30 NIV

A FRIEND CAME to me recently, suggesting a new church ministry. It was a worthy project but completely outside of my wheelhouse of abilities and time and the callings God has given me. Over the years others have had many ideas for what they think I should be doing with my life, and I have to chuckle. I mean, if God, as they say, gave them the idea, why wouldn't they simply move forward with it themselves?

God issues callings to his people. It's a sad commentary we find in Ezekiel 22:30—that God searched for someone to pray on behalf of the people, but he found no one willing to do that.

Praying for others is a privilege—something I love doing—whether I see the need on social media or hear of it through other means. It only takes moments to pray. Each of us can stand in the gap for others in prayer.

Lord, touch my heart with the needs of others around me. May I not neglect prayer on their behalf—especially that they would experience the life-giving salvation that you so freely offer.

Keep Looking Up!

We can give one minute to pray for someone as a need arises.

We Can Be a Signpost for God

Read Ezekiel 23–24

At that time your mouth will be opened; you will speak with him and will no longer be silent. So you will be a sign to them, and they will know I am the LORD. —Ezekiel 24:27 NIV

WHEN MY YOUNGER sister passed away from metastatic cancer, I didn't need friends who had all the answers or all the Bible quotes. The sweetest gift came from a teaching coworker who asked all the students to line the school hallway and just stand there as an expression of their care. Their simple, sympathetic silence is now a lovely memory.

When we listen closely to the Lord, he can help us understand what and what not to say. Even prophets are told to be quiet sometimes. God told Ezekiel not to say a word even when his wife died on the same day the temple burned. Then God sent a survivor, which was the sign Ezekiel could speak again.

Sometimes our presence is enough for someone in need. Sometimes God will give us the perfect encouraging words. In either case we can be God's signpost—an emissary of his love and care.

Lord, I ache when others ache and invite your Holy Spirit's presence to allow me to be a sign of grace and goodness that points them to you.

Keep Looking Up!

Weighing our words can lighten our speech.

SEPTEMBER 1

God's Word Comes to Us

Read Ezekiel 25–27

The word of the LORD came to me. —Ezekiel 27:1 NIV

YOU KNOW ABOUT those unexpected phone calls—the ones in the middle of the night that never bear good news. My friend called me yesterday to let me know the father of a former student passed away suddenly—a man much loved in our small community.

Bearing bad news is not easy. Prophets such as Ezekiel spoke and wrote the words the Lord gave them for the people and nations. They gave warnings, and sometimes they spoke of judgment and destruction to come. When we read such things, it's still hard to believe . . . but the prophecies of the Bible have been borne out in history—even promising the birth of our Savior, Jesus Christ.

God speaks to us through his Word each day, and we can have confidence that he will orchestrate our days with his guiding hand.

Lord, may I hear clearly from you throughout my day—from the rising of the sun to its setting. Stop me when something is not right. Pause me when I need to delay. And give me a clear go sign with a directional arrow for the right road.

Keep Looking Up!

Slowing down to listen to God can bring about clarity.

SEPTEMBER 2

God Raises Beauty from Ashes

Read Ezekiel 28–30

And then I'll stir up fresh hope in Israel—the dawn of deliverance!—and I'll give you, Ezekiel, bold and confident words to speak. And they'll realize that I am GOD. —Ezekiel 29:21 MSG

WE HAVE EXPERIENCED several major forest fires over our years of living in the Sierra. The devastation of forest and community is heartbreaking. But an unusual thing happens in the seasons after fires. Wildflowers, ferns, mosses, and other plants burst through the devastation—taking advantage of greater light and, oddly, the enriched soil from the burn. Beauty can rise from ashes.

When we experience devastation in our lives, that season can give us greater appreciation for the Lord. Despite the destruction of much of Israel and Judah, God made a promise to again raise the strength of his people. His prophets would again prophesy, and the people would listen and obey.

After the ravages of figurative wildfires in our lives, we can look for the beauty that arises from a greater sense of God's closeness and caring. And the challenges can actually grow personal strength in us that can be seen in beautiful joy on our face.

Lord, in the times that make me feel as though I am running through wildfires, help me rise with your strength and new focus to be an even better example for you. My faith walk may take me down paths I would not seek, but I trust you.

Keep Looking Up!

Taking times to breathe and rest can put hard times into perspective.

SEPTEMBER 3

God Provides Wise Counselors

Read Ezekiel 31–33

When this comes—and come it will!—then they will know that a prophet has been among them. —Ezekiel 33:33

ANY PARENT COULD have a sign hung in the home reading "I told you so." While I respected and loved my parents, I thought my way was best. They always told me I would be a good teacher, but I had to explore my own path and make my own mistakes. Imagine my surprise, years later, to find I loved teaching. I had no idea! Learning through experience, though, can be painful.

It's much simpler to listen to the counsel of wise people who know us. They may see strengths and weaknesses in us we overlook, and they might even help us avoid wasted years and difficult situations. It must have been hard for the prophet Ezekiel to have spoken God's words to the people around him and been totally ignored . . . and worse, ridiculed.

The expression "time will tell" helps us wait expectantly for God's counsel to come to fruition.

Lord, I have learned it is wise to weigh the counsel of those I respect. They know me and want the best for me. May the counsel I offer others be softened with encouragement and kindness.

Keep Looking Up!

Advice is cheap, but wise counsel is golden.

SEPTEMBER 4

God Seeks Us Out

Read Ezekiel 34–35

As a shepherd seeks out his flock when he is among his sheep that have been scattered, so will I seek out my sheep, and I will rescue them from all places where they have been scattered on a day of clouds and thick darkness. —Ezekiel 34:12

WHEN YOUR BEEF cattle are grazing in a pasture that is surrounded by a wooded area and has a winding creek hidden by willows, it can be tricky rounding them up in the fall to bring them back to the ranch. My husband and daughter do their best to gather them from hidden places before the cattle drive home.

It's hard to match up all the cow and calf pairs. Once a young calf got left behind because its mom had another and was probably disinterested in a second. But Craig found the little one and reunited it with its mom.

When the people of Israel were exiled to Babylon, they may have felt God abandoned them. But in today's reading we see that God promised to seek them all out and rescue them from scattered places.

Even today God still seeks us out and calls us his own.

In those times when I feel abandoned, God, remind me that you count me among your own, you will rescue me, and you will bring me back to a secure, safe place.

Keep Looking Up!

God's Word assures us that God is seeking us.

God Can Refresh Us

Read Ezekiel 36–38

So I prophesied as I was commanded. And as I was prophesying, there was a noise, a rattling sound, and the bones came together, bone to bone. —Ezekiel 37:7 NIV

WHEN MY HUSBAND served as a city councilman for four years, he took on more than fifty civil works projects to help revitalize the town. In that unpaid position he spearheaded efforts to build an outdoor events center and restore an old school building to house the museum, thrift store, and city offices—among other projects. Our little town came to life again.

With just a little effort, we can rebuild our spiritual lives as well. When God led the Hebrew exiles back to Jerusalem, they were in a spiritually dry condition—just like bones lying in the desert. But God's prophecy through Ezekiel indicated that God can restore even the spiritually dead.

When our faith is dry as scattered bones, we can ask God to refresh and fill us as we pray for renewed direction to serve him within our church community—bringing it new life too.

Lord, just as you gave Ezekiel the vision of the dry bones coming to life, I ask for your inspiration to fill me with a vision of how I might pursue spiritual refreshment. Teach me, Lord!

Keep Looking Up!

**Refreshment can come from Scripture,
a walk in nature, or worship music.**

SEPTEMBER 6

We Can Testify to God

Read Ezekiel 39–40

From that day forward the people of Israel will know that I am the Lord their God. —Ezekiel 39:22 NIV

I WAS DRIVING our family van down the western side of Donner Pass when chunks of hail suddenly fell. On a descent, I knew I needed to slow down and lightly touched the brake. But the car started to spin and sent us toward a concrete support for an overpass.

Save us, Lord, I quickly prayed and slowly steered into the spin. And we just missed the support.

It is no small thing to see your life pass before your eyes and then know God has saved you. Just as the Israelites returning from exile must have felt, you understand God's mercy protected you. They had been led as prisoners of war to Babylon . . . their future unknown. And now they would get to go home and give God the glory.

When we experience a life-saving miracle, we have the opportunity to testify to others about God's immense goodness.

Lord, thank you for rescuing me over and over. I give you honor and glory with my life and my words.

Keep Looking Up!

Thanking God publicly puts the honor where it's due.

The Lord's Glory Is All Around

Read Ezekiel 41–43

> Then the man brought me to the gate facing east, and I saw the glory of the God of Israel coming from the east. His voice was like the roar of rushing waters, and the land was radiant with his glory.
>
> —Ezekiel 43:1–2 NIV

AFTER I RETIRED from teaching, I began walking the hour wrapped around sunset—the half hour before sunset and the half hour after. After one particularly stressful day, I put on my walking shoes and headed out the door. As I mulled over the day's stresses, I noticed the sky turning purplish pink to the east. That didn't seem to make sense: the sun sets in the west! But as I continued to walk, the colors spread into the circle of skies around our bowl-shaped mountain valley. And my concerns flew away as I gave thanks for God's lovely gift.

The whole book of Ezekiel shifts from a negative tone to a delightfully positive one when God's glory appears in the restored temple in Jerusalem. It truly is a promise to us today too that God will fulfill his promises to us—with the final and joy-filled, triumphant return of his Son, Jesus, to the earth.

Until that time we can look around God's creation and see the glory he left for us to enjoy!

Lord, I am reminded of your radiant glory every time I see a sunrise or a sunset. The earth sings praise all around me—each day a precious gift. May your Word rush into me and fill me with encouragement today.

Keep Looking Up!

Gazing at a sunrise or sunset lifts the spirit.

God's Glory Fills Us

Read Ezekiel 44–46

Then he brought me by way of the north gate to the front of the temple, and I looked, and behold, the glory of the LORD filled the temple of the LORD. And I fell on my face. —Ezekiel 44:4

I LOVE ROCKS, and if it weren't for rattlesnakes who love them too, I would live on property with rock formations all around me. On a recent trip to Utah, we visited many national parks, including Arches, Bryce Canyon, and Zion. With each curve of the road, I joked, "There you are again, Utah, showing off." But I knew that God was the creator of such majesty.

Despite the beauty of God's world, I know that seeing the Lord and heaven will flatten me, face down, in the same way Ezekiel did when he saw the glory of the Lord filling the temple. He had experienced punishment, war, and exile in his lifetime—a lot of pain and rejection. But all of that must have paled in comparison to the privilege of seeing the glory of the Lord once again filling Israel's place of worship.

He is worthy of a worshipful face-plant.

Lord, as the world spins its crises one after another, I long for the glory, peace, and fulfillment of your presence. May my heart only grow in its desire to spend eternity with you.

Keep Looking Up!

Lying prostrate on the floor in prayer physically acknowledges God's glory.

SEPTEMBER 9

The Lord Is There

Read Ezekiel 47–48

And the name of the city from that time on will be: THE LORD IS THERE. —Ezekiel 48:35 NIV

AS I WALKED back toward my little town and saw the city limits sign, a series of thoughts came to me. What if the sign said, "The Lord lives here"? What if visitors to our town stopped and noticed people were different—kind, sweet-spirited, good-hearted? What if someone asked the clerk at the grocery store, "Why is this place different?" And the clerk responded. "Well, it's because the Lord lives here."

Later that day I read today's verse and learned that the expression "The Lord is there" (*Yahweh-Shammah* in Hebrew) sounds interestingly similar to the Hebrew pronunciation of Jerusalem: *Yerushalayim.*

Wouldn't it be lovely if your town and mine radiated with God's lovingkindness—so much that others found God's saving grace for their own lives because of having visited there?

I pray for that looking up perspective . . . and hope you will too!

Lord, I pray for my community, that each and every person would have a personal relationship with you and live out their lives loving and serving you the best way they can. May my community shine with your love, God!

Keep Looking Up!

When we demonstrate God's love,
others see his presence in our lives.

SEPTEMBER 10

God Gives Clarity

Read Daniel 1–3

He changes times and seasons; he removes kings and sets up kings; he gives wisdom to the wise and knowledge to those who have understanding. —Daniel 2:21

SOME OF THE heaviest praying seasons of my life were when my husband served on the county board of supervisors and the city council. Interpersonal dynamics, finances, differing priorities—all these created great stress for my guy, who was not at all interested in playing politics but simply wanted to get tangible results for our communities.

It may be a controversial saying, but I'll put it out there: prayer works. When we ask God for wisdom, he gives it. Daniel found this to be true when he was charged with interpreting the king's troubling dreams. He asked his three friends to pray for him and God revealed the answer to him in a night vision.

God does not hide from us, and he does not want us to live in confusion. We have access to the living God, and that access is more important than answers. Prayer works because God is at work in us.

I am so grateful, God, that you don't want me walking around in a cloud of confusion. You know my times and seasons, and you know the wisdom and precise direction that I need to navigate those times. I turn to you, Lord, for your guidance today.

Keep Looking Up!

Reading God's Word gives clarity to our lives.

SEPTEMBER 11

God Honors the Humble

Read Daniel 4–5

How great are his signs, how mighty his wonders! His kingdom is an everlasting kingdom, and his dominion endures from generation to generation. —Daniel 4:3

"GOD IS GREAT. God is good. And we thank him for this food."

That was a grace said over mealtimes at youth camps I attended. But away from the not-so-watchful eyes of camp counselors, all kinds of shenanigans went on. But that's probably true of many of us who say we follow Jesus. Our actions don't always live out our faith commitment.

It's easy to give lip service to God. Words fall off the tongue in rote fashion. That's the kind of behavior we see in Nebuchadnezzar, the king of Babylon. At several times during his reign, he praised Daniel's God publicly, but ultimately the king did not serve or worship the Lord and arrogantly boasted about his wealth and greatness.

Following the Lord means we submit our lives to his lordship and, with the help of the Spirit, determine daily to honor him with everything we say, do, and even think.

Lord, may I ever be mindful that anything I own or achieve is only because of your love and grace. May all I am and all I have honor you.

Keep Looking Up!

Boasting is only well received when it's all about God.

SEPTEMBER 12

The Lord Rewards Commitment

Read Daniel 6–8

He got down on his knees three times a day and prayed and gave thanks before his God, as he had done previously. —Daniel 6:10

I WAS ZIPPING through social media, responding with encouragement and notes that I was praying . . . without actually pausing to pray. When I caught myself, I stopped, closed my eyes, asked God to forgive me, and interceded for the people I'd sent notes to.

It's easy to let daily tasks sideline the disciplines of praying and reading the Bible. But the prophet Daniel demonstrated devotional disciplines. Even though King Darius signed a law that no one in his kingdom could worship anyone but him, Daniel risked his life by continuing to pray to God. His quiet defiance of the law and willingness to accept the consequences got him thrown into the lions' den, but the Lord saved him.

Practicing our faith openly means we trust God for how others perceive us. However, attending church and putting quiet time practices into place will bring about a reserve of strength we will need for any figurative lions' dens into which we are thrown.

Lord, sometimes I let the busyness of my days usurp those minutes I've committed to you. Thank you for your patience with me. You deserve to be first in my life.

Keep Looking Up!

The practice of scheduling and protecting quiet time makes it more likely to happen.

SEPTEMBER 13

God Hears Our Confessions

Read Daniel 9–12

> So I turned to the Lord God and pleaded with him in prayer and petition, in fasting, and in sackcloth and ashes. I prayed to the Lord my God and confessed. —Daniel 9:3–4 NIV

I HAD MADE a big mistake in regard to a student's English grade. I had mis-entered a score into the computer, resulting in a lower letter grade. When I told the student I was sorry and would quickly fix it, he said, "No worries, Mrs. McHenry. We all make mistakes."

We do all make mistakes, but some of them are not simple in their underlying causes. Sin may be at the root of many relational issues—which are harder to fix than simple grade mistakes. And when sin permeates an institution or an entire nation, such as during Daniel's time, much prayer is needed. Daniel pleaded with God, using a collective *we* when he confessed the nation's sin, and God responded that much atonement was still needed from the people.

We can be hope-filled and joyful because we know that God hears our prayers for ourselves, our communities, and our nation.

Lord, I see great needs around me and confess on behalf of my family and community that we have not followed you. I trust that you will forgive us and restore us to yourself.

Keep Looking Up!

Consistent prayers for our family will have effect.

SEPTEMBER 14

God Calls Us "My Loved One"

Read Hosea 1–4

Say of your brothers, "My people," and of your sisters, "My loved one." —Hosea 2:1 NIV

WE ALL HAVE characters in our families, right? My mother always says, "I don't need to watch soap operas. I have family." Someone might be called "troublemaker." Another, "slow" or "silly" or "lazy." Or worse. But those names can stick in our memories, hanging over us like harbingers.

Some people in the Bible had labels too, such as the wife of the prophet Hosea. The book of Hosea is an allegory to show God's unconditional love. The Lord told the prophet Hosea to marry an adulterous wife. Though she was continually unfaithful, Hosea nonetheless loved her, sought her out, and restored her to himself—just as God continually sought out his people Israel and still seeks us out today.

Despite our wanderings, God has special names for us: Chosen, Light of the World, and Child of God. Even when we mess up, he calls us "my loved one."

Father, you call me one of your people and your loved one. It's hard to feel worthy of those names. Thank you for the gift of your Son, Jesus, who paved the way for me to be part of your family.

Keep Looking Up!

The only labels that truly matter are those God has given us.

SEPTEMBER 15

God Desires True Repentance

Read Hosea 5–9

> Let us know; let us press on to know the Lord; his going out is sure as the dawn; he will come to us as the showers, as the spring rains that water the earth. —Hosea 6:3

"SORRY, MOM," MY kid said half-heartedly. "I'll clean it up later."

In looking for a missing shoe, I found a half-eaten cookie, candy wrappers, and other trash under the bed. I started to get upset, but then I remembered my own childhood and how when something of mine went missing, my parents would always say, "Look under your bed."

Apparently, room-cleaning methods are genetic. All would be forgiven, but I knew I'd stumble across the same kind of mess in the not-too-distant future.

Repentance means we not only apologize but also turn away from our bad behavior. We change. The prophet Hosea observed that the people of Israel did not understand the depth of their sins and thought God would not stay angry at them.

We can, however, step out of and away from our darkness to live in his light. That is true repentance.

Lord, while I know you love me and have forgiven me, I do not want to abuse your merciful nature. With each new rising of the sun, may I be that much closer to you so that I can enjoy your refreshment with a clean heart.

Keep Looking Up!

Obedience is just one good decision after another.

SEPTEMBER 16

God Invites Us to Sow

Read Hosea 10–14

Sow for yourselves righteousness; reap steadfast love; break up your fallow ground, for it is the time to seek the LORD, that he may come and rain righteousness upon you. —Hosea 10:12

MY RANCHER HUSBAND has a giant green tractor that breaks up the cold, early spring earth for planting hay crops. Then he drags a scraper behind his tractor to level it, followed by a cultipacker that firms up the earth. Finally, he goes over it one more time with a grain drill to drop the seed, cover it, and push the seed down firmly. Much of that he can irrigate with a large pivot, but the best water comes from the heavens.

Just as any crop takes a lot of effort, we also must continually sow good behavior to live a life that represents the Master Gardener well. With his help we can break up the fallow ground of our souls—rooting out sin that would choke us like weeds—and reap the sweet blessing of the peace that only comes from close fellowship with our Father.

Lord, I want to be in close fellowship with you each day. I don't want an up-and-down existence but instead a life that bears fruit—love, joy, peace, and other examples of righteousness. Rain your goodness over me.

Keep Looking Up!

Spiritual growth is a daily process of choosing God's will.

SEPTEMBER 17

God Brings Restoration

Read Joel 1–3

I will restore to you the years that the swarming locust has eaten.
—Joel 2:25

I HAVE A friend who lived through many years of her husband's emotional abuse before he walked away from the marriage. She had hung in there, hopeful for change, but things did not work out. Since then, though, she has gotten healthier, has redeveloped old friendships, and is experiencing a season of God's restoration.

We may notice that times of blessing cycle after hard seasons. When Judah experienced severe drought and then a locust plague, Joel called on the nation to repent: old and young alike. Despite the people's sin, the Lord pitied his people and restored the years of suffering with years of plentiful provision.

Receiving earthly plenty does not always happen. Yet as we reflect on the past years of our lives, we can remember the hard times as well as the blessings, giving praise to God for his faithfulness throughout each season.

Lord, I am in a season of weariness, with one struggle after another. I know time will pass and you will see me through this. I trust that you will restore the lost years.

Keep Looking Up!

God always restores us to himself when we are repentant.

SEPTEMBER 18

We Can Walk with God

Read Amos 1–4

Do two walk together unless they have agreed to do so?
—Amos 3:3 NIV

AS A HIGH school English teacher, I enjoyed teaching the art of argumentation to my juniors and seniors. They might never write a research paper or essay again, but daily they would need to be able to discern the truth of others' arguments and know how to stand up for what they believe.

One technique of argumentation is the use of the rhetorical question—one that has an obvious answer—to make a point. Often writers use rhetorical questions in multiples, and we find in Amos 3:3–6 that the Lord uses seven to show cause and effect. Because the people of God continued to turn away from him and choose other gods, they would face an invading disaster.

Does God love us? Yes. Does he care about our struggles? Yes. Does he want us to walk with him? Yes.

But walking with someone requires both parties to be in agreement. So if we want God to walk with us, we simply need to say yes to him . . . in obedience.

Lord, I choose you as my walking-through-life partner. I do not want to argue about where to go or what to do, but instead go your way, as you know the best way for me.

Keep Looking Up!

Saying yes to God's ways guides our daily walk.

SEPTEMBER 19

God Created Everything

Read Amos 5–9

> He who made the Pleiades and Orion, and turns deep darkness into the morning and darkens the day into night, who calls for the waters of the sea and pours them out on the surface of the earth, the LORD is his name. —Amos 5:8

WE LIVE AT five thousand feet elevation in the northern Sierra, and we joke that we are that much closer to heaven. The night skies are pitch black with stars so bright you don't need a flashlight to walk—although a skunk sprayed me one time, so night strolls are rarer now.

Sometimes we lay a blanket on our balcony or drive deep into our mountain valley with folding chairs to watch the autumn meteorite shows. Those occasions remind us of the magnificent glory of creation . . . and the Creator himself. Through the prophet Amos, the Lord refreshed the memory of the people of Israel that it was he who turns the night into day and pours the waters all over the earth.

While we fascinate and applaud ourselves with our own creations, a looking up perspective reminds us that our Creator is the only one worthy of our praise.

Lord, your creation should keep me in continual awe of your power. May absolutely nothing else ever slip into a place of worship in my life, so that you are the One True God I always serve.

Keep Looking Up!

Pausing to observe and thank God for the wonders of the night sky develops humility.

SEPTEMBER 20

God Rescues Us

Read Obadiah

Saviors shall go up to Mount Zion to rule Mount Esau, and the kingdom shall be the LORD's. —Obadiah 21

SOMEONE TOLD ME a student was bullying my son at school, but since my son hadn't mentioned it, I decided to pray instead of act. Then one day at a school rally, I heard that boy insult my son, and it occurred to me: *I would not tolerate bullying of any other student.* Because my job as a teacher required making school safe for all students, I gave that young man a firm warning.

In his Word God promises to protect his people. In the book of Obadiah we read that the Edomites to the southeast of the Dead Sea had bullied God's people continually. But we also see God's commitment to punish evil and restore hope to the people of the Southern Kingdom of Judah.

As God's people, we should intervene when we become aware of abuse situations. That kind of help could bring back joy and peace to someone in need.

Lord, give me clarity about how to help someone who is being bullied or abused. May I be that person who extends care and your love to others in need.

Keep Looking Up!

Love wins when God's people confront abuse.

SEPTEMBER 21

God Is in the Restoration Business

Read Jonah 1–4

And the people of Nineveh believed God. They called for a fast and put on sackcloth, from the greatest of them to the least of them. —Jonah 3:5

I'LL NEVER FORGET that phone call.

"Mrs. McHenry, you might not remember me, but this is Oscar. You taught me in the fourth grade."

Oscar went on to express his sincere apologies for being unkind to me—actions I didn't remember. Now in young adulthood, he had come to faith in God and wanted to make things right with people he had hurt.

Forgiveness can be a hard work—not only for the person apologizing but also for the victim. We see this lesson in Jonah. When the prophet escaped the belly of a great fish and finally followed God's call to preach to the evil Ninevites, they experience a dramatic spiritual turnaround and confess their sins. But Jonah couldn't let go of his hatred for them.

We don't want to be Jonahs. Instead, we can choose not to be offended and then forgive others and trust God to redeem their lives.

Lord, I don't want to hold grudges and anger, which can affect me emotionally and even physically. Help me choose not to be offended and just release the situation to your care.

Keep Looking Up!

I can choose to overlook and not act on a personal offense.

SEPTEMBER 22

God Says Peace Will Come

Read Micah 1–4

> He shall judge between many peoples, and shall decide disputes for strong nations far away; and they shall beat their swords into plowshares, and their spears into pruning hooks; nation shall not lift up sword against nation, neither shall they learn war anymore.
>
> —Micah 4:3

MY FRIEND WAS screaming awful words at me over the phone. She said I had not been there for her—that I was a hypocrite and had snubbed her. All because I'd just smiled and said hi to her at church rather than engage her in conversation—the same woman I had given a baby shower just weeks before. Anything I said only made her more angry. As a result, that friendship faded.

When we individuals cannot get along, how can we ever expect nations to live at peace with each other? As we learn from the book of Micah, God hates injustice and unkindness. He desires for people and nations to live in peace. But when sins of jealousy, selfishness, and idolatry permeate a culture, there will be conflict.

However, we can look forward to the days when God will reign over his kingdom, bringing peace to us all.

Lord, it hurts my heart when I see the discord around me—people tearing down other people, cultures divided, nations at war. May there be a mass exodus away from sin into your saving grace, so that peace reigns in our hearts and land.

Keep Looking Up!

Regardless of circumstances, peace begins when I live out my Christian faith.

SEPTEMBER 23

God Shows Us What Is Good

Read Micah 5–7

> He has shown you, O mortal, what is good. And what does the LORD require of you? To act justly and to love mercy and to walk humbly with your God. —Micah 6:8 NIV

MY FRIEND, WHO was the national director of a Christian health organization, has given me a lot of good counsel over the years, which could be summed up in five words: "Do the next right thing."

Doing the next right thing might be confusing in various situations because we have so many choices. Just a walk down the long toilet paper aisle in the grocery store shows why we're often overwhelmed by options.

But God teaches us what is good in this passage from the prophet Micah. When we are faced with a circumstance that seems unfair, God shows us that we should do the just thing. When we notice unkindness or someone who needs some loving care, we should demonstrate kindness to that person. The Lord will make clear what is the good way and what the Lord requires when we are walking humbly with him.

Lord, help me to do the next right thing in my life—acting justly, pursuing kindness, and walking humbly with you each day. Today and every day, may others see more of you in my life.

Keep Looking Up!

God shows us what is good in his Word.

SEPTEMBER 24

God Brings Good News

Read Nahum 1–3

Behold, upon the mountains, the feet of him who brings good news, who publishes peace! —Nahum 1:15

A PIECE OF good news just made my day. A friend told me prayers for her were answered: she had received the guidance from the Lord she needed to move forward.

Good news can encourage us at the perfect moment. Certainly, the prophets in the Bible would have wanted to share good news. But it was their calling only to warn and prophesy exactly what God told them to say. And often the words from the Lord were about tough times ahead. Nahum shared that God is a jealous God and gets angry when his people turn away from him. But good news was ahead for Nahum's Judah. The cruel Assyrians would be wiped out.

The very best news in God's Word is that Jesus came that we might have peace with God and that eternal life is just a repentant prayer away.

Lord, you know I am waiting for good news. Life has been such a struggle lately, but I trust that you will scale the mountains of troubles and encourage me.

Keep Looking Up!

Being expectant is a sign of faith.

SEPTEMBER 25

God Will Amaze Us!

Read Habakkuk 1–3

> Look among the nations, and see; wonder and be astounded. For I am doing a work in your days that you would not believe if told.
>
> —Habakkuk 1:5

I EXPECTED THE worst. Sharp gut pains shot through me. I was sure I had appendicitis. But after many hours of medical tests and waiting in the emergency room, I got a surprise.

"You don't have an appendix, Janet," the ER nurse said.

Yes, I'm laughing with you. Frankly, I'd lost track of the fact that in a prior surgery the surgeon had also removed my appendix.

When we have a long series of health or other issues, we just expect the worst, don't we?

Even the prophet Habakkuk was discouraged and complained in prayer: "How long, LORD, must I call for help . . . ?" (Habakkuk 1:2 NIV). After facing one assault after another, we begin to lose hope.

But we serve a God who wants us to be expectant in prayer. We can always keep looking up, and because he loves us, we will be amazed at what he does.

Amaze me, Lord! Show me your great works! I know that in this quiet season of waiting, you are doing something that will astonish me later. Thank you, God, for your faithfulness in my life. You are worthy of my trust.

Keep Looking Up!

Taking steps toward the best outcome shows a looking up perspective!

SEPTEMBER 26

God Sings over Us

Read Zephaniah 1–3

The LORD your God is in your midst, a mighty one who will save; he will rejoice over you with gladness; he will quiet you by his love; he will exult over you with loud singing. —Zephaniah 3:17

I FACED A significant health scare after a routine test. While I had been feeling fine—asymptomatic—the news of possible heart problems fueled days of anxiety. But after reading the Scripture focus above as well as other promises from God's Word, peace again settled over my heart, mind, and soul . . . filtering calm into my body as well.

We often can't escape the consequences of our actions, but we can always know that God loves us and even sings over us. During the reign of the good King Josiah, Zephaniah served as a prophet. When Josiah read the long-lost Book of the Law, there was a revival in Judah.

When hearts turn toward God, he rejoices over us. Consequences for our earlier sins may continue to play out, but even so, we have the companionship of a God who sings over us and quiets our hearts with his love.

Lord, you are indeed mighty to save me from myself and the mire I throw myself into with sin and misjudgments. But you are always with me and will not only save me but also rejoice gladly over me and quiet me with your love.

Keep Looking Up!

We can thank God for his companionship as we face struggles we have caused.

SEPTEMBER 27

We Are the Lord's People

Read Haggai 1–2

> On that day, declares the Lord of hosts, I will take you, O Zerubbabel my servant, the son of Shealtiel, declares the Lord, and make you like a signet ring, for I have chosen you, declares the Lord of hosts. —Haggai 2:23

I HAD BEEN prayerwalking for my community for many years when I began to understand that what I was doing was ministry. A sense of responsibility developed in me—that I *must* walk so that prayer was lifted up for the people in the homes, businesses, city and county offices, and schools I passed.

God may call one person to pray and another to serve the poor. In any case we get to do his work on earth. In Haggai's time a king would allow one or more selected servants to sign his name with a signet ring. That kind of ring had the king's unique symbol on it and was pressed into hot wax that served as a seal for a letter or other document. When we confess our sins and profess our faith, we are God's signet ring. We are his chosen ones, his people. And then we can turn and press God's presence into the world around us.

Lord, thank you for the privilege of serving you in my community. I pray I represent you well and am worthy of being your stamp on the world. As others observe me, I pray they see a glimpse of your goodness.

Keep Looking Up!

Representing Jesus can start with a simple question: "How can I serve today, God?"

SEPTEMBER 28

We Can U-turn Back to God

Read Zechariah 1–5

Therefore say to them, Thus declares the LORD of hosts: Return to me, says the LORD of hosts, and I will return to you, says the LORD of hosts. —Zechariah 1:3

AFTER CHURCH I walked up the aisle a bit to a friend and tapped her on the shoulder.

She jumped. "I didn't see you here!"

No wonder . . . she was facing the opposite direction.

That scene is what I picture when I read this Zechariah passage when the Lord says he will return to us if we return to him. The people had been running from God for a long time and wondering why things were going badly . . . when all they had to do was turn back to God.

I am often faced in the wrong direction too. I fret over my to-do list, the problems hanging over my head, and the prayer needs of those I love. In other words, I'm running in ten different directions mentally instead of into God's arms, waiting right behind me. All I need to do is turn around to him.

Lord, your Word says you will return to me when I return to you. I am sorry I don't maintain a reverential awareness of your presence in my life. I always want to face in your direction.

Keep Looking Up!

Confession helps us turn to see God.

SEPTEMBER 29

God Rains His Blessings

Read Zechariah 6–10

Ask rain from the LORD in the season of the spring rain, from the LORD who makes the storm clouds, and he will give them showers of rain, to everyone the vegetation in the field. —Zechariah 10:1

I CRIED FOR days after I lost both my wedding and engagement rings. Because a prong had weakened, I had taken them off and put them in my handbag. But after a short road trip to visit our son and his family, they were gone.

We didn't have the money for new rings, but my husband reminded me that years before he had found three rings in the street after we had come out of a movie theater. I had turned them in to the police department, but no one claimed them. Sure enough, the engagement ring fit, and Craig had his wedding ring sized down for me. I still pray my rings have blessed some young-in-love-but-broke couple.

When drought seasons—financial or otherwise—strike us, we can ask our Lord to pour down the sweet rain of his assuring presence . . . which he will.

Lord, I know you are aware of the need I have, and so I can trust you to bring about a refreshing season of favorable rain that will help my family and me right now. May our lives grow in faith as we see you provide.

Keep Looking Up!

God provides a way through our struggles because he is the Way.

SEPTEMBER 30

The Lord Is Our God

Read Zechariah 11–14

> They will call upon my name, and I will answer them. I will say, "They are my people"; and they will say, "The LORD is my God."
>
> —Zechariah 13:9

MY HUSBAND AND I were high school sweethearts. Our first date was the junior prom, and we steadily saw each other from our senior year through college. That's a lot of history together, and we share remembrances, jokes, and knowledge of each other's strengths and weaknesses. You could say we are each other's person.

The Lord also calls us his own and wants us to call him our God. Through the prophet Zechariah the Lord spoke to a faithful remnant who would rebuild the temple after the Hebrews' return from exile. But the book of Zechariah is also a sweet vision of Jesus's future kingdom on earth.

Keeping in mind that God cares about us and holds our hand in all challenges we face is great cause for continually looking up. We are his people, and he is our God.

Lord, here I am calling upon your name. You are my God and the Lord of my life. Hear my prayers, Father, because I will only turn to you.

Keep Looking Up!

Those who profess and follow Jesus are God's people.

OCTOBER 1

Giving Blesses God and Us

Read Malachi 1–4

Bring the full tithe into the storehouse, that there may be food in my house. And thereby put me to the test, says the LORD of hosts, if I will not open the windows of heaven for you and pour down for you a blessing until there is no more need. —Malachi 3:10

WITH BILLS MOUNTING up, we weren't sure the checking account would have enough to pay everything. And as we added things up, our financial resources and our costs didn't balance. Nonetheless, we wrote our monthly check to church because we knew that God would provide. Somehow. A week later we got a reimbursement check for exactly the amount we had given our church.

Giving financially to a church is important. The traditional tithe referred to in Malachi was a tenth of the people's earnings for produce and other products. This helped support the needs of the temple and those called by God to the priesthood.

Today's churches and Christian nonprofit groups still depend on people's generous giving. They don't particularly enjoy soliciting funds, so when we regularly give out of our love and respect for the ministry and for God, it blesses them. And we are blessed in return.

Lord, thank you for caring for my family and me. I am grateful for how you pour into our storehouse when we give to yours. I trust you for all the blessings in my life.

Keep Looking Up!

Giving out of gratefulness is the best place to start.

OCTOBER 2

God Sends His Son

Read Matthew 1–4

> All this took place to fulfill what the Lord had spoken by the prophet: "Behold, the virgin shall conceive and bear a son, and they shall call his name Immanuel" (which means, God with us).
>
> —Matthew 1:22–23

WAITING IS HARD, isn't it? We wait for traffic lights, doctor's appointments, a tax refund, a diagnosis. We wait for a marriage to improve, a prodigal's return, a job offer. I've never done waiting very well.

But God's people waited four hundred years after he spoke through the last prophets. His answer came loud and strong: Jesus. God sent his only Son, conceived through Mary, to fulfill roughly three hundred (or more, depending on who's counting) messianic prophecies. Jesus would be called *Immanuel*, which means "God with us."

The people struggled to know God through the stories of the patriarchs, through the leadership of judges and kings, and through the prophets. So God came to earth to walk among us, serve us, teach us, die for our sins, and then rise from the dead so that we might have new life. Jesus was a gift worth waiting for . . . and he still waits for us today.

Father God, you fulfilled all your promises by sending your Son, Jesus, to us. Thank you for this love gift that now binds my heart to yours eternally as a member of your family.

Keep Looking Up!

Daily we can take notice of God with us.

OCTOBER 3

Jesus Teaches on Prayer

Read Matthew 5–6

This, then, is how you should pray: "Our Father in heaven, hallowed be your name." —Matthew 6:9 NIV

I WASN'T RAISED knowing how to pray, other than by repeating memorized prayers. So when I began studying prayer in the Bible, I realized Jesus was a master teacher on the subject of prayer. In fact, his teachings on prayer are a significant portion of his teachings.

While we can certainly repeat the Lord's Prayer in our daily practices, it also serves as a model prayer for us. We can begin with praise. Then we can ask the Lord's will be done in our situation of concern. Jesus next teaches that it's perfectly fine to ask for our daily needs—but also to pray regularly for forgiveness and to extend forgiveness to others. Lastly, we can ask for protection from the enemy of our souls.

Jesus taught about prayer, provided prayers to us, and modeled practices of taking time to pray. His prayer life shows us prayer, in fact, works.

Our Father, who art in heaven, holy is your name. Your kingdom come; your will be done on earth and in heaven. Give me your daily bread, and forgive my sins as I forgive others. Help me overcome temptation with Jesus's help.

Keep Looking Up!

Time taken for prayer is never time wasted.

OCTOBER 4

We Pray to a Big God

Read Matthew 7–9

Ask and it will be given to you; seek and you will find; knock and the door will be opened to you. —Matthew 7:7 NIV

COLLEGE TUITION WAS a big ask. With four kids lined up, we would have seventeen straight years of at least one person in college . . . without savings set aside. That may seem irresponsible to some, but when your family qualified for free school lunches, the need was real.

When our oldest was a senior in high school, a group of parents and their senior students met several times for prayer together. We prayed for their plans, for our hopes and dreams as parents, and for God to provide. By the end of the school year, the needed financial aid was in place. We still look back at that season as a miracle in the making.

In the Sermon on the Mount, Jesus taught us to pray big. I call this beyond-your-reach prayer. We can pray beyond our imagination, beyond our abilities, and beyond our resources because we have a big God.

Lord, you are good and give good gifts to your children. I have a big need right now, so with this prayer I am asking, seeking, and knocking for you to answer in a big way.

Keep Looking Up!

Prayer should be the first response to a need, not a last resort.

OCTOBER 5

Jesus Carries Our Burdens

Read Matthew 10–11

Come to me, all who labor and are heavy laden, and I will give you rest. —Matthew 11:28

I NEVER PLANNED anything but sleep for the two weeks after school got out. Since I was an English teacher with stacks of papers to grade and organized all the year-end senior events, I was wiped out. I compare those days to those after my several surgeries. Both took so much out of me.

Life can exhaust us, can't it? But we have a Savior who understands what it's like to walk this earth. After travels and teachings and healings, Jesus must have been exhausted. What did he do? He prayed. Then he invited all who were weary and burdened to come to him to find rest.

When we have overwhelming burdens that drain us, we need a season of recuperation. Thankfully, we can dump our concerns on Jesus by releasing them through prayer, trust him for the results, and allow the sweetness of rest to fill us with joy again.

Lord, I am exhausted and weighed down with so many needs—my own and those of others. But I give them now to you, knowing that you will carry the burdens and me through this season of life.

Keep Looking Up!

We can symbolically surrender our prayers to God by writing them down.

OCTOBER 6

Jesus Is Lord of the Harvest

Read Matthew 12–13

Other seeds fell on good soil and produced grain, some a hundredfold, some sixty, some thirty. —Matthew 13:8

I ONCE ASKED a high school valedictorian how she found academic success.

"It wasn't all that hard. I just listen." She went on to explain that she had a desire to learn and to succeed, so she listened to her teachers for the purpose of understanding. Clearly also gifted with a good brain and work ethic, that young woman went on to become a veterinarian.

In his parable of the sower, Jesus explains a principle of teaching others about his being the promised Messiah. Some won't listen. Some don't follow through. Some allow the world to choke out faith. But some embrace Jesus as Savior and Lord and pursue a life that produces fruit such as peace and joy.

We also can be sowers of the faith simply by sharing our faith story and the gospel message with others. Then we can pray expectantly for God to bring about an abundant harvest of souls.

Lord, may I be a sower. I want to share freely my story of redemption in such a way that others hear, understand, and allow that seed of faith to grow.

Keep Looking Up!

Sharing our faith is simply telling our story.

OCTOBER 7

Jesus Prioritized Prayer

Read Matthew 14–17

And after he had dismissed the crowds, he went up on the mountain by himself to pray. —Matthew 14:23

AFTER I RECEIVED news of my friend's death, I just wanted to be alone and pray. But company arrived, and the next days were filled to the brim with gatherings and such. As dear as those folks were to me, solitude with God was what I needed.

So I resonate with the series of incidents after Jesus learned Herod beheaded John the Baptist—Jesus's relative. Jesus tried to get away by boat to a place he could be alone, but thousands sought him out. Nonetheless he healed the sick and fed them through yet another miracle. Finally, he was able to find quiet up on a mountainside, where he prayed.

Jesus modeled for us the importance of seeking solitude for prayer. Despite the busyness around him, he prioritized time alone with his heavenly Father. Those quiet times of prayer will prove to be greater sources of joy than anything the world might hand us.

Father, in the same way your Son, Jesus, found times and places of solitude to be with you, I know that despite the demands in my life, I also can prioritize prayer that's more than an on-the-go experience. Help me not slack on this, Father.

Keep Looking Up!

Blocking out daily time for prayer is how it gets done.

OCTOBER 8

God Does the Impossible

Read Matthew 18–20

But Jesus looked at them and said, "With man this is impossible, but with God all things are possible." —Matthew 19:26

MY SON WAS praying for a miracle. Recuperating from extensive knee surgery in February, he desperately wanted to play on the golf team less than two months later. So I joined him in that prayer for a miracle, and sure enough, he was able to walk those five-mile-long courses in April.

We read several times in the New Testament of God doing the impossible: the conception of Jesus through Mary, the miraculous healing of a boy, and this story about God's salvation for man. The rich, young ruler walked away from Jesus discouraged because he knew he could not give up his life's riches to follow Jesus. But we know we have every chance in the world for eternal life because we serve a God who can do the impossible.

The truth is we need not put our trust in the miracle but in God, who is able.

Lord, I need a mountain-moving miracle. You know the person and you know the situation. I have seen you do the miraculous, God, so I put my faith in you alone for this heart-changing request.

Keep Looking Up!

Prayer is a step of faith that God can do anything.

OCTOBER 9

We Sing Hosanna to God

Read Matthew 21–22

And the crowds that went before him and that followed him were shouting, "Hosanna to the Son of David! Blessed is he who comes in the name of the Lord! Hosanna in the highest!" —Matthew 21:9

"HELP!" MY DAUGHTER cried when the tractor accidentally ran over her hip and leg.

Her son ran to get my husband, who called 911, with rescuers responding in minutes. An hour later in the emergency room, doctors said it was a miracle she was alive, much more that none of her bones were broken. A couple weeks later she was on the ranch again.

We've all known cries for help—literally and otherwise. Perhaps we've fallen or gotten into an accident . . . or just need a hand to help us. It's interesting that the word *hosanna* actually means "save, we pray." When Jesus entered Jerusalem on the donkey colt, the people were shouting prayers for their salvation—inspired by the same words in Psalm 118:25, "LORD, save us" (NIV).

Today we might consider *hosanna* a dual prayer—both praise to the Lord who hears and saves us and a petition for his help.

Lord, hear my hosanna! I give you honor and glory and praise for the great God you are to hear me. And I ask for your help—in crises and also just in the dailiness of life's challenges. You are my all in all!

Keep Looking Up!

Every day we can sing our hosannas to the Lord Most High.

OCTOBER 10

We Can Get Ready for Jesus

Read Matthew 23–24

Therefore, stay awake, for you do not know on what day your Lord is coming. —Matthew 24:42

MIKE WALKED INTO my classroom with paperwork in his hand.

"So sorry," I said, "the deadline for that scholarship was yesterday."

"But, I thought it was today. I guess I lost track." And he left, shaking his head.

It's easy to put things off. We get distracted and lose sense of deadlines or personal goals we have. Often it seems as though an event is in the far distance . . . and then suddenly we realize we've let an opportunity slip by.

Such could be true of the Lord's second coming to earth. Jesus teaches at the end of Matthew 24 that no one knows when his return will occur, so it's simply best to be ready.

But how? Perhaps we simply pursue Christlikeness each and every day and hold on to an attitude of expectancy: that Jesus will come again.

Father God, only you know the hour and place where your Son, Jesus, will return to earth. May I be awake and alert to your personal promptings in my life and take advantage of opportunities to serve you and share my faith with others.

Keep Looking Up!

Reading the Bible each day helps us prepare for Christ's second coming.

OCTOBER 11

We Can Pray God's Will

Read Matthew 25–26

And going a little farther he fell on his face and prayed, saying, "My Father, if it be possible, let this cup pass from me; nevertheless, not as I will, but as you will." —Matthew 26:39

TWENTY-SOME YEARS AGO I couldn't decide if I should go to a conference, so in a moment of silliness, I thought about flipping a coin. And then I stared at it in my hand. Heads, I'd go. Tails, I wouldn't. I really didn't know what was right.

Then I realized I could pray a two-sided coin prayer: God, I really want to go to this conference, but if you don't think that's the best choice right now, I'll trust you and stay home.

That was the kind of prayer Jesus prayed in the Gethsemane garden: his best human prayer for his life versus God's will. Our Father understands such a prayer—that we have human heart's desires and desires for God's purposes. Sometimes the two happily intersect but sometimes those two-sided coin prayers are polar opposites.

No matter the outcome, praying to be aligned to God's will puts us joyfully in alignment with his plan.

Lord, you know the desire of my heart, but you also know I want my life to be in sync with your plan for me. So I pray, not my will but yours be done because I know the end result will bring glory to you . . . and that's all I need.

Keep Looking Up!

Praying "thy will be done" trains our heart to look for God's plan.

OCTOBER 12

Jesus Is with Us Always

Read Matthew 27–28

And behold, I am with you always, to the end of the age.
—Matthew 28:20

I FELT REALLY alone in the basement of that large hospital, awaiting my back surgery. The nurses had scooted my husband off to the waiting room, and I lay there, shivering.

But in stepped Pastor Ron with his characteristic grin and "I found you!" He had driven an hour from our town and somehow had located me in the hospital bowels at six in the morning—just to pray for me.

After Jesus was resurrected from the dead, he stayed with the disciples for forty days, teaching them and exhorting them to make disciples of all nations. Such a charge would have been daunting, certainly, but Jesus promised that he would be with the disciples always.

Just as Jesus was with his disciples as they spread the gospel far and wide, he is with us wherever we are today.

Lord, you do not leave me alone and shivering with worry. You promise you will never leave or forsake me. Buoy me with your courage as I step out of my comfort zone to live my life fully for you and the sake of your kingdom.

Keep Looking Up!

No matter our circumstances, we can know Jesus is always with us.

OCTOBER 13

The Father Affirmed Jesus

Read Mark 1–3

And a voice came from heaven, "You are my beloved Son; with you I am well pleased." —Mark 1:11

ALTHOUGH I WAS just doing a question-and-answer session with a writers' group, the emcee gave me a long and much-too-kind introduction. But it did give the audience a sense of the kinds of works I had written, so they would know who I was.

What must be the best ever introduction came from God himself. His Son, Jesus, had arisen out of baptism waters when several things happened. First the heavens were torn open, and the Holy Spirit descended on Jesus like a dove. Then those watching heard the following: "You are my beloved Son; with you I am well pleased." Jesus's heavenly Father made it clear that this was no ordinary baptism—the man rising out of the Jordan River was God's Son.

Some might wonder if God still speaks today. One thing we can know: we can always find his words in the Bible.

Lord, I sense your presence and leading in my life. Thank you for how you communicate to me through your Word. I am ready to be a witness for you with whatever you have for me.

Keep Looking Up!

Many find journaling about God's Word helpful to discern his voice.

Jesus Healed Women

Read Mark 4–5

And he said to her, "Daughter, your faith has made you well; go in peace, and be healed of your disease." —Mark 5:34

AT THE ARCHAEOLOGICAL site of Magdala in Israel—town of Mary Magdalene—you find the Women's Atrium in a modern building dedicated to Jesus's life and Christian worship. One of the large murals in the atrium depicts the scene of the bleeding woman who was healed by touching Jesus's garment. It is a moving work of art that acknowledges the dignity of women who suffer physically simply because they are women.

Jesus went out of his way to heal women and children—those who did not have status in that culture. He invited women to his teachings and included them in his parables. He protected and defended them. The bleeding woman was healed the moment she touched Jesus's garment. He didn't need to pause from his mission to heal the ruler's daughter. But Jesus stopped, called the bleeding woman "daughter," and spoke peace over her.

Jesus heals us with life and dignity.

Lord, your words breathe life into me. You challenged cultural practices to extend honor to women and others often ignored or discriminated against. May your kingdom come here to earth as we live out the kind of love you demonstrated.

Keep Looking Up!

Jesus's healing gift of salvation is for everyone.

OCTOBER 15

Jesus Gave to Others

Read Mark 6–7

> When he went ashore he saw a great crowd, and he had compassion on them, because they were like sheep without a shepherd.
>
> —Mark 6:34

EVERY MONDAY AFTER my weigh-in and health meeting, I stopped at Taco Bell for a quick on-the-road bite for my hour's drive home. There was always a man sitting outside next to a shopping cart filled with what I guessed were all his earthly possessions. I shook my head as I zipped through the drive-through. *Poor guy.* Then one evening I realized my feelings amounted to nothing and ordered several burritos for him—something I did thereafter every time I saw Joe.

Jesus always acted on his feelings of compassion. After learning his kin, John, had been beheaded, Jesus wanted to get away, but he saw the people and their hurts and stopped to teach and heal the needy masses. And when the sun began to set, he multiplied five loaves and two fish into a miraculous dinner for thousands.

Some will say not to give anything to the homeless on street corners, but responding to the nudges in my heart gives me joy.

Lord, may I see other people and their needs through your eyes. Fill me with your compassion and love and give me clarity about when and how to give.

Keep Looking Up!

Giving granola bars to the homeless is one way to help them.

OCTOBER 16

Jesus's Touch Changes Us

Read Mark 8–9

> Once more Jesus put his hands on the man's eyes. Then his eyes were opened, his sight was restored, and he saw everything clearly.
>
> —Mark 8:25 NIV

AFTER MY BACK surgery, healing came gradually. I had to recuperate from the operation, but I also had to wean myself off the painkillers I had been on for months. I quit in two days' time and was surprised that when I was completely off any medication, the pain was gone.

Healing may not be an overnight miracle. It may take time. When Jesus healed the blind man at Bethsaida, it took two touches from Jesus to heal the man's sight.

We may find God heals us in stages. We may need medication or a surgery, but then we may need a long recuperation time with physical therapy. Even when we have physical healing, we may still need an emotional healing that helps us shift into a healthy and confident mindset about our abilities. One thing is for sure: a touch from Jesus changes us!

Lord, I need your touch. I am hurting and need a change in my life. Help me heal. Help me grow. And help me clearly see the life you have for me.

Keep Looking Up!

Our life changes when Jesus touches us with healing.

OCTOBER 17

Jesus Welcomed the Children

Read Mark 10–11

When Jesus saw this, he was indignant. He said to them, "Let the children come to me, and do not hinder them, for the kingdom of God belongs to such as these." —Mark 10:14 NIV

MY BROTHER-IN-LAW GARY loved children. When he arrived at a family event, he'd head right for wherever the kids were and play whatever game they were playing or engage them in something else fun. He called my youngest Wilson—after the volleyball manufacturer and the Tom Hanks movie *Cast Away*—for a reason we never understood. He soaked up the joy of children and left them with wonderful memories of Uncle Gary.

Jesus loved children too and beckoned them to himself when the disciples tried to shoo them and their parents away. Perhaps Jesus blessed them or answered their questions or even taught them a bit. In any case, his welcoming them in a crowd of adults demonstrates to us that Jesus valued everyone and understood that the kingdom of God was not just for adults but also for children.

And just as Jesus welcomed children, we should too.

Lord, may I also be the kind of person who notices children, gives them a big smile, engages them in conversation, and values their presence. And may I learn something about simple faith through them.

Keep Looking Up!

Smiling at and talking to children in public helps them feel a part of our world.

OCTOBER 18

Jesus Sums Up the Law

Read Mark 12–13

> Love the Lord your God with all your heart and with all your soul and with all your mind and with all your strength. —Mark 12:30 NIV

I WAS JUST an English teacher filling in for a quarter for the on-leave Science 8 teacher. And those eighth graders challenged me from day one. Right away a boy asked if I knew what DNA was.

A beat later I said, "Deoxyribonucleic acid." So that took care of that.

Teachers are always challenged, and religious leaders continually confronted Jesus with seemingly unanswerable questions. In today's reading a leader asked Jesus what the most important commandment was, probably knowing there were hundreds of statutes in the law in addition to the Ten Commandments. But Jesus summed up the Ten Commandments as well as all those hundreds of laws with two: love God and love people.

If we love God with all our heart, soul, mind, and strength, we will interact with others with love. And God's Word teaches us how to love God and love people.

Lord, I simply want to love you with all of my heart, all of my soul, all of my mind, and all of my strength. And may that kind of love overflow toward others, so they are drawn to you.

Keep Looking Up!

Love is expressed in words and in actions.

OCTOBER 19

Jesus Praised a Woman

Read Mark 14

And truly, I say to you, wherever the gospel is proclaimed in the whole world, what she has done will be told in memory of her.

—Mark 14:9

I HAD A fun series of emails that afternoon at school. A former student wrote, saying she was bored in her college English class because the teacher was explaining how to write a cited research paper . . . and she already knew how because of me. We joked back and forth online for a few minutes, then I had to get back to teaching my current students about citations and such.

It's fun being remembered. Jesus said Mary would be remembered wherever the gospel was preached throughout the world because she had poured costly perfume on him. While some of the disciples are now known for bickering with one another and others for turning away from Jesus, Mary is remembered for her devotion.

When we serve others on Jesus's behalf, those others will remember us for faithfully following him.

Lord, I give you my time, talents, and treasure in adoration of you. May my testimony be a beautiful thing in your eyes—that others see me as your loving follower.

Keep Looking Up!

Many consider time the greatest gift someone could give them.

OCTOBER 20

Jesus Lifts Our Burdens

Read Mark 15–16

> Very early on the first day of the week, just after sunrise, they were on their way to the tomb and they asked each other, "Who will roll the stone away from the entrance of the tomb?" —Mark 16:2–3 NIV

WHO DOES THE heavy lifting in your family? I am blessed that my rancher hubby not only lifts literal tons of hay every day to feed his cattle but also does the heavy lifting around the house, like carrying boxes and shoveling snow.

When Mary Magdalene, Mary the mother of James, and Salome went to the tomb where Jesus's body lay, they naturally had a question. Who would roll the large stone away from the tomb so they could anoint Jesus's body? Those stones were either circular or plug-shaped and weighed thousands of pounds. The women did not have the physical strength to move one.

But the tomb was open when they got there. And they found that Jesus had risen from the dead!

Today Jesus is still a heavy lifter for us. He pushes our burdens out of the way or carries them for us. He turns burdens to joy.

Lord, you do not ask me to do what is humanly impossible. But you are always there when I face the immovable. I trust you, Lord, to roll away the stones and to continue to manifest your greatness to me.

Keep Looking Up!

When heavy burdens weigh us down, we can pray for the Lord to remove them.

OCTOBER 21

We Can Give Our Life to God

Read Luke 1–2

And Mary said, Yes, I see it all now: I'm the Lord's maid, ready to serve. Let it be with me just as you say. Then the angel left her.

—Luke 1:38 MSG

I HAVE A friend who, with her husband, has ten kids—three of their own and seven adopted. What they've done in raising—including homeschooling—those children is one of the greatest gifts to the world I can imagine. They could have easily slid into years of living with an empty nest but instead filled it to overflowing.

That generosity of spirit is how I picture Mary, Jesus's mother. She was greatly troubled when the angel announced God had chosen to bring his Son into the world through her. But then she acceded, "Let it be with me just as you say." As her Son would later do, she laid down her life, which otherwise might have been a lovely, quiet one. Instead, she watched Jesus step into ministry and then onto the cross.

Submitting ourselves to God may not bring a life of comfort, but following God's calling will bring great fulfillment.

Lord, may it be to me as you have planned. I open up my hands to whatever you give me, and I know that may be hard, but not stepping into your promises for me would leave me with regrets. I trust you.

Keep Looking Up!

We can trust God for the calling he has on our lives.

OCTOBER 22

Jesus Models How to Say No

Read Luke 3–4

Jesus answered, "It is said: 'Do not put the Lord your God to the test.'" —Luke 4:12 NIV

I HAD JUST started a healthy eating program to lose some weight when I walked into the teachers' room and found a giant bakery box filled with doughnuts. The treat was a thoughtful gesture from my boss, but I knew that just one bite would start my day on a downward spiral.

We all have temptations in our lives. I don't need to list them—you probably have a couple that immediately come to mind. My weakness is anything sweet, so I have to remind myself often how Jesus used Scripture to rebuke Satan's several attempts to lure him into his control. The temptation does not need to be literal bread for me to say, "I do not live by bread alone."

The story of Jesus's temptations reminds us we have the power of the Spirit to say no to anything that might pull us away from a life that follows his example.

Lord, your Word is a powerful weapon to speak truth in the face of temptation. May I be faithful to memorize it so that it's ready to use when the enemy tries to steal my joy.

Keep Looking Up!

Memorizing strategic Bible passages makes God's truth available when we need it.

OCTOBER 23

Jesus Teaches on Mercy

Read Luke 5–6

Judge not, and you will not be judged; condemn not, and you will not be condemned; forgive, and you will be forgiven. —Luke 6:37

I WANTED TO eat my words the moment after they'd escaped.

My friend sighed heavily. "Janet, if I had wanted your advice, I would have asked for it. I just wanted a little prayer support."

She was right. What I had said sounded judgmental, unkind, and insensitive, and I apologized to her.

Instead of going into problem-solving mode as soon as someone expresses a problem or even a prayer need, I need to remember to weigh my words. While we can have difficult face-to-face encounters, today's technology multiplies opportunities for offense to be doled out and received. So it's always timely to remember Jesus's teachings about judgmental attitudes and behavior and offer mercy and grace instead—forgiving when someone offends us. And also asking for forgiveness when we have been unkind.

It takes a couple seconds to hurt someone but as long as a lifetime to make amends.

Lord, thank you for modeling mercy and forgiveness. People are not perfect, and that certainly includes me. Help me be less judgmental—changing my critical eye to one of loving-kindness.

Keep Looking Up!

Asking forgiveness can start with simple words: "I was wrong when I . . ."

OCTOBER 24

Jesus Quieted the Storm

Read Luke 7–8

And they went and woke him, saying, "Master, Master, we are perishing!" And he awoke and rebuked the wind and the raging waves, and they ceased, and there was a calm. —Luke 8:24

THE STORM OVER Alaska's Inland Passage was significant enough to rock our cruise ship noticeably. But we had chosen a room in the middle of the ship, so we didn't experience as much rolling as others around the perimeters did.

Just as the center of the boat was stable, we want to be centered in our faith for the figurative storms of life. And centering comes from studying and meditating on God's Word. Even though his disciples had already seen Jesus perform many miracles, they panicked in the storm on the Sea of Galilee. The fishermen among them took seriously storms that arose quickly. Jesus asked them, "Where is your faith?" (v. 25). Worry dissipates and faith grows as we are better centered in God's character and promises.

Jesus answered their prayers and quieted the howling wind and raging waters. And he will hear our prayers today too as we turn to him in faith.

Lord, you created our atmosphere and its weather. You bring tempests, and you bring calm. When life storms out of control, I ask that you center me securely with you, trusting you for whatever the outcome may be.

Keep Looking Up!

Repeating "Be still and know" (Psalm 46:10), can calm us when we are stressed.

OCTOBER 25

Jesus Beckons Us to Listen

Read Luke 9–10

> But the Lord answered her, "Martha, Martha, you are anxious and troubled about many things, but one thing is necessary. Mary has chosen the good portion, which will not be taken away from her."
> —Luke 10:41–42

I HAD PICKED up my kids' Hansel and Gretel trail of scattered stuff, cleaned the house, prepared the dinner, and was lighting the candles when the first batch of company knocked on the door. *Rats!* I glanced at my watch. They were ten minutes early. Then I remembered why I was putting together such a fuss—*for them*—and opened the door with a smile.

I love hospitality, but sometimes I skew its focus when I get bogged down in the details. The best part of inviting people in is sitting down, soaking up conversation, and getting caught up with each other's lives. Jesus taught Martha the value of listening to his teachings. But he also taught us that in order to learn, we need to quiet our hearts and listen to him.

As we get overwhelmed with life's screaming details, we can hit life's pause button, drop to our knees, and soak up what Jesus will teach us. He knocks at our door and loves sitting down with a listening ear.

Lord, my calendar is screaming at me, and I feel overwhelmed with an endless list just for today. I need your assurance and wisdom, so I will quiet my wild heart and hands to read your Word and pray.

Keep Looking Up!

Quiet time seeking God is the best-spent time of the day.

OCTOBER 26

God Doesn't Overlook Us

Read Luke 11–12

What's the price of two or three pet canaries? Some loose change, right? But God never overlooks a single one. And he pays even greater attention to you, down to the last detail—even numbering the hairs on your head! So don't be intimidated by all this bully talk. You're worth more than a million canaries. —Luke 12:6–7 MSG

WE HAVE AT least two terrible blots on our parenting record. My husband and I formerly worked together in his business a half hour away. We always had our children with us, and they busied themselves playing in an extra room or outside. One time each of us thought we had our older daughter with us, and both drove home separately. A neighbor there watched her carefully until we realized our mistake. You'd think we'd learned but history repeated itself with our younger daughter years later. Our girls still tease us about this.

Though we are forgetful creatures, God never forgets us. In today's teaching Jesus says not only are we not overlooked—he pays great attention to every last detail of our lives.

When today's culture would overlook us, we can remember God keeps us in the forefront of his mind and the center of his heart.

Lord, if I feel forgotten, I will remember that you number me among your own and that I have great value in your sight. You love me, so I need have no fear or doubts about my worth.

Keep Looking Up!

God not only loves us, he values us!

OCTOBER 27

God Welcomes Us Home

Read Luke 13–15

But while he was still a long way off, his father saw him and was filled with compassion for him; he ran to his son, threw his arms around him and kissed him. —Luke 15:20 NIV

I TAUGHT A lot of prodigals—troubled teens often shuffled from one parent to another to a grandparent or other relative. Some of them ended up sleeping on a friend's couch, and we housed one for a while. We all make stupid decisions at some point, but knowing loving arms are waiting for us helps us find home again.

There is much to learn from the story of the prodigal son. We could dwell on the younger son and his impulsive, careless decisions or we could focus on the older son and his jealousies. The most important character, though, is the father. He was waiting for his son to return. He lovingly welcomed the prodigal son home. And then he celebrated the young man's return.

This speaks clearly of our heavenly Father's merciful character. Even when we mess up, he welcomes our repentant return and pours love into us.

Lord, I could list a litany of my mistakes today. But here I am saying I need you and your embrace of acceptance and love. Thank you for your compassion that overlooks what I have been and understands what I could be.

Keep Looking Up!

Reaching out to prodigals makes it easier for them to return home.

OCTOBER 28

God Rewards Persistence

Read Luke 16–18

And he told them a parable to the effect that they ought always to pray and not lose heart. —Luke 18:1

MY HUSBAND MANAGED a business years ago and helped facilitate new hires. One fellow who applied for a mechanic's job kept showing up day after day . . . until he was finally hired. I told that story year after year when my students were doing mock job interviews.

Persistence in prayer pays off too. In another parable Jesus tells how a widow persists in asking an unjust judge to decide in her favor. Finally, he consents. And Jesus teaches that we have an even better situation in prayer because we pray to a good judge: our God.

Some wonder why we have to even ask God more than once to fulfill our needs. It's not that God doesn't care or doesn't want to answer us. Our going to God consistently in prayer changes us and teaches us to rely on God for everything.

Father, you are a good Judge. You make decisions that further your kingdom—in me and in the world as a whole. There is no better place to advocate for my loved ones or even me than with you. Thank you that you hear my prayers, Lord.

Keep Looking Up!

Photos placed in our homes can remind us to pray persistently.

OCTOBER 29

God Provides Resources through Us

Read Luke 19–20

And they said, "The Lord has need of it." —Luke 19:34

WE HAD AN old Buick we bought from my parents. Mom called it Beulah, and it served us well until we got a more practical car for mountain travel. After our youngest used Beulah in college, we donated the car to our church's CARS ministry that helped single moms and widows with car repairs. Beulah found a new home with a grateful single mom.

Sometimes the Lord may have a greater use for the things we own. When Jesus was about to make his entry into Jerusalem the week he would go to the cross, he directed his disciples to seek out a donkey colt for that triumphal walk. The disciples told the owners of the colt, "The Lord has need of it."

We could meet others' needs simply by giving away clothing or housewares or furniture . . . or even a car named Beulah.

Lord, help me learn to live simply and give generously. After all, you gave up your Son, and he gave up his life. As I learn of others' needs, may I consider how I might have the resources to help.

Keep Looking Up!

Sharing with others brings double joy.

OCTOBER 30

We Can Give God Our All

Read Luke 21–22

> Jesus looked up and saw the rich putting their gifts into the offering box, and he saw a poor widow put in two small copper coins.
>
> —Luke 21:1–2

GROWING UP, WE five kids wore hand-me-down-and-over clothes—the "over" clothes from families with kids bigger than we were. We took a lunch to school because my folks couldn't afford hot lunch. But every week I saw Mom and Dad's faithfulness as they placed their church offering in that round, brass collection plate.

Jesus noticed giving too. One day he watched as the rich put their gifts into the offering box and then a poor widow put in her couple pennies. Jesus knew her gift was a sacrifice greater than that of others because she gave everything she had—which was what Jesus eventually gave too: everything he had . . . his whole life on the cross.

There's no rule for giving, but I've found that if God prompts me to give, the joy I receive helps me realize I've gained, not lost.

Lord, thank you for giving me the best offering ever: your Son, Jesus. I understand that everything I have comes from you, so may I hold loosely to what you've given me in case you want me to steward it for someone else.

Keep Looking Up!

We can give our best because Jesus did just that for us.

OCTOBER 31

God Wants Us to Forgive

Read Luke 23–24

And Jesus said, "Father, forgive them, for they know not what they do." —Luke 23:34

"SORRY!"

That kind of apology said on the fly never seemed genuine or effective, so I used to teach a formula for my children and students.

I was wrong when I ______________. Will you forgive me?

That demonstrates acknowledgment of the offense, a sense of regret, and an attempt to restore the relationship.

But we are also called to go deeper than that. In his first prayer from the cross, Jesus asked his Father to forgive those involved with his crucifixion. It can be assumed, then, that Jesus also forgave those who brought about his death.

Holding an offense against someone can only build anger, resentment, and bitterness in us. If someone *makes* us angry, we have allowed the power of that situation to alter us. Letting it go frees us to love that person and be a witness to the fact that faith works, because Christianity is the only faith that addresses forgiveness.

Lord, help me keep my relationships clean. When someone hurts me, prod me to forgive—even if the other person doesn't acknowledge the problem. And if I hurt someone, nudge me to own my mistake and apologize sincerely.

Keep Looking Up!

Even when they do know what they're doing, forgiveness is healing.

NOVEMBER 1

Jesus Is the Word

Read John 1–2

In the beginning was the Word, and the Word was with God, and the Word was God. —John 1:1 NIV

THE BIBLE IS active and effective in speaking truth into our lives. One reason I know this is when my husband was a college freshman, a new friend challenged him to read the Bible to decide for himself if Christianity made sense. Craig bought a Bible, then read from Genesis through Revelation . . . and believed Jesus was God, the Messiah, and his personal Savior.

In today's reading from John, we learn that Jesus was the written Word in the flesh. He was both fully God and fully man. While he came to earth through his mother, Mary, he never lost his divine nature; however, he also was able to experience all the senses and emotions that humans undergo. Creation came through him but he also underwent his physical, earthly creation.

We can fully trust in a Savior who understands what it is like to walk this earth and experience the kinds of pain we encounter.

Father God, it assures me to know that your Son, Jesus, experienced loss, betrayal, rejection, and physical death, so that when I cry out in prayer, I can know that the Living Word hears and understands my cries.

Keep Looking Up!

We understand God's love for us when we read through the whole Bible.

Jesus Spills Living Water

Read John 3–4

> Jesus said to her, "Everyone who drinks of this water will be thirsty again, but whoever drinks of the water that I will give him will never be thirsty again." —John 4:13–14

A FRIEND OF mine once had a long conversation about faith with an airplane seatmate. Then God nudged her to give him her Bible—a dear one she had marked up. She knew he would find the answers to his questions there. They exchanged business cards, and later she learned the man had given his life to Christ, sharing his testimony with others.

You never know how life-changing a conversation can be. The longest one recorded in the Bible between Jesus and another person was with a Samaritan woman when Jesus stopped to get a drink of water at a well. Jesus said he was living water—the Messiah—and that conversation was life-changing not only for the Samaritan woman but also for the people of her whole town, who also believed.

When our joy overflows like a river filling a tiny cup, it can bring life to those we know and even strangers on a plane.

Lord, your living water refreshes my soul. May I never forget that others are thirsting for your saving grace, so that I do not neglect to share with them that you are my Messiah and Lord.

Keep Looking Up!

The overflowing joy of salvation is part of our faith story.

NOVEMBER 3

Jesus Asks an Important Question

Read John 5–6

When Jesus saw him lying there and learned that he had been in this condition for a long time, he asked him, "Do you want to get well?" —John 5:6 NIV

LIFE HAD GOTTEN busy, and I had been neglecting my health for many months, allowing weight to slip back on. It wasn't a surprise then when results from blood tests didn't come out optimally. I didn't need medication, but I did need to eat healthier foods and get more exercise. It was time to get well.

One of the most profound questions of all time is the one Jesus asked to the invalid at the Bethesda pool. The man had been lying there for thirty-eight years, waiting for someone to put him into the healing waters. "Do you want to get well?" Jesus asked him. When the man said he did, Jesus told him to get up and walk, which he did . . . healed!

Jesus's question is still relevant for us today. Do we want to get well spiritually? Emotionally? Physically? Choosing faith and being obedient to God are our first steps toward wellness.

Lord, I do want to get well. Instead of lying in my own state of passivity, I will stop placing blame on anything but myself and take steps to help myself get stronger.

Keep Looking Up!

One step toward wellness is to answer Jesus's question with "Yes!"

NOVEMBER 4

Jesus Teaches about Mercy

Read John 7–8

> Jesus stood up and said to her, "Woman, where are they? Has no one condemned you?" She said, "No one, Lord." And Jesus said, "Neither do I condemn you; go, and from now on sin no more."
>
> —John 8:10–11

THE DECISION WAS easy. I knew the student had plagiarized his research paper because I'd found the original source online. Both he and his parents had signed an agreement that stated they understood plagiarized papers got zero points. So he should have gotten a zero. But I told him he could do the paper again, with a loss of points. "That's mercy," I said.

We learn a lot about mercy from Jesus's interactions with others. At the temple one day the religious leaders were ready to stone a woman for adultery. When they asked Jesus what he would do, he suggested anyone who was without sin could throw the first stone. The men walked away. And Jesus told the woman to walk away from sin.

Jesus did not come here to condemn us; he came to bring life. Just as Jesus extended compassion and mercy to others, we can too.

Lord, I confess I have been a stone thrower. I am quick to judge others—to see their mistakes rather than their potential. Help me to see others the way you do and show them your mercy.

Keep Looking Up!

Taking time to understand someone builds empathy in us.

NOVEMBER 5

Jesus Gives Abundant Life

Read John 9–10

I came that they may have life and have it abundantly. —John 10:10

I SHOOK MY head as I looked at the pile of bills. We were having a lean month financially. I found myself biting my fingernails when I strolled to the kitchen back door and watched my kids chasing each other in the backyard. An abundance of four kids—all different, all talented in some way, all blessings. Suddenly a smile replaced my frown, and I knew God, out of his abundance, would provide.

Abundant life was what Jesus promised. A thief steals and destroys, but Jesus came to give us abundant life. While we may think of abundance in terms of wealth and worldly success, Jesus brought something even better—the opportunity for us to have a personal relationship with the living God and life eternal. Our earthly perspective then changes, and we begin to notice the blessings God has given us.

And we see that earthly possessions will never match up to God's lavish love.

Lord, forgive me for not acknowledging the abundance of life you have given me. I could spend all day listing the blessings in my life, as well as the privilege of being called your child.

Keep Looking Up!

Abundant living starts with a looking up perspective.

NOVEMBER 6

Jesus Wept

Read John 11–12

Jesus wept. —John 11:35 NIV

MY MOTHER SAYS I can cry at the drop of a hat. I'm not sure I'd cry if my hat dropped, but I do cry spontaneously without a forethought. The other day I cried because a former student was sad. I cried over a silly rom-com movie this week. And I'll probably cry tonight at the last home basketball game, for which I'll keep score.

I take comfort in knowing that Jesus wept too. Even though he knew Lazarus was dead, and even though he knew he would raise his friend to life again, Jesus wept. He also wept over Jerusalem before entering the city for the last time (Luke 19:41).

God gave us a full gamut of emotions: joy and sadness, delight and fear, satisfaction and anger. Sometimes those emotions surprise us and even challenge us. The joy I find behind tears is that my Lord Jesus understands my tears . . . and me.

Lord Jesus, you understand the wide range of my emotions because you created me and experienced those emotions yourself here on earth. Comfort me in those times of sadness. Redirect my anger and fear to your peace that passes understanding.

Keep Looking Up!

While tears express our sadness, they may also spring from pure joy.

NOVEMBER 7

We Can Abide in Jesus

Read John 13–15

If you abide in me, and my words abide in you, ask whatever you wish, and it will be done for you. —John 15:7

MY HUSBAND DECIDED to leave the meandering path and head straight up the mountain instead. But after a frustrating hour, he was a bit lost. When he found the trail again, he reached his destination and then reconnected with the rest of the family shortly after that.

We may feel lost at times too. We stray from routines of Bible study and prayer. Then life creeps in and its concerns overwhelm us because we're not equipped to handle the detours. The key to feeling emotionally and spiritually steady is to abide in Christ—stay as glued to him as a branch on the vine. Apart from Jesus, our vine, we are fruitless.

When we stay close to him, our prayers are synced with God's heart. And we joyfully experience his love, grace, and purpose.

Lord, I want to remain in your love. Straying from you makes me feel incomplete, unloved, and powerless. I will stay connected to your Word, so that your joy flows from you to me.

Keep Looking Up!

The joy of Jesus comes from abiding in him.

We Team Up with Jesus in Prayer

Read John 16–17

> I do not ask for these only, but also for those who will believe in me through their word, that they may all be one, just as you, Father, are in me, and I in you, that they also may be in us, so that the world may believe that you have sent me. —John 17:20–21

DO YOU HAVE prayer partners—friends or family you can call or text with a quick prayer request and know they will pray for you? I have a bunch! It's reassuring to know others are advocating for me with the Father.

Even if you don't feel comfortable sharing prayer requests with others, you have a heavenly advocate. Jesus prayed not only for himself and for his disciples but also "for those who will believe"—in other words: you! When you chose to follow Jesus, you were included in his priestly prayer—the longest of his prayers recorded in the Bible.

Praying for those who will believe teams us up with Jesus, who still intercedes for us with the Father (Hebrews 7:25).

Jesus, you prayed for me! That just stuns and humbles me. May I live out your prayer as I love others on your behalf. May we all be one, as you and the Father are one, as we continue to advocate for those who will believe.

Keep Looking Up!

Prayer unifies us with each other and Jesus.

NOVEMBER 9

Jesus Provides for His Mother

Read John 18–19

When Jesus saw his mother there, and the disciple whom he loved standing nearby, he said to her, "Woman, here is your son," and to the disciple, "Here is your mother." From that time on, this disciple took her into his home. —John 19:26–27 NIV

WHEN MY MOM decided to move to a senior living apartment, I worried whether she would be able to stay in touch with her many circles of friends. But as it has turned out, she not only sees them on occasion, she also has made new friend circles right where she lives.

God has a way of helping us find family wherever we end up. Jesus modeled this when—from the cross—he arranged for his mother, Mary, to live from that point on with his disciple John. As a good son, Jesus made sure that his mother would have care after his death.

The Lord may ask us to care for others who aren't in our blood family. The Bible teaches us to look after widows and orphans (James 1:27). But joy grows when our family lines expand.

Lord, I am so glad I am a part of your family. Help me to be responsive to the needs I see around me, just as your Son, Jesus, and disciple John provided for Mary's care. May your kingdom love and family grow through me.

Keep Looking Up!

Welcoming others into our family is a loving act.

NOVEMBER 10

Jesus Provides a Big Catch

Read John 20–21

He said to them, "Cast the net on the right side of the boat, and you will find some." So they cast it, and now they were not able to haul it in, because of the quantity of fish. —John 21:6

I DIDN'T GET a student teaching spot in my kids' school district. No one wanted to take me on—even though I would have lightened their load. So I applied at a school a half hour away from home across our large mountain valley, was interviewed for the prospective volunteer position, and was invited to take the job.

Like the disciples, sometimes we need to throw the net on the other side of the boat. After Jesus's resurrection he observed the disciples fishing on the Sea of Galilee. When he asked them if they'd caught anything, they told him no. So Jesus said to put the net in the water on the other side of the boat, and they caught so many fish they weren't able to haul them all into the boat.

Jesus has plenty for us too—though we need to stay close to him, seek him for daily direction, and then alter our plans for his. He will show us a better way.

Lord, you have the best plans and always provide for me. I will stay open to you because I know you will help me use my time and resources wisely.

Keep Looking Up!

Jesus sees our problems and helps us find the best solutions.

NOVEMBER 11

The Spirit Is God within Us

Read Acts 1–3

> For the promise is for you and for your children and for all who are far off, everyone whom the Lord our God calls to himself.
> —Acts 2:39

I WILL NEVER forget our young son walking down the church aisle and telling the pastor he had asked Jesus into his heart. No one had prompted or pushed him. He was, in fact, the first of his peers to ask God to be the Lord of his life. Each of our four kids did the same, and we pray their children also will someday.

When we repent of our sin and profess Christ as Savior and Lord, God promises his Holy Spirit will then live in us. While Jesus came to earth as Emmanuel, God *with* Us, the Holy Spirit is God *within* those who put their faith in him. This promise will stand true for our children and our children's children when they also believe in Christ.

As we allow the Holy Spirit to live within us, we can draw upon his power to bring about personal change in our lives and experience strength and joy for each day.

Holy Spirit, thank you that you reside within me. Convict my heart of any sin remnants. Guide my steps. And give me boldness to share about your life-giving strength.

Keep Looking Up!

We can ask the Spirit for spiritual insight and guidance.

NOVEMBER 12

Disciples Share the Good News

Read Acts 4–5

> But Peter and John answered them, "Whether it is right in the sight of God to listen to you rather than to God, you must judge, for we cannot but speak of what we have seen and heard."
>
> —Acts 4:19–20

MY FAMILY TELLS a story about how, after wrapping a tie for my dad for his birthday, Mom said to us kids, "Now don't tell your father about the tie. Keep it a secret."

But when Dad came home from work, my brother blurted, "Dad, I'm not going to tell you about your birthday tie."

Good news is hard to keep in, isn't it? Even though threatened with imprisonment or worse, the disciples could not stop sharing that Jesus was the Christ—the Messiah the Jews had been waiting to arrive for centuries. Even when authorities told the disciples to stop, they said they had to obey God rather than men in that regard.

The thing is the Good News is still good news for us today. When we experience the vitality, strength, and joy God brings us each day, we should not keep that powerful testimony to ourselves. Because many need just that.

Lord, although it makes me a little nervous to share my faith, I know what I say need not be perfect. All I need to do is tell my story about how you changed my life from hopeless to hopeful.

Keep Looking Up!

A testimony is simply a story of how God has changed us.

Stephen Radiated Faith in God

Read Acts 6–7

And gazing at him, all who sat in the council saw that his face was like the face of an angel. —Acts 6:15

OUR OLDEST HAS the ability to change the tenor of a room. Her smile and laugh turn others' frowns in the opposite direction. She radiates the love and joy of Jesus and loves being with others. She definitely reflects the sign she made for her classroom: "Get excited, people!"

Radiance is hard to resist. When the ever-expanding number of disciples couldn't stop sharing about Jesus, one man's radiant passion became a threat to the religious authorities. Even though Stephen was doing great wonders and signs among the people, the authorities framed him with wrong accusations and false witnesses. But even during his execution, Stephen asked the Lord not to hold their sin against those stoning him. Radiant faith knows heaven holds more for us than does the earth.

We may never face deadly persecution, but even when others criticize our faith, we can lean into God's strength and bring him glory.

Lord, I don't know if I am as strong as Stephen, so I must completely rely on you to give me strength for any kind of persecution I might face. I trust you to fill me with joy, no matter what I face.

Keep Looking Up!

In faith trials we can rely upon Jesus, who provides our radiance.

NOVEMBER 14

God Chooses Paul . . . and Us

Read Acts 8–9

> But the Lord said to him, "Go, for he is a chosen instrument of mine to carry my name before the Gentiles and kings and the children of Israel." —Acts 9:15

CHOSEN. ONE OF my greatest thrills as an educator was when seniors came to me to show me their acceptance letters. Whether to the military, college, or trade school, it didn't matter. All were important, and whatever their final decision was, they knew they were chosen.

God has a calling for each of us. He even chose Paul, who had persecuted Christians, to preach to the Gentiles, foreign officials, and children of Israel. It took a literal loss of sight and Jesus's direct and convincing words to Paul to wake him up from his spiritual and mental blindness. But upon that dramatic calling, he passionately began spreading the gospel message throughout the Mediterranean area.

We who believe are also called to testify to his saving grace—to our influence circles of family, friends, business, and community. It is a privilege and joy to step into that calling.

Lord, just as you chose Paul, you have chosen me to do the work you have planned for me here on earth. I may not have the same gifts, but I do have a story to tell about how you encourage and help me each day.

Keep Looking Up!

Each of us can share our faith story—starting with our family.

NOVEMBER 15

God's Good News Is for All

Read Acts 10–11

So Peter opened his mouth and said, "Truly I understand that God shows no partiality." —Acts 10:34

OVER THE YEARS my children asked many times which child was my favorite.

And I always replied in the same way my parents did: "I love you all just the same." And it's true! While each of the four is different in personality and in strengths, I hope and pray I have not shown partiality to one more than the others.

God does not show partiality. Anyone from any nation or culture who makes a decision to follow Christ is acceptable to the Lord. In the early church this idea was revolutionary because at first they believed that the Messiah, Jesus, was only for the Jews. But with Peter's vision, God made it clear that the good news is for all people.

It is joyous news indeed that we need not fit into a mold of what a Christian should look like or do. God loves us all.

Father, you are the model parent, loving each of us just the same. You want all people of all nations, cultures, races, and backgrounds to choose a personal relationship with you by embracing your Son, Jesus, as Savior and Lord. May we, your church, remember that.

Keep Looking Up!

Suspending judgment of others provides a grace space for faith.

NOVEMBER 16

God Sends His Angels

Read Acts 12–13

And behold, an angel of the Lord stood next to him, and a light shone in the cell. He struck Peter on the side and woke him, saying, "Get up quickly." And the chains fell off his hands. —Acts 12:7

OCCASIONALLY I HAVE a strong sense of God's protection. I was delayed from leaving our house for several minutes by a phone call, then by someone else who just happened to stop by the house to leave something for my husband.

While I was initially a little frustrated and concerned about being on time for my appointment, relief settled in when I came on a highway accident that must have occurred just minutes before I came onto the scene. Several cars were piled up—one on its side and another upside down. I felt bad for those involved and prayed for those standing by the side of the road waiting for help.

When Peter was jailed unjustly for speaking boldly about Christ, an angel appeared and opened the prison doors for his release. Sometimes heaven touches earth and provides unexpected favor. We just need to look for it.

Lord, favor me with angelic protection as I travel. As I serve you, keep me safe. Thank you for all the ways you guide me around danger.

Keep Looking Up!

Approaching travel prayerfully helps us see God's hand guiding us.

NOVEMBER 17

God's Ways Are Best

Read Acts 14–15

Barnabas took Mark with him and sailed away to Cyprus, but Paul chose Silas and departed, having been commended by the brothers to the grace of the Lord. —Acts 15:39–40

A GROUP OF local people had a different idea about an aspect of the ministry, so they left their church and started another one. While that move initially seemed divisive, it served to expand the ministry in our rural, isolated area. Now churches are planted in all corners of our mountain valley.

A similar experience happened with the disciples. Barnabas had been ministering with Paul and wanted to include Mark with them, but Paul didn't agree. So Barnabas and Mark headed to Cyprus to spread the gospel message there, and Paul enlisted Silas to travel to the north to strengthen the churches there.

God has ways of expanding his kingdom through us. While we always want to maintain peace and unity, the Lord may provide opportunities for us to serve in new ways or new places. We may not understand his purposes, but his ways are always for the better!

Lord, I trust you for all the mysterious ways you use your people. I am open to how you want to use me and where you would send me. Please use my gifts for your purposes.

Keep Looking Up!

We can pray for God's ways to win out over human desires.

NOVEMBER 18

God Things Are Everywhere

Read Acts 16–17

> One who heard us was a woman named Lydia, from the city of Thyatira, a seller of purple goods, who was a worshiper of God. The Lord opened her heart to pay attention to what was said by Paul. —Acts 16:14

I STOPPED BECAUSE the name of the town was McHenry, and I wanted to get something to drink before driving to my Mississippi event. As I enjoyed taking pictures of McHenry signs here and there, a man politely asked me what I was doing, and our conversation continued for about an hour. Because he is related to the original McHenry clan that founded the town, we now stay in touch.

Coincidence or circumstance? Looking at Paul's story in Acts, we notice that many people he encountered experienced dramatic change. When he, Silas, and Timothy went to the riverside for a place of prayer, they met Lydia who, with her household, chose baptism and provided housing for the traveling preachers.

When you watch for what God is doing in your life, you begin to see God's fingerprints through circumstances. And you erase words like *random* or *coincidence* from your vocabulary because God's fingerprints are all over our lives.

Lord, what a joy it is to speak about you and serve others in your name! May I be spiritually aware and responsive to the circumstances you provide and share your love naturally.

Keep Looking Up!

God will provide opportunities for sharing his love.

NOVEMBER 19

God's People Are Near

Read Acts 18–19

And the Lord said to Paul one night in a vision, "Do not be afraid, but go on speaking and do not be silent, for I am with you, and no one will attack you to harm you, for I have many in this city who are my people." —Acts 18:9–10

I RECENTLY DID a little road trip to visit the last three of the US states I had not yet seen: Louisiana, Mississippi, and Alabama. Yes, I've visited all fifty states now! It was a thrill to see the Deep South and meet some of its lovely people. I didn't worry about driving from place to place, because I knew God would be with me and I had people here, there, and about everywhere whom I could call on for help.

One joy-filled result of embracing the faith is how our friendship circles expand. Even though Paul faced opposition in his missionary travels to Corinth, the Lord assured him not only of his presence but of the presence of his people there.

Knowing there are those close by who will help and support us provides assurance that all will be well—no matter where we find ourselves.

Lord, I know I never need to feel afraid, because you are with me and others who call you by name are close by. I need not be silent about my faith, because you will provide protection as I trust you for the results.

Keep Looking Up!

We can build up others of the faith all over the world with simple, encouraging words.

NOVEMBER 20

God Calls Us to Finish Well

Read Acts 20–21

What matters most to me is to finish what God started.
—Acts 20:24 MSG

HAVE YOU EVER taken on a job, only to wonder, *What was I thinking?* I worked as a legal secretary for ten years, and the beginning was rugged. I had no mentor or helper and had to manage the accounting responsibilities as well. The tasks became immense and much more challenging than I thought, but I muddled through and grew during that season of my life.

A calling can be like that too. God called Paul to preach to the non-Jewish peoples throughout the Mediterranean coastal areas. That meant difficult travels, opposition to his message, imprisonment, physical abuse, and more. Nonetheless, he told the church elders at Ephesus that what mattered most to him was fulfilling the calling that the Lord put on his life to testify that Jesus had come to earth to save the lost.

Our calling may not be as dramatic, but our greatest fulfillment is to finish well.

Father God, I want to finish well. Thank you for planting me right where I am, so I can serve you here and now. Despite any difficulties or even the inadequacies I feel, I know you will help me as I seek your daily strength for the tasks ahead.

Keep Looking Up!

Finishing each day's work is an offering to God.

NOVEMBER 21

Paul Lives for God

Read Acts 22–23

> And looking intently at the council, Paul said, "Brothers, I have lived my life before God in all good conscience up to this day."
>
> —Acts 23:1

I HAD A shock of a lifetime when a gentleman walked into my classroom with the state superintendent of schools and presented me with a teacher-of-the-year award. The man was from a tech school. A former student had nominated me—a student I thought didn't like me.

Sometimes you won't know how people perceive you. You may not know if you are having a positive effect on others through your work. But your responsibility is the same. You just have to speak the truth and do the best to live that out.

When Paul spoke before the Roman authorities, he simply told his story about his encounter with Jesus and his conversion from Judaism to faith in Jesus. While Paul admits in his letter that he was not perfect, he lived his new life of faith with integrity.

We never know whom we will touch with our faith story, but we can spread our joy by simply being the best version of ourselves each day.

Lord, may I be able to say I have lived my life before you in all good conscience. May I never turn down your assignment—whether that be to serve in ministry or simply tie a child's shoes—all to your glory.

Keep Looking Up!

Daily we have opportunities to be a billboard for Jesus.

NOVEMBER 22

Paul Testifies about Jesus

Read Acts 24–26

But this I confess to you, that according to the Way, which they call a sect, I worship the God of our fathers, believing everything laid down by the Law and written in the Prophets. —Acts 24:14

WHILE THE OLD Testament can seem like a long, drawn-out story, I love reading through it. Its pages of laws have helped me understand the need for a Savior. And reading about the kings and prophets has helped solidify that Jesus was truly the one who fulfilled all those prophecies.

Knowing God's Word helps us testify about Jesus. Because of his study, Paul could clearly argue for the validity of Jesus as Messiah each time he was asked to testify in his defense—the people in Jerusalem, the chief priests and council, the governor, a second governor, the king, and then Caesar. While each challenge seemingly added another layer of frustration, there was also a new opportunity to testify about Christ.

When we struggle with frustration after frustration and with delay upon delay, we can pray that with each layer we shine with a witness of joy.

Lord, what refreshment and joy you sent to the earth when Jesus was born! The people waited so long for a Savior. Everything in your Word points to him, and I pray that my life will as well.

Keep Looking Up!

The challenges of waiting may bring witness opportunities.

NOVEMBER 23

God Rescues Us

Read Acts 27–28

On seeing them, Paul thanked God and took courage. —Acts 28:15

WE HADN'T PAID attention to the gas gauge and found ourselves on the side of the interstate miles from the nearest gas station. Newly married, we felt vulnerable. But then a long-haul trucker pulled over. Not only did he pick us up, he took time out of his evening to drive back down the freeway and loop around again to our car. We thanked him—and God—immensely.

We've probably all benefited from a rescue or helping hand. Paul received help on the island of Malta after the ship carrying him as a prisoner was wrecked in a storm. Then fellow believers in Rome took care of him when he was under house arrest. Many times people stepped in to minister to him in his quest to share the gospel.

While life can feel like a figurative shipwreck, we can always know God is present with us in those tough circumstances.

Lord, thank you for the people you sent me when I needed a rescue. Even though some of my shipwrecks have been at my own hand, your mercies cover me, and so I give you praise.

Keep Looking Up!

God is our shelter and help in time of need.

NOVEMBER 24

There Is Power in God's Gospel

Read Romans 1–3

For I am not ashamed of the gospel, for it is the power of God for salvation to everyone who believes. —Romans 1:16

I HAVE AN icebreaker question I ask new folks who visit our church: "Have you lived in Reno very long?"

After they answer, they typically say, "How about you? Have you lived here very long?"

Eventually our conversation segues from church-going to matters of faith and personal testimony.

We need not be ashamed of our faith and talking about the gospel message. Paul, the writer of the letter to the Romans as well as many other letters in the New Testament, experienced a dramatic conversion to Christianity. His personal transformation compelled him to spread the good news throughout the known world.

While it can feel a little uncomfortable talking about Jesus, it's not hard to think of an icebreaker that naturally leads into a discussion about our faith.

Lord, I am not very bold to talk about my faith, but I do know that making a decision to follow you is the best decision someone can make. Give me courage to speak about you with love.

Keep Looking Up!

Sharing the gospel message is love in action.

NOVEMBER 25

We Hope in Jesus

Read Romans 4–7

> We rejoice in our sufferings, knowing that suffering produces endurance, and endurance produces character, and character produces hope, and hope does not put us to shame. —Romans 5:3–5

MY SISTER NAN always had the sweetest expression on her face that invited others to know her. She conversed easily with strangers and within minutes they were friends. Nan was her most beautiful, though, in the last stages of her cancer—with a continual grin on her face. She knew that while life on earth was precious, her passing to heaven was like moving from a basement apartment to an ocean-view penthouse.

Living hopefully means we understand that someday there will be an end to suffering and struggle. Hope gives us a reason to endure through life's trials, because then our character becomes a greater reflection of our Savior in whom we hope.

I look up with hope because, if I look around, the world has nothing eternal to offer me. Hope does not disappoint. Hope does not bring me shame. Hope is the exercise of my faith in Jesus.

Lord, I lift my eyes to you, the object of my hope. See me through the suffering ahead. Be my strength as I endure. Build character in me. And may my hope be contagious so others grasp onto it as well.

Keep Looking Up!

Jesus is our hope—a hope that can grow by researching God's promises of heaven.

God Works All for Good

Read Romans 8–10

And we know that in all things God works for the good of those who love him, who have been called according to his purpose.
—Romans 8:28 NIV

I DID NOT understand at first why I lost my teaching job. We faced a significant loss in income at a time when my husband had just started ranching full time—barely meeting expenses in the best of months. But when I got a teaching position just around the corner from our home a couple months later, I realized if I had not been laid off, I would have been under contract to the other school district. And that meant I would not have been able to take the new position.

The circumstances of our lives often baffle us . . . but they do not surprise God. When we are his, we can trust that his sovereign hand moves the events of our lives in a way we could never manipulate ourselves.

Yes, we will face hardship and loss. But God can bring about good as we look to and trust in him.

Lord, you work all things together for good in my life. Despite the struggles and hardships I've gone through, my faith and trust in you have increased. I pray others find their highest calling by following you.

Keep Looking Up!

We can look for God's good in all situations.

NOVEMBER 27

God Can Transform Us

Read Romans 11–14

Do not be conformed to this world, but be transformed by the renewal of your mind, that by testing you may discern what is the will of God, what is good and acceptable and perfect. —Romans 12:2

I OFTEN THINK that the latest new clothing design should be in my closet or that the latest decorative object should find its way to my living room. While I don't particularly love shopping, there is a sense of striving or discontent in me at times that makes me think I need something I don't have.

These kinds of lures from the world can have a strong pull on us. And this is not a new phenomenon. Paul was aware that Roman society could greatly influence the Christian believers in Rome. There were statues and temples to Greek gods. Immorality was rampant. Philosophers emphasized the idea that reason was preeminent over faith. Paul wanted believers to seek godly lives that rose above the depravity of typical Roman culture.

Living lives that reflect Jesus is easier when we daily focus on our Lord Jesus—thinking about him instead of how to gratify earthly longings (Romans 13:14).

Father, I am sorry that I let the world drag me down sometimes. I simply need to look to you for all that I need instead of seeking the momentary pleasures the world offers. Transform my mind and heart, God, as I seek you.

Keep Looking Up!

Transformation begins when we seek the things of God before the things of earth.

We Can Be Witnesses for God

Read Romans 15–16

Let each of us please his neighbor for his good, to build him up.
—Romans 15:2

I CAN BAKE a pie. It's not magic, really. I call it "following directions." It's fun to knock on the door of a new neighbor and deliver a pie—a delicious calling card. It breaks the ice and helps to start out a new relationship.

The world can be a brutal place, full of criticism and abuse. The kindness of Christ can reign in our hearts, though, when we set aside our own concerns. In Paul's letter to the Romans, he told the readers to please their neighbors, to build them up. As we extend kindnesses to those who live near us, we create open doors for opportunities to share our faith with them.

While some neighbors may drive us a little crazy with some of the things they do or don't do, a full measure of patience, tolerance, and kindness is a good recipe to create community.

Lord, you have planted me exactly where you wanted me—in this house, in this neighborhood, in this city. May I be the best possible example of a Christ follower, so others are drawn to you.

Keep Looking Up!

Waving hello is a simple way to start a relationship with a neighbor.

NOVEMBER 29

Our Body Is the Spirit's Temple

Read 1 Corinthians 1–4

Do you not know that you are God's temple and that God's Spirit dwells in you? —1 Corinthians 3:16

AFTER A LONG season of sedentary work and very wintry weather not conducive to walking, aches and creaks had snuck into my body. So I found an exercise DVD for strength training and flexibility that would make me healthier.

Earlier we read that Solomon built the temple his father David designed (1 Chronicles 28) for the Name of the Lord God (1 Chronicles 22:6–10). Later in Psalms we read that God designed each of our bodies (Psalm 139:13)—the new temple in which God's Spirit dwells. When I don't take care of my body, I imagine that dismays God because the consequences often distract from the work and witness he has prepared for me.

I don't want to abuse the Spirit's place of habitation. While there are many unpreventable diseases, there are others I can bring on by choosing unhealthy practices. So I will focus on doing that which helps, not abuses, my body.

Lord, I understand that a steady diet of junk food is not going to be good for me. Help me make good choices in food and exercise, so I can make the most of this life you gave me.

Keep Looking Up!

Choosing a healthy lifestyle is respecting the Spirit's temple.

NOVEMBER 30

God Wants Victory for Us

Read 1 Corinthians 5–9

"All things are lawful for me," but not all things are helpful. "All things are lawful for me," but I will not be dominated by anything.
—1 Corinthians 6:12

I REGRETTED THE gossip as soon as it left my mouth. Even though what I said was true, I should have kept my critical remarks to myself. The information would have come out eventually, but it didn't need to come from me.

Although we know Christ died for our sins and although we know God loves and has forgiven us, my reverting to fallen behavior doesn't do him, his kingdom, or even me any good. Paul saw that the Corinthians weren't experiencing freedom from their sinful behavior, and the same may be true for us today.

One reason people don't embrace Christianity is they see hypocritical behavior (saying one thing and doing another). If I gossip, I'm demonstrating that faith in Christ hasn't changed me—that it doesn't work. God understands that change is a process. His well of forgiveness will not run dry, and we can offer a fresh drink to someone else.

Lord, I ask forgiveness for things I've done that don't reflect the freedom and goodness you want for me. I also ask forgiveness for an attitude of indifference in this regard. Show me daily how to make decisions that foster growth.

Keep Looking Up!

A day is a series of opportunities to make good choices.

DECEMBER 1

God Says, "Love!"

Read 1 Corinthians 10–13

Love bears all things, believes all things, hopes all things, endures all things. —1 Corinthians 13:7

I HAVE A friend whose teenaged son was so out of control one day that he used bad language at his dad and took a swing at him. In response her husband put his arms around his son and just held him until his anger subsided. Many years later, that young man now calls his dad for business advice.

People will take all kinds of swings at us—verbally and otherwise. But in the thirteenth chapter of 1 Corinthians, Paul lays out an essay of what Christian love truly looks like. It is patient and kind, and it is not any of the following: envious, boastful, arrogant, rude, selfish, irritable, resentful. It holds up truth and lives out love.

Love is more than a feeling. Daily we put it into action as we do our best to emulate our loving Savior who gave his all for the sake of love.

Lord, I want love to permeate all that I say, do, and even think. I want love to trigger my responses and take over my thought life. I want to love others so well that they know it comes from you.

Keep Looking Up!

Christian love is demonstrated.

DECEMBER 2

God Gives Spiritual Gifts

Read 1 Corinthians 14–16

Pursue love, and earnestly desire the spiritual gifts.
—1 Corinthians 14:1

IT NEVER OCCURRED to me to pursue teaching, but when I began a junior church program for kids, I found I loved breaking down challenging concepts into life-changing ideas relevant for young people. Then I started teaching Sunday school for adults. And one day someone said, "You have the spiritual gift of teaching." I was never more surprised!

Paul writes of spiritual gifts in his letters. In Romans 12 he lists prophecy, service, teaching, exhortation, giving, leadership, and mercy. In 1 Corinthians 12 he adds wisdom, knowledge, faith, healing, miracles, discernment, tongues, and interpretation of tongues.

It's exciting to think God would entrust us with spiritual gifts to build up the church and serve him in the world. No one gift is more important than another, just as each part of the human body is essential. You are needed and valued!

Lord, thank you for the spiritual gifts you have given me. May I not disregard them, but desire them, develop them, and use them for the building up of your church.

Keep Looking Up!

Using our spiritual gifts builds up the body of Christ.

DECEMBER 3

God Is Good for His Promises

Read 2 Corinthians 1–4

For all the promises of God find their Yes in him. That is why it is through him that we utter our Amen to God for his glory.
—2 Corinthians 1:20

I WAS CONFUSED about God's promise to me—the one for a house. Several years earlier I had prayed, "Lord, if you give us a house, it will be yours for ministry." A short time later I read this verse in Isaiah 32:18 and knew it was God's promise to me: "My people will abide in a peaceful habitation, in secure dwellings, and in quiet resting places."

A year after we built our house, it flooded. The same happened a year later—but even worse. These struggles confused me because I thought God provided our home for ministry. However, the losses caused us to raise our house four and a half feet, which resulted in our redesigning the garage into a guest house . . . now used often for ministry.

God is good for his word. Paul wrote to the Corinthians that all the promises of God—all the prophecies of a messiah—were fulfilled in Jesus Christ. All the questions of how and when and where were realized in a Yes answer: Jesus. Is Jesus the Messiah? Yes. Is he the Savior? Yes. Can he bring life everlasting to whoever believes in him? Yes.

When we say yes to Jesus, we receive his promise for eternal life.

Lord, over and over I have seen your faithful hand in my life. Surely, disappointments and twists occur, but in the end, I know you are near, you love me, and you care.

Keep Looking Up!

God's promised Yes is in us if we have Jesus in our heart.

DECEMBER 4

We Are New in Christ

Read 2 Corinthians 5–9

Therefore, if anyone is in Christ, he is a new creation. The old has passed away; behold, the new has come. —2 Corinthians 5:17

I REMEMBER THE first time I put glasses on. In the sixth grade, I suddenly saw that trees and leaves had edges. Greens and browns didn't blend into each other in a haze but had definitive lines. Everything looked new and fresh.

Did you experience a similar feeling when you put your life into God's hands? That's what happened with me. I didn't want the same things anymore: I wanted to do whatever the Lord laid out for me. I wanted to learn more about faith and could actually understand the Bible when I read it. And whereas I'd always sort of worked at life and school half-heartedly, I had a new desire to do my best.

When we make a commitment to follow Christ, we have a new starting point. All the sin and mistakes of our past are gone, and we can step into an exciting, joy-filled calling to serve God.

Lord, it is heartwarming to know that the old mess of me is gone and that I am a new creation in your eyes. Show me life as you see it—with the full potential of a joy-filled walk with you!

Keep Looking Up!

One way to leave the former life behind is to say, "I used to do that."

DECEMBER 5

God's Grace Is Sufficient

Read 2 Corinthians 10–13

But he said to me, "My grace is sufficient for you, for my power is made perfect in weakness." —2 Corinthians 12:9

THE FIRST TIME I stood as a teacher in front of a classroom of teenagers, I was scared to death. *Am I wearing something stupid? Does my hair look okay? Will the words come out right? What if they ask me something I can't answer? Help me, Lord!* I felt some of the same angst a half dozen times daily for the next twenty-six years. But it was fun. My students extended me grace . . . a lot.

Being out of our comfort zone is not a bad thing. When we are thrust into a new job or new ministry or new experience, we have to rely upon the Lord. And when we depend on him, he gets the glory from that situation, because we know any success did not come from our own strength or abilities but was only filtered through his grace.

And those become teachable moments as we sit in God's classroom.

Father, you know that I do not like being out of my comfort zone. Even so, I do know that your grace is sufficient and that your power is made perfect through my weakness. So I look expectantly to you for that grace.

Keep Looking Up!

It's perfectly all right to admit we don't know something.

DECEMBER 6

God Establishes Our Worth

Read Galatians 1–3

For am I now seeking the approval of man, or of God?
—Galatians 1:10

MOM ALWAYS COOKED for a crowd—a crowd of individuals. She made coleslaw because that was Craig's favorite. Macaroni salad, Pete's favorite. Potato salad, my favorite. Green salad, Roberta's favorite. And two kinds of scalloped potatoes—with and without cheese. Everyone was happy, but Mom was probably exhausted.

Mom gave out of her love for others—and still does! If we only give to earn others' approval, we can lose sight of what God would have us do. Exhaustion can ensue—making us feel overlooked and even used. And often we become crushed when someone doesn't return kindness for our hard efforts.

The good news is that our identity is in Christ. He defines our worth, so that we don't have to prove our worth to him or others. Serving those we love is honorable, but serving for the purpose of earning others' love can strip away the joy.

Lord, I own my people-pleasing tendencies. Remind me to look up to you for my worth. And help me develop relationships not so much through performance but through mutual respect and love.

Keep Looking Up!

The examination of motives can reveal people-pleasing tendencies.

Keep in Step with the Spirit

Read Galatians 4–6

But the fruit of the Spirit is love, joy, peace, patience, kindness, goodness, faithfulness, gentleness, self-control; against such things there is no law. —Galatians 5:22–23

WHEN I LEARNED my first name means "God's gracious gift," it struck me that I did not live up to it. So I began choosing a character quality—such as grace, love, joy, peace—as a yearly focus word. I study what the word means, how it's used in Scripture, and how others have used it, including poets and lyricists. The challenge has helped me grow as I focus on the fruit of the Spirit and other Christlike qualities.

A measure of our growth as Christians can be studied as we consider the fruit or results of the Spirit listed in our focus verse today. Do I actually demonstrate love? Joy? Peace? Patience? Now there's a good one! Paul challenged the Galatian Christians to set aside negative behaviors and keep in step with the Spirit.

And when we keep in step with someone, we have the same pace and outcome . . . or fruit. And arrive at the same destination!

Lord, I pray that my life produces fruit—tangible outcomes for your kingdom but also character outcomes—not for my sake or glory but so others see you in me.

Keep Looking Up!

Memorizing Scripture can help us grow spiritual fruit.

DECEMBER 8

God Gives Abundantly

Read Ephesians 1–3

> Now to Him who is able to do exceedingly abundantly above all that we ask or think, according to the power that works in us, to Him be glory in the church by Christ Jesus to all generations, forever and ever. Amen. —Ephesians 3:20–21 NKJV

WHEN I SERVED as an academic advisor to juniors and seniors, I would ask them what their dream job was, but I asked them like this: "What would you love so much that it wouldn't seem like work?" Coming from a town of less than a thousand in an isolated, rural area, they often had a hard time dreaming big, but I felt it was my job to come alongside them to help them the best way I could.

Sometimes it's hard to dream big, isn't it? We are often nearsighted in thinking—immediately considering our limitations of abilities or finances. Paul's prayer that precedes Ephesians 3:20 asks the Father to give the Ephesians spiritual strength and power so they would fully understand the breadth, length, height, and depth of Christ's love.

Moving forward with that kind of assurance, we can step into the abundance God has planned for us.

Lord, you are able to give more abundantly than I can ask, think, or imagine. I do not ask for power or riches but simply for your wisdom and that your purpose for me would be fulfilled.

Keep Looking Up!

The biggest kind of dream starts with this question: What could God do?

DECEMBER 9

God Provides Armor

Read Ephesians 4–6

Put on the whole armor of God, that you may be able to stand against the schemes of the devil. —Ephesians 6:11

BOTH OUR BOYS played catcher on their baseball teams. They'd suit up with a chest protector, shin guards, and a catcher's helmet to be ready for about anything a wild pitch, foul ball, or throw might do. I wasn't as wise when I played catcher in a family baseball game one summer evening and ended up with a broken nose. The next time I put on the gear.

We need protection for our Christian walk too. Paul taught the Ephesians how to prepare for spiritual battles—true for us today too. Our defensive weapons are truth, the righteousness we have in Christ, peace, faith, and salvation, and then we have God's Word, which provides an offense for the devil's temptations.

We cannot strengthen ourselves, but when we feel weak against the enemy's attacks, we can draw upon the Lord's strength and power.

Lord God, suit me up with your spiritual armor. May I live in the truth of your Word, ready to claim victory because of the faith I have in your righteousness and salvation.

Keep Looking Up!

Praying in Jesus's name is a powerful weapon.

DECEMBER 10

God Can Change Our Mindset

Read Philippians 1–4

Finally, brothers and sisters, whatever is true, whatever is noble, whatever is right, whatever is pure, whatever is lovely, whatever is admirable—if anything is excellent or praiseworthy—think about such things. —Philippians 4:8 NIV

IT'S NOT IN my nature to be positive, but God is changing me. I worked well as an English teacher because I could immediately assess what was wrong with a student's writing. But I'd have to make myself pause to write several positive reactions too before giving it back to the student. I also notice if pictures are crooked and even rearrange items in store displays.

Today's verse is one that has helped me. When I find myself in a negative mindset, I will recite the verse over and over until I remind myself of the good of a situation. In this letter to the Philippians, we see Paul understood that our thoughts can overflow into negative behavior and speech.

I was surprised at a recent conference when I met up with a longtime friend who said, "You are such a positive person!" God truly can change us with his Word.

Father, help me choose joy and shake negativity by focusing on what is true, noble, right, pure, lovely, admirable, excellent, and praiseworthy! In other words, you!

Keep Looking Up!

Memorizing today's verse provides a weapon against negativity.

DECEMBER 11

We Work for the Lord

Read Colossians 1–4

Whatever you do, work heartily, as for the Lord and not for men.
—Colossians 3:23

ONE SUMMER I worked as an intern for the Army Awards Branch in Washington, DC. When my supervisor showed me my desk, I was stunned. There were hundreds of unopened letters from surviving kin, asking about awards they thought their child or spouse deserved. Every day I researched and wrote letters. My last day on the job I took a final look at my desk. I had done my best to clear it off . . . and prayed someone would not leave the letter writing to the next summer intern.

Doing our best is important. While Paul was writing to bond-servants in today's verse, it applies to us today. We all have work to do that reflects not only on us but also on the Lord. Others see us, and while we need not obsess about doing something perfectly, we should always want to do our best. After all, Jesus gave his best.

Lord, thank you for the work you have entrusted to me. Whether that's doing laundry or teaching kids or shoveling snow, I will do it all to the best of my ability. Give me strength and wisdom, God.

Keep Looking Up!

We can do our best when we're doing what God would have us do.

DECEMBER 12

God Encourages Our Prayers

Read 1 Thessalonians 1–5

Rejoice always, pray without ceasing, give thanks in all circumstances; for this is the will of God in Christ Jesus for you.

—1 Thessalonians 5:16–18

AS A HIGH school English teacher and mom of four kids, I struggled to find time to pray. I dozed off in the morning and at bedtime never finished before falling asleep. But when I began the practice of prayerwalking, I found that wherever I was, there was a reason for prayer, and I learned to pray through my day. Then when I began reading through the Bible each year, I started allowing Scripture to inspire my prayers.

There are various types of prayers. Paul mentions several in his first letter to the Thessalonians. We can rejoice—praising God for his good character. We can intercede for those in need and pray for our own needs too. And we can give thanks for all the good . . . and the challenges too. Prayer is our spiritual lifeline that keeps us in touch with the Father who loves us.

Lord, I give you honor and praise for your faithfulness, compassion, and grace. And I thank you for all the blessings you have poured out on my family and me, as well as the tough circumstances, because they draw me closer to you.

Keep Looking Up!

When we count our blessings, we can include the challenges that shape us.

DECEMBER 13

We Can Stay in Touch with God

Read 2 Thessalonians 1–3

To this end we always pray for you, that our God may make you worthy of his calling and may fulfill every resolve for good and every work of faith by his power, so that the name of our Lord Jesus may be glorified in you, and you in him, according to the grace of our God and the Lord Jesus Christ. —2 Thessalonians 1:11–12

"PRAYING FOR YOU!"

That is on my signature on emails I send. I see each contact during the day as an opportunity to pray.

It was the writer Paul who challenged me to pursue a praying lifestyle years ago when I read "pray without ceasing" in his first letter to the Thessalonians. I formerly had the focus that people were problems—that they drew something out of introverted me each day. So I studied Paul's letters to see how he prayed for the churches.

He prayed for grace, peace, their faith, their witness. Paul prayed for strength for them and gave thanks for them. Despite their mess-ups, or even because of them, he wrote that they were in his prayers continually. His strength only grew because of his prayer life.

Like Paul, we have the opportunity to pray for those we influence and those who will follow them. What a joyful legacy!

Lord, it is a joy to pray for others. Hear my prayers, God, on behalf of others who are hurting and need you. May their faith grow as they also seek you.

Keep Looking Up!

As a good friend would, God says, "Stay in touch!"

DECEMBER 14

God Can Use Us All

Read 1 Timothy 1–6

> Let no one despise you for your youth, but set the believers an example in speech, in conduct, in love, in faith, in purity.
>
> —1 Timothy 4:12

I MET A young woman last summer who some years before started a ministry to the wives of military men. The women support each other in entrepreneurial business pursuits, train each other in leadership qualities, and provide community for women who find themselves moving their families from place to place—all to glorify the name of Jesus. She's a fearless young woman who loves teaching God's Word.

Just because someone is young does not mean they can't be a powerful leader. Samuel, David, Josiah, and Jeremiah were young when God called them to lead. In his first letter to Timothy, Paul encouraged the younger man to be an example and step into leadership. While it may seem intimidating to work or serve with others who are older and more experienced, God will always equip us for his calling. Wisdom can come with age, but it can also come when we are young.

Lord, thank you for this reminder that you can use all kinds of people—old or young, rich or poor, educated or not. May I be an example in speech, in conduct, in love, in faith, and in purity.

Keep Looking Up!

God can use us right now no matter our stage of life.

DECEMBER 15

God's Word Teaches Us

Read 2 Timothy 1–4

All Scripture is breathed out by God and profitable for teaching, for reproof, for correction, and for training in righteousness, that the man of God may be complete, equipped for every good work.

—2 Timothy 3:16–17

EVERY ONCE IN a while someone will ask me, "Who mentored you in your faith?"

My answer usually surprises them. "The Bible."

While I wish I had a mentor through the earlier seasons of my faith, that person never came into my life.

Even when we don't have someone older to teach us the Bible, we can dig into God's Word on our own and allow the Holy Spirit to teach us. We can read a chunk of Scripture, then look at any study notes in our Bible or even a commentary. Joining with others to study the Bible is also faith-building. I love my Bible study sisters and take notes like crazy when they offer their insights.

It's also helpful to consider how to put the Bible into practice, as Paul suggests here that the Word is living. We can use it to teach others and to correct our own behavior.

Lord, thank you for your Word that breathes truth into me. May I remember that it is living and active—effective for equipping me, teaching others, training my family and me for any battles ahead, as well as correcting me. I am grateful for it.

Keep Looking Up!

Every day the Bible can teach us something new.

DECEMBER 16

God Wants Us to Encourage Others

Read Titus 1–3, Philemon

For I have derived much joy and comfort from your love, my brother, because the hearts of the saints have been refreshed through you.
—Philemon 7

I JUST RECEIVED a note from a friend who said she was praying for my health matter. What humbled me was that I knew she had an aggressive form of cancer. I had meant to send her a card but kept forgetting. Her kindness touched my heart—that she cared about me enough to encourage me, and also that she rose above her own suffering to do so.

Words encourage us. Paul always prefaced his letters—some of which would provide some correction for the recipients—with thanksgiving for them and mentions of his prayers for them. He noted their positive characteristics and his appreciation for them. Our positive words can lift up our discouraged friends and also soften any serious discussion to follow.

Sharing our expressions of care and appreciation—as Paul did—may encourage someone we love just when she or he needs it.

Father, I have derived much comfort and joy from your love. I pray for greater awareness of how I can pass that comfort and joy to others so that they are encouraged.

Keep Looking Up!

A short thinking-of-you note is always appreciated.

DECEMBER 17

Jesus Advocates for Us

Read Hebrews 1–4

> For we do not have a high priest who is unable to sympathize with our weaknesses, but one who in every respect has been tempted as we are, yet without sin. —Hebrews 4:15

I HAVE A couple prayer buddies I can text at any time and know they will be praying for me. In the last week we have sent prayer request texts back and forth relating to upcoming travels, family concerns, and medical tests, and answers to those prayers. It is comforting to know that at least two others will be advocating with God for me, and it's a privilege to partner with them in their needs too.

We have a heavenly prayer partner too. We learn in Hebrews 1 that Jesus serves as our high priest in advocacy for us. And just as close earthly friends would, he understands our pain and worries because he also experienced temptation and many forms of suffering during his thirty-three years of life here.

So we can approach the throne of grace with confidence because our Savior, advocate, and prayer partner—Jesus—joins us in prayer.

Lord God, hear my prayers for your mercy and grace. Help me in my time of need. I am not sinless, but I trust in your Son, Jesus, and put myself in your hands.

Keep Looking Up!

We can always remember that Jesus is interceding with the Father on our behalf.

DECEMBER 18

We Grow Up in Christ

Read Hebrews 5–8

> Therefore let us move beyond the elementary teachings about Christ and be taken forward to maturity, not laying again the foundation of repentance from acts that lead to death, and of faith in God.
>
> —Hebrews 6:1 NIV

I KNEW VERY little about the Bible when I first committed my life to Christ, but a friend invited me to meet with her to learn more about the faith. So that's how it happened that my first Bible study was on the book of Romans. We figuratively skipped elementary teachings and dove deeply into the richness of theology. That semester's study laid important foundations for my Christian walk.

Having a strong foundation keeps us standing through life's storms. The writer of Hebrews emphasizes several principles. First, repentance and faith are our faith footings. We are saved by God's grace through faith in Christ, not by rituals or good works. Another is that though we don't earn our way to heaven, it's important to put sin behind us—otherwise it's as though we mock Jesus's painful suffering for our sins.

Growing up in faith means that we joyously follow Jesus, so others are drawn to the faith.

Lord, I do want to grow up spiritually. I don't want to collapse every time bad news surfaces. Instead, I want to build a foundation of faith that weathers the storms of life.

Keep Looking Up!

Growth occurs when we incorporate daily spiritual disciplines.

DECEMBER 19

God Loves Our Fellowship

Read Hebrews 9–10

> And let us consider how we may spur one another on toward love and good deeds, not giving up meeting together, as some are in the habit of doing, but encouraging one another—and all the more as you see the Day approaching. —Hebrews 10:24–25 NIV

THE PANDEMIC WAS devastating in many ways, including church attendance. About one-third of our own church is still watching church online, as opposed to attending in person. And I miss those faces! While we can get the same meat from a sermon either way, the time worshiping together and visiting afterward is precious.

When we don't spend time with other Christ followers, discouragement and even depression can begin camping out in our heart, mind, and soul—and that's a roadblock for personal growth. When we meet together in small groups for study and prayer and fun, we do life together. We become part of others' lives and can encourage one another. The writer of Hebrews challenges us to meet even more as Christ's second coming grows closer.

Fellowshipping with others is delightful practice for the joyous eternity we will all spend together in the presence of our Lord.

Lord, fellowshipping with others is such a privilege! I get to sing songs of praise with them. I get to serve and minister and encourage them. I get to receive their love. Thank you for stirring up faith within me through other believers.

Keep Looking Up!

Attending church is the best way to start a week!

DECEMBER 20

Jesus Paces Our Race

Read Hebrews 11–13

> Let us run with perseverance the race marked out for us, fixing our eyes on Jesus, the pioneer and perfecter of faith.
>
> —Hebrews 12:1–2 NIV

"WANT TO RUN a triathlon with me?" my son asked.

No, I didn't really want to run a triathlon, but I did want to spend time with him. So I settled for a mini version of the swim-cycle-run event, and my two daughters and a grandson joined us too. The early spring lake waters were frigid, but I won first for my age category! All right, I was the only one in my category, but it still was a win.

Life is an endurance run, isn't it? However, the author of Hebrews writes that we have a cloud of heavenly witnesses to inspire us. Each day may seem like a tough lap, but when we fix our eyes on Jesus, who sets the course for us and paces us, we can consider our lives victorious.

Eventually we will win the prize of heaven and hear God say the words, "Well done, good and faithful servant."

Lord, I love the promise that Jesus will perfect my faith. May I run with endurance this race called life as I look forward to the finish line, where he will greet me.

Keep Looking Up!

We can endure with joy because we know Jesus did.

DECEMBER 21

God Helps Us Endure

Read James 1–5

Consider it pure joy, my brothers and sisters, whenever you face trials of many kinds, because you know that the testing of your faith produces perseverance. —James 1:2–3 NIV

MY HEART QUICKENED as we drove into our corner of the mountain valley late that winter evening. A fire appeared in the distance, and fearing the worst as we drove nearer, we saw it was a hay barn on Craig's ranch, about a mile from our home. Although there was a lot of loss, firefighters saved most of the metal structure. And once again, the Lord deepened our faith as we trusted him for the income loss.

As we look around, we see no one escapes struggle. And while some can point fingers at God and get angry about the trials they face, the truth is that those who trust him have not only a companion for that valley experience but also a Comforter (Jeremiah 8:18 NIV), a Shepherd who guides us (Psalm 23:1–3), and a Stronghold when we feel weary from struggles (2 Samuel 22:3).

We simply look to him for each step of the way so that his miraculous endurance sees us through.

Lord, help me consider it all joy when I encounter various trials. I know that the testing of my faith will bring about perseverance and a new strength that will bring honor to you.

Keep Looking Up!

God helps us and is with us through all the trials we face.

DECEMBER 22

Jesus Fulfills His Promises

Read 1 Peter 1–5; 2 Peter 1–3

> The Lord is not slow to fulfill his promise as some count slowness, but is patient toward you, not wishing that any should perish, but that all should reach repentance. —2 Peter 3:9

I COULDN'T WAIT to get married. Then when I was married, I couldn't wait to have kids. After the kids came, I couldn't wait to get a house. Seasons and years passed with various sorts of waiting periods. And at this writing I can't wait to get a medical procedure behind me.

It seems we are always waiting for something, doesn't it? As life and its sorrows and tragedies fill our days, we may also be longing for the Lord's second coming so we can put earthly pain behind us. In Peter's second letter to believers scattered in Asia Minor, he affirms Christ's promise that he will come again, noting that with the Lord one day is as a thousand years and a thousand years as one day.

In any waiting period we need not twiddle our thumbs. Instead, let's continue to pursue God's calling on our lives—loving God and loving others.

Lord, you are worth the wait. And because you are good for your promises, any delay that I may feel in this waiting time is simply a season for me to draw closer to you and serve you with joyful abandon.

Keep Looking Up!

Any waiting season is an opportunity to anticipate how God will fulfill his promises.

DECEMBER 23

Jesus Is the Bridge to Life

Read 1 John 1–5

If we confess our sins, he is faithful and just to forgive us our sins and to cleanse us from all unrighteousness. —1 John 1:9

AS A TEENAGER I talked back to my mother once. After a scolding from my dad, I learned my lesson. When I apologized, though, everything was all right again. And it struck me how great my parents were—that they did not allow offenses to brew but simply cast them aside like vapor that disappears in the air.

Our heavenly Father forgives like that too. The disciple John writes that when we confess our sins and ask God to forgive us, he not only forgives us, but provides a clean slate for us. While others might hold grudges against us for a misplaced comment, God does not. Because we have committed our lives to following Christ, he himself is our clean slate—his death and resurrection provide the means for our salvation.

That doesn't mean we are sinless. We're just seen as forgiven in our Father's eyes. In other words, Jesus—more particularly his sacrifice on the cross—is the bridge for coming to God.

Father, thank you for sending your Son, Jesus, that I might be freed from the bondage of my sins and accepted as clean in your sight. I am free from blame and free from shame because of your grace.

Keep Looking Up!

Confessing quickly puts sin in the past.

DECEMBER 24

Love Points Others to God

Read 2 John; 3 John; Jude

And now, dear lady, I am not writing you a new command but one we have had from the beginning. I ask that we love one another.
—2 John 5 NIV

AFTER A FRUSTRATING weekend of kids not behaving while we visited my parents, they were still giving me a hard time when I asked them to help load the car to go home. After I yelled at them, my dad ushered them to the car and said, "Janet, I know it's not easy raising kids, but just love them."

Those words have echoed since then in my memory and sound much like the counsel from the apostle John, who in his gospel referred to himself as "the disciple whom Jesus loved." What Jesus laid out for us to do was simple: love God and love one another. When we demonstrate love for one another, our actions represent our love for the Lord. Others pay attention to our loving acts and are drawn to those who do them—and thus to our inspiration, Jesus.

When we love God, we walk it out by loving others.

Lord, if I say I follow you, that means that I must emulate your loving-kindness. And the payback is incredible: satisfaction and deep-seated joy that fills me and spurs me on to do more.

Keep Looking Up!

We can be instruments of love through small, daily gestures.

DECEMBER 25

Jesus Is God's Promise Fulfilled

Read Revelation 1–3

"I am the Alpha and the Omega," says the Lord God, "who is and who was and who is to come, the Almighty." —Revelation 1:8

MY MOM NEVER wanted a thing for Christmas, other than having her family go to church with her on Christmas Eve. For her, the best celebration of Jesus's birth was going to church to sing traditional Christmas carols and worship the Lord with other believers.

There is a reason Jesus is called the Alpha and the Omega. *Alpha* is the first letter of the Greek alphabet—Koine Greek being the original language of the New Testament—and *Omega* is the last Greek letter. Jesus was with the Father at the beginning of creation, he is with God now, and he will rule over human history until its very end.

He also has been with us in our faith walk since the first day we put our trust in him and will be with us in heaven when our time comes. Jesus is the first and the last and everything in between.

Heavenly Father, when you sent your Son, Jesus, to earth, you fulfilled centuries of prophetic promises to your people. He is my Alpha and Omega—my faith's beginning and fulfillment.

Keep Looking Up!

On Christmas Day today we can know Jesus is the best gift—the Alpha and the Omega.

DECEMBER 26

Jesus Hears Our Prayers

Read Revelation 4–7

And when he had taken the scroll, the four living creatures and the twenty-four elders fell down before the Lamb, each holding a harp, and golden bowls full of incense, which are the prayers of the saints. —Revelation 5:8

I WAITED MANY years for God to answer my prayers to restore the marriage of friends. I had seen him repair our own marriage, so I knew there was hope. Every time I got in my car to drive an hour to the nearest city, I prayed, and I prayed on the way home too. A couple years later their love returned, stronger than ever.

We may wonder if God hears our prayers. Where do they go, we ask—to outer space or a filing system? Sometimes it feels as though our prayers have gone to a dead letter office, unread. But in his revelation John saw golden bowls filled with incense made of the prayers of God's people. Whereas Jewish tradition held that the chief angels presented prayers to the Lord God, in Revelation 5:8 we read that the heavenly chorus presents them to Jesus.

Our prayers bring about a sweet aroma in heaven.

Thank you, Lord, that you hear my prayers. Help me be patient as I wait for your timing. Help me be humble to accept your answer. Help me turn to you continually in a looking up posture.

Keep Looking Up!

Our best first response is prayer.

DECEMBER 27

Jesus Will Come Again

Read Revelation 8–11

> Then the seventh angel blew his trumpet, and there were loud voices in heaven, saying, "The kingdom of the world has become the kingdom of our Lord and of his Christ, and he shall reign forever and ever." —Revelation 11:15

MY HUSBAND RAN for local offices three times—and won only once. He was also appointed for office three times. Elections, politics, and government decisions often aren't much fun and can cause divisions between people that sometimes never heal. One good thing about politics, though, is this: it can make us long for Jesus's return to earth to reign forever!

The trumpets will resound when Jesus comes again, because trumpets have historically been blown when a king is enthroned. That final trumpet sound will announce the end of rule by nations. Jesus will be the King of Kings and Lord of Lords and will reign over all the earth forever. Handel's "Hallelujah Chorus" that men and women have sung since 1742 will see its fruition in the second coming of Jesus.

Until then, we can rest in the promise that Jesus hears our prayers.

Lord, you are the King of Kings and the Lord of Lords. Your kingdom will reign on this earth forever and ever, just as you reign now in my heart and in the hearts of those who follow you.

Keep Looking Up!

A praise-filled life knows Jesus is near.

DECEMBER 28

Jesus Is the Victor

Read Revelation 12–14

> And I heard a loud voice in heaven, saying, "Now the salvation and the power and the kingdom of our God and the authority of his Christ have come, for the accuser of our brothers has been thrown down, who accuses them day and night before our God."
>
> —Revelation 12:10

MY HUSBAND IS a big fan of classic Western novels and films. The antagonist villain provides conflict for the not-perfect hero, the protagonist, who often is on a quest to save a town or a group of people. The lines are clear in those good-versus-evil stories, and the good guys and gals always win.

Godly justice will finally fall into place when Jesus comes again to reign on the earth. He will strip Satan—the enemy of God and accuser of those who follow Jesus—of any strongholds he has planted. Satan will no longer be able to accuse and blame, tempt and torture, and will lose his role as a prosecutor of sorts.

This is joyful news! Justice will reign on earth as the Lord God fulfills his final promises. And all of heaven will sing praise!

Lord, I can't imagine what that scene will look like when your Son, Jesus, comes again to earth! May all of heaven and earth lift praises when your salvation and power and kingdom come, defeating death and bringing life eternal.

Keep Looking Up!

Praying "your kingdom come" anticipates God's promise.

DECEMBER 29

God Sets Us Free

Read Revelation 15–17

And they sing the song of Moses, the servant of God, and the song of the Lamb, saying, "Great and amazing are your deeds, O Lord God the Almighty! Just and true are your ways, O King of the nations!" —Revelation 15:3

I'LL NEVER FORGET the sense of freedom I felt after having back surgery. I could sit again! I could stand. I could hold a book in my hands and read. While I needed some time to recuperate from the actual pain of surgery, the extreme back pain was gone. I was delivered.

Those who have experienced freedom from pain or an addiction or abuse know what it's like to sense deliverance from the weight of that captivity. We see that kind of celebration in today's reading when the angels play harps and sing the song of Moses, which praises the Lord God for the deliverance of the Israelites from captivity in Egypt.

When we embrace Jesus as our personal Savior, we are freed from our sin and can celebrate that it no longer has a hold on us. And someday we too will celebrate being with him in heaven.

I celebrate you, Lord God! Great and marvelous are your works. You are the Almighty, King of the nations, and just and true are your works. May all nations worship and adore you.

Keep Looking Up!

Starting prayer with praise puts God in his rightful place.

We Give Praise to God

Read Revelation 18–19

Hallelujah! For our Lord God Almighty reigns. Let us rejoice and be glad and give him glory! For the wedding of the Lamb has come, and his bride has made herself ready. —Revelation 19:6–7 NIV

I LOVE THE wedding scene in the play *Our Town* by Thornton Wilder. In an aside the busybody character, Mrs. Soames, rambles about how the wedding is perfect and lovely, that she loves a good wedding. She brings a smile to audience faces.

We clap and cheer, sing and dance at weddings. The future is bright and hopeful. But that cheer is a dim glimpse of the hallelujahs believers will shout when Christ returns to earth for his church. In his vision, Revelation writer John saw the church represented as a bride dressed in pure white linen presented to the Lamb, who is Christ.

Many times we read shouts of "Hallelujah!"—meaning "Praise the Lord!"—in Revelation, the only place the word is used in the New Testament. Praising God helps us grow in spiritual maturity because it helps us understand the Lord is our all-powerful Creator, and we, his created beings.

Lord in heaven, you are worthy of all my hallelujahs! I give you honor and praise and glory and pray that my worship gives you joy.

Keep Looking Up!

Praise ushers us into the presence of God.

DECEMBER 31

God Will Wipe Away Our Tears

Read Revelation 20–22

He will wipe away every tear from their eyes, and death shall be no more, neither shall there be mourning, nor crying, nor pain anymore, for the former things have passed away. —Revelation 21:4

A RECENT MEMORIAL service I attended did not have the typical, somber music associated with such ceremonies. Instead, there were a half dozen songs you would typically hear at a vacation Bible school or summer camp for kids—smile-inducing songs the memorialized man used to play for children. While there were tears among the hundreds who paid tribute to the pastor who died, there was also much joy and laughter. A saint had gone home.

We all wonder what heaven will be like. Peace will take on new meaning as we enter the place Jesus has prepared for us. And not only will we have a place to live right next to Jesus, we will have new bodies, new emotions, and new experiences of God's presence. We will leave life's struggles and pain behind, and any tears will come only as a result of joy beyond any human experience we've had.

Today we can be encouraged that our Lord is with us each step of our way there. Hallelujah!

Dear Lord, I long for the day when you will wipe all my tears away and remove all my physical and emotional pain. Come soon, Lord Jesus! Come soon!

Keep Looking Up!

Praise takes away the power of despair and replaces it with joy.

Closing Prayer

Lord, I thank you for the promises in your Word. As I read each page, I see how you are good and true to fulfill each and every promise. Even when humankind was not faithful, you still pursued a relationship with your creation—eventually sending your Son, Jesus Christ, as an offering for our sin.

May I continue to grow in grace and understanding as I study your Word. I dedicate my life, Father, to love and serve you forever. In Jesus's name, amen.

Acknowledgments

I AM GRATEFUL to God for a village of people who made *Looking Up!* possible:

- My literary agent, Janet Grant, who saw its potential to encourage others to find joy in and pray through the Bible. Thank you!
- The amazing folks at Our Daily Bread Publishing, whose passion it is to spread the Good News throughout the world. Thank you!
- The wonderful editorial team of Dawn Anderson and Sarah De Mey, along with terrific support from Janyre Tromp, Linnae Conkel, and others—all of whom worked meticulously to keep this book theologically sound. Thank you!

Lastly, I am thankful to the Lord God, who birthed this idea in me and came alongside me in its writing and editing seasons. To him be all honor and glory and praise!

About the Author

JANET HOLM MCHENRY started reading through God's Word each year about twenty-five years ago and leads a Facebook Bible Girls group, which reads through the Bible each year. A national speaker, she has written twenty-seven books—including Bible studies and books on prayer. Her book *PrayerWalk: Becoming a Woman of Prayer, Strength, and Discipline* has encouraged thousands to walk and pray for their communities. Janet coordinates the prayer ministries for The Bridge Church in Reno, Nevada, and is on the state leadership team for the National Day of Prayer in California. She and her husband, Craig, have lived in the Sierra Valley in Northern California for more than forty years. There they raised their four children, Janet formerly taught high school English, and Craig is a cattle rancher. A graduate of UC Berkeley, Janet loves to connect with readers, and you can contact her through social media or her website: https://www.janetmchenry.com.

Spread the Word by Doing One Thing.

- Give a copy of this book as a gift.
- Share the QR code link via your social media.
- Write a review of this book on your blog, favorite bookseller's website, or at ODB.org/store.
- Recommend this book to your church, small group, or book club.

Our Daily Bread.

Connect with us.

Our Daily Bread Publishing
PO Box 3566, Grand Rapids, MI 49501, USA
Email: books@odb.org

renew, refresh, reclaim

In a world that disappoints again and again, your heavenly Father does not. Wherever you are today and whatever your situation tomorrow, know on a whole new level that God is with you, He is for you, and He will never fail you.

Well-loved author, blogger, and women's ministry speaker, Lori Hatcher is here to help renew, refresh, and reclaim your confidence in the rock-solid truths about God.

Our Daily Bread Publishing®

Connect with us.

Our Daily Bread Publishing
PO Box 3566, Grand Rapids, MI 49501, USA
Email: books@odb.org